Memoirs of a Less Travelled Road

Marcel Trudel, *circa* 1940

Memoirs of a Less Travelled Road

A Historian's Life

Marcel Trudel

TRANSLATED FROM THE FRENCH BY
JANE BRIERLEY

Véhicule Press

Published with the generous assistance of The Canada Council for the Arts, the Book Publishing Industry Development Program of the Department of Canadian Heritage, and the Société de développement des entreprises culturelles du Québec (SODEC).

Cover design: JW Stewart
Cover painting: "House in Chambly" (detail) by Maurice Cullen, courtesy K.E.Y. Stewart
All photos courtesy of the author.
Set in Adobe Minion by Simon Garamond
Printed by AGMV-Marquis Inc.

The original book, *Mémoires d'un autre siècle*
was published by Les Éditions du Boréal, 1987.

Dépôt légal, Bibliothèque nationale du Québec and the National Library of Canada, fourth quarter, 2002.

CATALOGUING IN PUBLICATION DATA

Trudel, Marcel, 1917-
Memoirs of a less travelled road : a historian's life
Translation of Mémoires d'un autre siècle.
ISBN 1-55065-156-0

1. Trudel, Marcel, 1917-. 2. Historians–Québec (Province).
I. Brierley, Jane, 1935- II. Title

FC151.T78A38 2001 971.007202 C2001-901035-4

A DOSSIER QUÉBEC BOOK

Published by Véhicule Press
P.O.B. 125, Place du Parc Station
Montréal, Québec H2X 4A3

www.vehiculepress.com

Canadian Distribution: LPG Distribution 800.591.6250
U.S. Distribution: Independent Publishers Group 800.888.4741
www.ipgbook.com

Printed in Canada on alkaline paper.

Contents

Translator's Foreword

I FIRST READ MARCEL TRUDEL'S *Mémoires d'un autre siècle* shortly after they were published in 1987. His name was familiar to me because I had consulted some of his works while translating Serge Gagnon's study, *Quebec and its Historians: the Twentieth Century*, and *A Man of Sentiment*, the memoirs of Philippe-Joseph Aubert de Gaspé (1786-1871). I had bought Dr. Trudel's book at Montreal's annual Salon du Livre, intrigued by its title and always interested in finding new avenues to Quebec's past. Later, seated in my favourite chair, I was immediately captivated by the world in which I found myself. As the author so aptly points out, he and his generation were born into a world of the eighteenth century. This world existed, almost in a time warp, while the aftermath of war, revolution, and the Great Depression held most of Europe and North America in its grip.

Marcel Trudel was born on May 29, 1917, in a rural village deep in the hinterland north of Trois-Rivières, about halfway between Montreal and Quebec City. His father was a carpenter by trade. The early death of his mother resulted in the breakup of his family. His father left to find work in Montreal, and the nine children were parcelled out among relatives. It was then that Trudel's life first took the less travelled road—a paraphrase of a line of Robert Frost's poem that seemed to me an apt title for the translation of this book—for "that . . . made all the difference."

The motherless child found himself adopted by an elderly aunt and her husband, whom she had married late in life. His step-uncle was a thoughtful man who had seen something of the world while working for the railway, and who had a love of reading and a great reverence for the printed word. In this way young Trudel early discovered the joys of reading. It opened unexpected paths that were to lead him far beyond the confines of the small village that was his home until he left to become a boarder in Trois-Rivières at the age of eight. Although lonely and unhappy at first, this bright little boy began the long road through the clerical schools and colleges of his day, developing a determination to succeed, a passion for learning, and a certain skepticism that shaped his future. He also encountered a number of road blocks that changed the direction of his subsequent life and career as an eminent historian and trail-blazer in the study of New France. Here, however, I will leave readers to discover these things for themselves.

I have had the privilege of meeting Marcel Trudel, now in his eighties, several times: once for a first encounter—a delightful lunch in Montreal at a favourite restaurant of his, another time at his Boucherville home to confer over photographs which he graciously gave permission to use in this English edition of his memoirs. We later met to go over my questions about the first half of the translation manuscript, which he had careful earmarked for our discussion with yellow self-stick paper tabs, a small indication of the painstaking methodology for which he is well known in his research. When I sent him the second half, I made sure to return the courtesy with similar little tabs.

The honours and awards that have come Marcel Trudel's way are many. One has only to type his name into a web browser to find the details. Yet although he has travelled far, he has never forgotten the village of his roots. After being so close to the details of his life and career in the year and a half it took me to translate his memoirs, I was touched recently to read, on the website writeup for the Prix Léon-Gérin awarded him in 2001, that he had founded a scholarship in memory of his adoptive parents, Théodore Baril and Mary Trépanier, to help a young student from his native village, Saint-Narcisse-de-Champlain, go to university. These memoirs are another legacy, the kind of conversational, three-dimensional account of an era that should delight future historians.

A Word of Thanks

I would like to express my appreciation to the Canada Council for the Arts for funding assistance for this translation. Also my thanks go to the author, Marcel Trudel, for generously taking time to discuss aspects of his memoirs, including brief additions and clarifications for readers unfamiliar with the background.

I am grateful to my late husband, John E.C. Brierley, for supplying much of the English terminology connected with Quebec Civil Law, to my son Tim for advice on ancient Greek and Latin material, and my daughter Sarah for her cheerful presence at various times during the preparation of this book.

September 2002

For my granddaughter Catherine

Preface

Montaigne's ridiculous project of depicting himself.
–Pascal

Montaigne's charming plan of depicting himself.
–Voltaire

If it were only necessary to live an extraordinary life in order to write one's memoirs, mine would not keep the reader interested beyond the title page. I have been neither a cardinal nor a prime minister, a member of parliament, nor even an alderman. My career has been spent in teaching and research, far from the well-travelled path. Once or twice I happened to step into the limelight in an attempt to influence public opinion, but I withdrew each time, feeling I'd made a fuss for nothing. It was then that I remembered the words of Pascal, the subject of my dissertation for the *licence ès lettres*: "I have discovered that all human evil comes from this, man's being unable to sit still in a room."

All the same, at seventy I can serve as a living document of twentieth-century Quebec, especially in the years before the Quiet Revolution, and of the education given the adolescent that I once was, this young man's outlook, how he became a historian, the battles he fought, the storms he encountered almost each time he published a book, the sense of some satisfaction in work accomplished and yet an awareness of his weaknesses. I will weigh these things in the balance, fully confident that for once the critic will not be hostile.

Like other memoirs of my generation, mine should teach readers now in their twenties or thirties about a kind of society that has only recently vanished—a society they can barely imagine. I used to tell my young students how I was brought up like someone living in the eighteenth century, how we stayed in our *collège classique*—our secondary boarding school—over the Christmas holidays, how we had to present notes proving we had been to confession, how we had to raise our hats to every cassock we passed in the street, and how I, a layman, had to submit my writings to a religious censor for approval. My students would look at me as though I had just emerged from the caves of Lascaux—and yet, so short a time ago, this society was still with us.

These memoirs might never have seen the light of day had it not been for Pascal-Andrée Rheault, who urged me to write them. With funding from the Canada Council for the Arts, she spent months analyzing my work and the development of my career. There followed hours of conversation, duly recorded, which we planned to publish just as they were. A publisher was found, and then—as often happens in publishing—the project was called off. I put aside the tapes, knowing I could come back to them if they were still of interest, and chose the traditional, chronological form of memoir: *le récit au fil de la plume*. This too is a kind of conversation, but with a reader who has no chance to intervene throughout this long monologue.

1

Born in the Eighteenth Century

"WHAT ARE A HUNDRED YEARS—a thousand years?" asked Bossuet, trembling. What we call the Old Régime or the French Régime, which ended for us French-speaking Canadians in 1760, is scarcely yesterday and almost today.

In my student days, the nuns of Quebec City's Hôtel-Dieu were still singing an annual mass for the Hundred Associates of 1627. Our grandparents knew the grandsons of men who had fought on the Plains of Abraham. Ignace Boucher de Grosbois was born in the days of François de Laval, first bishop of Quebec, and his grandson died in the ninteenth century. Even more amazing is that I myself as a youth, and even in recent years, lived under institutions established during the French Régime. My actions were often influenced by the mentality of that era. The men of my generation are in many ways men of the Old Régime.

Physically speaking, we are indeed men of the Old Régime. You have only to measure us against archeological skeletons like those, dug up recently, of people who wintered over on Île Sainte-Croix in 1604. We bear a family resemblance. Just visit one of those French hamlets from which our ancestors set out three short centuries ago. Their brothers have left a parallel line of descent. It's great fun to discover Trudels, Fortins, and Tremblays that could be our twins. The ancient mould is still turning out the same product. The flaws are the same, too. A family from the Perche region is afflicted with ocular myopathy (the eyelids won't stay open). Family members settle in Canada, the affliction passes from father to son, and we see it today in their progeny along the Lower Saint Lawrence, who must wear *lunettes à béquilles* (literally "glasses with crutches") equipped with supports to keep the eyelids up. I've seen a shoemaker in Kamouraska who relied on a less scientific solution: a plaster stuck to his eyebrow kept each eyelid open all the time, resulting in a constant stare.

Does the Old Régime still survive? We could find the answer by exploring the folklore that survives in songs, tales, and maxims handed down from generation to generation since the earliest days of New France, by a people with an oral tradition that exists quite outside of books. To put it simply, we have only to listen to ourselves speak.

As a schoolchild I said *siau*, like everyone, for *seau*—a bucket. For *poil* I said *poël* as in the old adages: "C'est aujourd'hui la Saint-Michel que tous les ânes changent de *poël*" ("Today is the feast of St. Michael when all the donkeys change their coats"), or "À Noël, les jours allongent d'un *poël*" ("At Christmas, the days get a hair's breadth longer"). We used to say *moé pis toé* for *moi puis toi* (me and you). In the eighteenth century, the names Isabelle and Élisabeth were often interchangeable—a confusion that occurred in my family. Like everyone else, I would say "Je me suis *enfargé*" to express "I got entangled" in something or "mixed up" in some problem (*les enfarges* are hobbles used to keep animals from wandering). If I left with someone, I said "partir *quand et lui*" instead of "partir *avec lui*" and "*mais qu'il* viendra" for "*quand il* viendra" (when he comes). An oft-told story concerns a French-Canadian at the Sorbonne who was required to critique an excerpt from Montaigne and was roundly told off for not mentioning the arcane usage of *quand et* and *mais que*. Since the student used these expressions in his everyday speech, he hadn't bothered to mention them.

And what about the use of the subjunctive past, a legacy of the Old Régime if ever there was one? My country-born father, who left the rural line school at the age of twelve, rejoiced in its use and would roll its hissing endings off his tongue with a sibilant relish that left you almost breathless. Do you remember the raccoon carriage rug made of pelts sewn together that we used to call a *robe de carriole*? Why a *robe* (gown) since it wasn't one? When I taught history, I eventually discovered the explanation: the Amerindians of three centuries ago used to sew eight, ten, or twelve beaver pelts together to make a blanket in which to wrap themselves. The French traders called it a *robe*, hence our *robe de carriole*. What about other reminders of the Old Régime such as *une bonne secousse* for *longtemps* (a long time), *se greyer* for *se préparer* (to prepare), *être paré* for *être prêt* (to be ready)? We say *nous barrons nos portes* as did our ancestors of the Old Régime, when a door was locked by using an actual bar. We *embarquons* (embark) in our cars, even though they don't float, although they are occasionally known to *verser* (tip over) like a canoe. People used to say *une légume*, using the feminine article, because the gender of the word had not been settled; nowadays you hear the expression *grosses légumes*, giving a feminine adjective to what has become a masculine noun.

Our *fèves au lard* (baked beans and pork) aren't a survival from the Old Régime, but a nineteenth-century blessing from the United States. However the French Régime did give us equally nourishing food: *lard* (bacon), the main source of cooking fat of my youth, and dried peas prepared in the soup that earned us our "peasoup" nickname. We also have the indigenous foods that French colonists learned to eat—hare, bear, and moose, which my generation ate and wish they still could. The colonists concocted the *tourtière*, a mixture of *tourte* (the now extinct passenger pigeon) or partridge and hare, with lard. We still have the *tourtière*, greatly shorn of its ancient glory, for it lacks the tourte and partridge. In my family we ate *sagamité*, prepared more hygienically than in the Huronia of the Recollet missionary Gabriel Sagard. For dessert, we ate the same wild strawberries, raspberries, and blueberries, as well as maple syrup and maple sugar, and had dinner at noon and supper at nightfall like our forebears of the Old Régime.

And what about the clothes of that era? Paniers and crinolines survived among us until the twentieth century, although certainly less voluminous. An old aunt of mine kept hers in memory of her wedding. We wore moccasins for snowshoeing, and these *souliers sauvages* (Indian shoes) were used for canoe trips instead of *souliers français* (French shoes), the high-heeled men's footwear that would have punctured the birchbark of our craft. Searching my earliest childhood memories, I can remember that night caps were worn by men as well as women. Men's nightcaps, made famous in Molière's *Le malade imaginaire*, were still worn on winter nights in those rural houses where the fires were only rekindled early in the morning.

In the main, however, it was religious apparel that prolonged the visible sense of the Old Régime. The priests of my youth wore clerical bands hanging from the necks of their cassocks, and these *bavettes* (bibs) were also seen beneath monks' chins. The original nuns' habits in the old orders had to hide their hair, as Bishop Saint-Vallier considered curly hair indecent. Only the parts of the face used for seeing, breathing, and eating were visible. The nineteenth century did bring one change, however. Sartorial vanity led the Ursulines and the Dames de la Congregation to stiffen their wimples and veils with starch. As a result, the good sisters had a little bell-tower rising up from their foreheads, differing from the original habit. I think there must have been a move to restore these historical monuments to their former style, for the little steeples suddenly disappeared.

Many of our past and sometimes present ways of life are legacies of the French Régime. Give anyone who wants to make a whirlwind tour of the St. Lawrence Valley a copy of the map drawn by Jacques-Nicolas Bellin in the first half of the eighteenth century. The basics are all there, from Anticosti Island, Sept-Isles, and the Gaspé Peninsula, to Montreal. The useful place-names on both shores haven't changed. In the Charlevoix region, for example, our tourist can find Tadoussac, Pointe-aux-Alouettes, Baie-des-Rochers, Port-au-Persil, Port-au-Saumon, Cap-à-l'Aigle, and La Malbaie. Using this map, he or she can go up the Richelieu River, stop at Île-aux-Noix, and move on to Lake Champlain, Île Lamothe (now Isle La Motte), Grande-Isle (now Grand Isle in the Hero Islands), and even the little Rivière-au-Sable that has become Ausable Chasm in English. The visitor to the Upper St. Lawrence will reach the region of the Taronteaux Indians (hence Toronto). If the home of the Outaouais (Ottawa) Indians is the visitor's destination, Bellin's map will show the same Rideau River as depicted on current maps.

The territorial divisions of the Old Régime are still with us as well. While the Hundred Associates of 1627-1663 didn't invent the lines or *rangs* of the Canadian seigneurial system, it was they who laid them down for many of our regions. The land granted by seigneurs was divided into long, thin rectangles, generally oriented toward the northwest. Many of them are to be found on both banks of the St. Lawrence. If you stand on a height of land on the Île d'Orléans looking down the island's north slope toward the Beaupré shore, you can see the same geometric quilt that our ancestors observed and that Gédéon de Catalogne drew on his map of 1709. There are also plenty of ancient seigneurial boundaries. A Charlevoix property that I know well still has a fence known as a *trécarré* that separates the former seigneurial domain from the land *en censive*—that is, land granted to the tenants (*censitaires*) under certain conditions. South of the St. Lawrence between Quebec City and Montreal you can still find a boundary marker indicating the end of the old seigneurial lands and the beginning of the Townships of the British Régime, a frontier still known the by old name of *le fronteau*. I was born on a line road called Grand'Ligne. This was the long line drawn from the St. Lawrence into the back country to mark the northwestern boundary of the Jesuit seigneurie of Batiscan. If you look at a Quebec electoral map, you will see ridings in the Assomption-Joliette region that still have the northwest/southeast orientation of the old seigneuries. The same is true of the Lower St. Lawrence, where the borders of the first ridings were drawn along seigneurial boundaries. We are possibly the last to witness this phenomenon. With the rapid urbanization of rural areas, municipal subdivisions are being made according to other strategies and the traces of the seigneurial régime are fast disappearing.

Certain old forms of juridical organization have hung on tenaciously in Quebec. Sometimes it is just a fragment of some institution, rather like a sliver of glass that someone has forgotten to toss out. For example, more than a hundred years after the seigneurial régime was abolished, a number of Quebec residents (in the thousands, according to a 1967 news story) continue to pay *rentes* in virtue of a seventeenth or eighteenth-century seigneurial concession. These payments are now gathered by municipalities, not the seigneurs' descendants. A Laval University colleague who settled in Beaumont went to make his payment, a matter of a few cents, and was handed a receipt with the august wording: "For seigneurial rentes."

We were among the last to use the weights and measures of the Coutume de Paris. Weight was calculated in the old avoirdupois ounces, sixteen-ounce pounds, hundredweights of a hundred pounds, and tons of two thousand pounds. For volume we had the *roquille*, the *demiard*, the *chopine*, the *pinte*, and the *minot*, as well as the *corde* of wood (four by eight feet) that is still in use. Country folk continue to measure length in *perches* (rods), linear *arpents* (still legally accepted), and *lieues* (leagues). With the aid of a ruler applied to my knuckles, I learned that twelve inches equal one foot. Nowadays children learn the metric system—but to the thwack of a ruler, I wonder? We still call a dollar a *piastre,* but this Spanish coin used during the French Régime has been officially extinct since 1851. As for measuring time, when I was an altar boy serving mass for the Ursulines of Trois-Rivières, the nuns recited the office with an hourglass perched on the prayer stool. This was no antiquarian caprice, but a functional means of timekeeping. In law, the thirty years' statutory limitation cited in the Coutume de Paris was still recognized. When it came to measuring someone's worth, a benchmark from the Old Régime was still with us. An old aunt who had only gone to the "little school" on the line road said to me one day, "That fellow's no Croix-de-Saint-Louis," unaware that the French Régime's highest military decoration hadn't been awarded since the British Conquest.

Until a relatively recent change in the Quebec Civil Code, we were the last generation to be married in community of property, exactly as laid down in the Coutume de Paris, where the lucky husband had the privilege of administering the couple's assets without being accountable, except upon separation or death. He was simply asked to manage the family finances wisely, *en bon père de famille*—the expression still used by old notaries and rendered in official English as "a prudent administrator." Under the Coutume a woman was a perpetual minor. Despite abundant provisions for her protection, she was restricted to her minority status and unable to act as a witness before a notary. Before marriage, her father guaranteed her a *dot* and her husband pledged her a dower or "widow's portion." Once married, she was under the authority of her husband, who was described as "lord and master" of the community. In Bishop Saint-Vallier's *Catéchisme du Diocèse de Québec* (Paris, 1702) and *Rituel du Diocèse de Québec* (Paris, 1703), all the husband was asked to do for his wife was to love her (not so bad at that!), whereas the wives were asked—and I quote—"to be submissive in everything to their husbands as to God. Because the husband is the leader of the wife as Jesus Christ is the leader of the Church, she must fear & respect him." This situation remained unchanged right up to our own day. Until very recently, a woman automatically married under the regime of community of property unless a marriage contract was drawn up specifically making the wife "separate as to property." Assured of a *dot* by her father and a widow's portion by her husband, most women remained under their husband's tutelage. If a child needed an emergency operation, it was the father who gave his consent, not the mother. Quebec law was changed only a few years ago, obliging the cherished husband to share some of his privileges.

In one respect modern women have had to catch up with those of the Old Régime. It was customary for women to sign their maiden names (which remained their legal names then as now), even after marriage. Nineteenth-century women, still subject to their husbands as the Church is to Christ, began using their married names. This habit became so entrenched that even in recent times women who wanted to use their maiden names after marriage encountered all sorts of problems.

Despite the husband's traditional legal power over his wife, I witnessed the age of the matriarch in my youth. It may have begun before 1665, but this was the year in which Bishop Laval assigned the mother a religious role as part of the Confrérie de la Sainte-Famille (Brotherhood of the Holy Family).

She was given responsibility for winning over her husband to God, raising the children in the fear of the Lord, teaching them their prayers, and making sure they said them every day. The performance of these tasks eventually established a spiritual matriarchy, and until my generation religious education was the mother's domain. We have only to look at our literature on this topic to observe the phenomenon, and especially the attitude that gave the highest consideration to a priest's mother, not his father. I can remember ordination banquets where the mother received all the credit for her son's vocation. The speechmakers forgot to address their eloquence to the poor father, relegated to the role of mere breadwinner. This matriarchy extended to things material, a situation that arose under the French Régime. The fur-trading economy took the man from home and hearth, and the woman filled his shoes. For a good part of the year she took charge of the farm. When a lumber economy replaced the fur trade, the woman retained her role as deputy-in-chief. I've seen farms where, to all intents and purposes, the husband only came home occasionally, rather more annoyed than otherwise at having to leave the lumber camps or the *drave* (the log drive) for an occupation that didn't pay. The master was in fact the woman, and she reigned over the rural family for three centuries.

As we used to say, "When you marry, you must make a will." I did this like everyone else, and listened as the notary read the following: "Firstly, I give my soul to God and my body to the earth." This was what Bishop Saint-Vallier recommended in 1703. Indeed, with regard to my body I had no choice but to be buried. It is only in the last few years that Roman Catholics in Quebec could be cremated or could choose to leave their remains to colleagues in the faculty of medicine for teaching purposes.

After death the inheritance had to be shared. Sometime in the 1980s I was explaining to my young historians the text of a 1662 *partage de succession*, referred to in English as a partition of succession. This one involved a house owned "in indivision," which meant it was owned jointly by several heirs. For example, one would get a quarter of the ground floor, a quarter of the cellar, a quarter of the attic, and a quarter of the courtyard. The others would receive the same. A similar case occurred in my own family. A young man was considering marriage. His mother declared before a notary that the future husband would possess a bedroom in her house, but that in this room half the clothes closet would belong to his sister, who would therefore have free access to the nuptial chamber. The future bride (my cousin) refused to live in such public quarters and preferred to let the whole matter drop.

Another survival of the old legal framework was the *donation* of parents to one of their children. The old age pension had not been established then, and the old folk had no choice but to give themselves and their property away in return for bed and board for life—something they did until quite recently, following the same ritual and often under the same conditions as in the Old Régime. A deed of gift *inter vivos* of 1750 could, with minimum changes, be dated 1950. It dealt with the same social problem, in any case. The difficulty experienced by mother-in-law and daughter-in-law in 1950 was no different from that over which a royal judge in Quebec City might have ruminated two centuries earlier in New France.

The inveterate habit of bartering in rural areas—that is, of paying for consumer goods with other consumer goods or hours of labour—can be traced back to the French Régime. Interest on a mortgage was often paid in kind: merchants supplied their wares in return for potatoes, cords of wood, or maple sugar. The closed economy of the French Régime has only just disappeared. I knew a family that practised subsistence farming in the strictest sense. They made everything, from bread to the children's shoes. When, on rare occasions, they needed something from the village shop or had to pay for schooling, the father took along produce to sell rather than his wallet. On New Year's Day, however, the parents departed munificently from the rule and bought oranges for the children. This closed economy was the result of determined effort rather than natural development, but it had been practised without a break from one generation to another.

In our parish we had a survival of the French Régime's military organization. This was the militia captain. As in New France, the captain organized volunteer military exercises on Sundays. We learned to shoot, to present arms, and march in step. When conscription came into effect in 1942 the same thing happened as in 1760: the militiamen were no longer there to serve His Majesty! I can't tell you how long our parish had possessed a militia captain. The title, attached to one family, became its last name, so that when speaking of the individual we never used either his given or family name. It was always Monsieur Capitaine, or Madame Capitaine when speaking of his wife. And of course we went raspberry picking with "the little Capitaines."

Above all, however, it was through religion that the man of my generation seemed like one of the Old Régime. In the French Régime, one had to be a practising Catholic to exist in civil society. Until recently, baptism was still the only way to acquire civil status after birth for Catholics in Quebec. Only a priest could perform the ceremony and testify to the baby's entry into civil society with a baptismal certificate (not a birth certificate). When the French-Canadian teenager registered for the first time at a classical college, his application had to include his baptismal certificate. When he wanted to marry the woman of his choice, he was obliged to take part in another religious act: marriage before a priest. In Quebec Civil Law, as in the Coutume de Paris, marriage was a religious act with civil consequences, since the marriage contract didn't take effect until after the religious ceremony. Marrying, like being born, required the priest's signature for entry into the registry of civil status. Ecclesiastical law decreed that the marriage could only be dissolved by the death of one of the partners, and this, until recently, was the sole ending accepted by the Coutume de Paris and Quebec Civil Law.

Having entered civil society by means of a religious act, there were only two ways for a Catholic to leave it (apart from civil death as punishment for an infamous crime like murder). Either you joined a religious order, which in certain cases meant civil death (hence the expression *dire adieu au monde*) or you were buried with due solemnity by a priest who then signed a burial certificate. This was the recognized proof of death and it took the place of the official death certificate common in other jurisdictions. Change came only during the Quiet Revolution of the 1960s, after which birth, marriage, and death certificates issued by civil authorities became the official confirmation of these three landmarks of civil status.

Considering the role of religion in civil status, it is no surprise to find that the parish church had remained the social centre of the community since the Old Régime. In the early days of radio my father set his watch, not by the official time signal, but by the verger ringing the Angelus. We never knew who was right—the radio or the verger! Church bells told the whole community that a baptism or wedding was in progress, that the curé was bringing Holy Communion to a sick person, that someone had just died, or that a fire had broken out. In my youth the parishioners' association had to meet in the church and nowhere else. Political gatherings could only take place around *le husting*, a covered platform on church property. I can still remember the *criée des bancs*, with parishioners bidding competitively for pews in their anxiety to acquire prestige, just as their forebears had done under the French Régime. We looked up far more to the churchwardens whom we saw every week than to the municipal councillors. The wardens sat enthroned upon their bench on Sundays in full view of the assembled parishioners, whereas the mayor and councillors were lost in the congregation. The advent of radio, television, and public halls soon shifted Quebec society from its traditional parish-focused outlook, and the churchwardens lost their prestige to municipal politicians.

Certain special dates from the old church calendar have survived. One of these, Saint-Jean-Baptiste Day, June 24, was considered the official start of summer when I was young. No one was allowed to swim before then. Saint-Pierre Day, June 29, was an important date for gardeners. Saint-Michel Day, September 29, was the day when curés were replaced, and All Saints' Day, November 1, was the day for settling accounts.

Sunday was the most important day of the week, and as of old it was strictly observed as a day of rest. Since the entire parish gathered on that day, you had to wear your good clothes, hence the expression "Sunday best." You also had to attend high mass and, later in the afternoon, vespers. According to Bishop Saint-Vallier, attendance at vespers was obligatory because of the Church's "dominical" commandment. As a child I went to vespers regularly. My parents spoke disparagingly of the few villagers who lingered in their porch rocking-chairs instead of attending the afternoon service. At my classical college, even non-boarders went to vespers as a matter of course.

Christmas was a strictly religious holiday. Although we had a *réveillon* on Christmas eve, there were no Christmas trees inside or outside. At most there was a *crèche*—a manger scene with the Holy Family. We left out shoes (*petits sabots de Noël*) or stockings that were duly filled with candy, but this was through the kind offices of Saint Nicholas, not today's secular Santa. As in the eighteenth century, presents were exchanged on New Year's Day and we called them *étrennes*. I don't think the traditional paternal New Year's blessing came to us from the Old Régime. I haven't found it referred to in any source. Saint-Vallier's *Rituel* doesn't mention it, although it lists fifty-seven blessings (even one for animals with cattle plague and another for driving out evil spirits from people "possessed.") However the *gâteau des Rois* or Epiphany cake is an Old Régime tradition. We didn't celebrate Halloween, a festival brought here by the British, but there was Mardi Gras on the eve of Lent, as in the Old Régime. We would dress up in typical costumes and run about from house to house indulging in various bits of tomfoolery. Lent was no longer the forty meatless days of an earlier era, although the number of daily meals allowed remained the same. We ate one full meal a day plus a little meal known in Saint-Vallier's day as a *collation*. Beginning at the end of the nineteenth century, we had the right to "a few mouthfuls of bread," as described in the *Discipline du diocèse de Québec*. In our day this amounted to two ounces. In the spring *Quatre-Temps* (special seasonal fasting days), when my parents would not have wanted to miss Sunday mass, farmers used to bring a bowl of seed grain to be blessed according to the old ritual. Going home from mass, I saw a farmer mix this seed into his larger store so that all of it would share in the blessing.

Part of this seed would return to the Church through the custom of paying the *dîme* or tithe. For my generation this was another familiar religious institution dating from the French Régime. The Church introduced it into New France in 1663, and the French government approved this move in 1667, setting the rate at one-twenty-sixth of the harvest. Even today, Catholic farmers must pay the tithe. Payment was a moral duty, but recalcitrant parishioners could be forced to comply by the civil courts. Come fall, I have seen my uncles pass by, their carts heaped with grain destined for the curé's barn. However, even in those days this wasn't really appropriate for our society. Villagers didn't harvest crops, and for them the tithe was replaced with a poll tax equalling a day's wages. This created an unfair situation. My father paid only a day's wages while my uncles delivered one-twenty-sixth of their grain harvest. Another awkward aspect of the tithe was that curés were obliged to become grain merchants. In very much the same way, early Canadian Jesuits had to sell the furs given to their mission.

Strictly speaking, my generation received the religious training of the French Régime. When my parents were about twelve, they attended catechism classes in preparation for their first Holy Communion. This ceremony took place at what was termed "the age of discretion," which according to Saint-Vallier "usually began no sooner than the age of ten and no later than fourteen." Once they had passed their catechism examinations, schooling was over and they were on the labour market.

Saint-Vallier's *Catéchisme* was replaced in the nineteenth century, but the content remained unchanged. The questions and answers that we learned were often those of 1702, word for word:

"Who created us and brought us into this world?"

"God."

"Why did he bring us into this world?

"To know, love, and serve Him, and in this way to acquire eternal life."

"What is God?"

"God is the Creator of Heaven and Earth, and the Lord of all things."

Parts of my childhood catechism had long been obsolete. I'm not speaking here of dogma, but of Church rules. In the Old Régime, the Church forbad meat not only on Friday, but Saturday as well. An omelette with bacon on Saturday would have been a mortal sin. This changed in 1844, when the archbishop of Quebec responded to the pressure of public opinion and "regretfully" allowed Catholics to eat meat on Saturday. Even so, it seems laws are written in stone and take ages to wear away. As a child I learned the saying, *Vendredi, chair ne mangeras, ni le samedi mêmement* ("No meat on Friday nor on Saturday"). Nobody ever explained to me why we shouldn't have meat on Saturday when we regularly ate sausages on that day.

As in the Old Régime, we had to know a certain number of prayers in Latin, the language of the Church. These daily prayers are given in Saint-Vallier's *Catéchisme*: the graces to be said before and after meals, the *Pater*, *Ave Maria*, *Credo*, *Confiteor*, and even some litanies. In the families of my childhood there was always someone who could recite Latin prayers and litanies. As these were always said in the kitchen, what was called "kitchen Latin" was in the right place. Incidentally, these family prayers were just as long as those of Saint-Vallier's time.

Marriage had its place in this world of devotion. According to Saint-Vallier, marriage was ordained "not for pleasure but for the procreation of children." The married state ought first to "give a new degree of sanctity" to the relationship and then "communicate a spirit of chastity." The rigid morality surrounding what was coldly referred to as "conjugal duty" affected our parents and even ourselves, and was as exacting as it had been under the French Régime. As late as 1938 a Quebec City priest and doctor of theology published a "supplement to the official catechism" entitled *Catachèse des 6e & 9e commandements de Dieu*. Certain parts of the adult human body were, he wrote, "dangerous to look at or touch," and he therefore divided the body into the following categories: decent (the face, hands, and feet), less decent (the chest, back, thighs, and arms), and indecent (sexual or genital organs and the neighbouring parts of the thighs). The good abbé forgot the head, neck, and legs, an omission that might cause serious concern to the more scrupulous among us.

With the body thus carved up for moral purposes, we can understand why dancing was frowned upon, especially between two people of the opposite sex. Saint-Vallier weighed in heavily on this subject in a pastoral letter of 1691. If you look at the 1879 edition of the *Discipline du diocèse de Québec* you can read, under "Dancing," a long diatribe against mixed dancing attributed to "Saint-Vallier, 1691." My parents were therefore forbidden to dance together by this two-hundred-year-old commandment. The shadow cast by the olden-day bishop even affected me in Quebec City in 1940, when dancing was still forbidden by the Church. Responding to episcopal pressure, the city council had banned dancing within the city limits, so we had to go to the suburbs to dance.

The theatre fell under a similar shadow. Bishop Saint-Vallier divided comedies into two groups—those that were "by nature absolutely bad and criminal in themselves," and others "that were not absolutely bad in themselves." He explicitly denounced *Tartuffe* in a pastoral letter of 1694, a condemnation repeated word for word in the 1859 edition of the *Discipline*. We performed many Molière comedies at college, but never, absolutely never *Tartuffe*! It is fairly significant that this play was only performed in French Canada for the first time in 1952, nearly three centuries after Molière wrote it.

Death permeated the religion of the French Régime. We read in Saint-Vallier's *Catéchisme* that after evening prayers "one must try to arrange oneself in bed in the manner of a person about to be buried." My parents had a little nineteenth-century Canadian work among their books of devotion, and in it I found the same advice: "When you retire, consider the bed as your coffin, the sheets as your shroud, and sleep as the image of your death." How often the same precaution was preached to us at college, constantly reminding us that we might not live to see the morrow—a thought that gave us many a sleepless night. My generation heard the terrible sermons on death preached on November 2, All Soul's Day, and at the end of our retreats. We lived with death.

For centuries we observed the burial rites of the French Regime. Since embalming was the privilege of the wealthy, the common people of the Old Régime went to the grave as nature made them. Those who died during the summer had to be buried the next day—sometimes on the same day. In winter the problem didn't arise. The body was dressed in brand-new clothing, including a fine new pair of ankle boots, and laid out on planks supported by trestles, hence the expression *exposer sur les planches*. A veil covered the face, for only priests and members of religious orders, according to Saint-Vallier, had the right to have their faces uncovered in death. The room in which the body was laid out was entirely hung in black. I have seen this rite as a young child: it served as a lesson to those who loved life.

What lay behind all this was the great preoccupation of the Old Régime and my generation with eternal salvation. You have to remember the all-embracing presence of religion in the classroom. Prayers, the rosary, and pious readings took up time that nowadays would normally be devoted to the regular program. Classes were frequently interrupted to take us to chapel or church. October was rosary month, November the month of the dead, December brought the novena of Saint-François-Xavier, March was the month of Saint-Joseph, May the month of Sainte-Marie, June the month of the Sacred Heart—not to mention special observances on the first Friday of each month. This preoccupation with eternal salvation was especially evident in the last will and testament of the French Régime. Making a will was first and foremost a religious act, as exemplified by its statement of fidelity to the Roman Catholic Church, charitable bequests, and numerous invocations. Our main concern before dying was to make sure of the soul's salvation. It had been drummed into us in our youth by such biblical aphorisms as "For what is a man profited if he shall gain the whole world and lose his own soul?" (although the desire to gain the whole world didn't often loom large). We were also warned in the celebrated canticle to "Ponder this well: without salvation there is no help for you."

In our classical college we were very close to the French Régime in many ways. We rose at five in the morning and were allowed to sleep in an extra half hour on holidays, just like students in the seventeenth-century Quebec Seminary established by Bishop Laval. Our uniform—an abridged version of the old-fashioned cassock worn by students in the days of the seminary's founder—included a buttoned, calf-length coat, tied at the waist with a woollen sash like those worn by priests.

Laval considered recreation a serious matter, and so it was for us. Recreation time began and ended in prayer. My parents' little book of devotion warned me that "to play deliberately and uniquely for pleasure and amusement amounts to sensuality." This mentality is aptly illustrated by the ancient adage, its source unknown to me, reminding us that "Time to play is not time for amusement." Those who preferred to walk while philosophizing were rather frowned upon, and we bore in mind the stern jingle, "Rarely alone, never two, always three."

In teaching establishments, as with Bishop Saint-Vallier's dances, boys and girls were kept strictly apart—and in strictly separate buildings. My school days were long past before the first woman appeared on the staff of a classical college. The matter was the subject of exhaustive discussion. The object of this deliberation was, believe it or not, a staff nurse for the boys! In the colleges of my day, no woman ever taught boys, no man taught girls. Such were the directives set forth in 1859 by the *Discipline du diocèse de Québec*, which hearkened back to at least 1700 and Saint-Vallier's rules. When we put on a play the most willowy boys with as yet unbroken voices were dressed up as luscious little women, and morality was thus preserved.

This cloistering mentality was carried even further. Some colleges accepted boarders only. Day pupils were allowed to attend if some illness made it necessary for them to live at home, but they weren't permitted to play with the boarders. I knew of one historic convent in Quebec City where even the little weekly boarders were kept separate from the full boarders. The little girls were all from the same social background, sometimes even from neighbouring families. Once inside the convent, however, all contact was strictly forbidden in order to ward off any influence from the outside world. This was exactly the spirit governing education in eighteenth-century Quebec.

During the French Régime, parishioners who made their annual confession outside their home parish had to provide their own curé with a certificate signed by the confessor. In my college the same rule applied, although we needed confession vouchers not once a year, but twice a month.

Forgiveness for all sins didn't necessarily apply to students of classical colleges, for if sin called for divine mercy, it also called for exemplary punishment. Under the French Régime, a public fault called for public penance. This is why parishioners could be seen on their knees at the church door during high mass, a custom that continued into the early nineteenth century. The expression *se tenir sous la cloche* (literally, stay under the bell) describes this performance of public penance. The classical colleges that I attended subscribed to the same principle. For a public fault, the guilty party, whether in the first or last year of his baccalauréat, had to kneel before the assembled students or sometimes listen to the public announcement that he had been expelled like a black sheep. Indeed, "showing someone the college door" was a highly popular remedy. For less serious cases there was the time-honoured practice of "striking" persuasion. The whip was used in the Jesuit college of the French Régime. The Jesuit superior Jérôme Lalemant noted in his *Journal* that two pupils (from noble families) were whipped for having disobeyed an order during a quarrel over who had precedence, the colony's governor or the bishop. Corporal punishment was considered a salutary lesson—at least for whoever was on the receiving end. It was an accepted form of discipline in my elementary school, where the nun who taught us always kept a strap tucked in her bag. The principal of my classical college wielded a stout cane.

During the French Régime and for a long time under British rule, Quebec Seminary pupils didn't go home for the summer holidays. They passed the summer months on a farm belonging to the seminary, protected from evil by a set of rules that governed the entire day's activities. One or two study hours were set aside each day for homework. In my time we spent Christmas and Easter at our classical college and had just begun to be allowed home for a monthly day off, on condition that we returned the same day. Boarders today are *obliged* to go home for the entire weekend! We still had homework for the holidays, but this custom was already on its way out. Almost the only thing left was a research project in the natural sciences (referred to as "the little sciences"), with a report to be given when school reopened in September.

When it comes to the subjects I was taught, I am the most fortunate of men. My generation was still governed by the *ratio studiorum* of the Old Régime, based on Greek and Latin studies. We had to learn hundreds of lines of Latin and Greek poetry. The goal of this education was to produce the upright man (*l'honnête homme*) by giving us a well-balanced range of knowledge. The program was sustained by the Cartesian spirit and classical theory (the sacred rules of the three unities in theatre and the division of all discourse into three parts). Difficult mental gymnastics were the order of the day in the *ratio studiorum*. All subjects were obligatory: there was no picking and choosing. Since we had spent several years learning Latin, we studied philosophy in this language, our textbook being a three-volume Latin work.

While at college we were familiar with the public exercises of the Old Régime. These exercises are mentioned in the *Journal des Jesuites* in connection with young Louis Jolliet, who in 1666 gave a speech on the problems of philosophy. Under British rule, seminary students continued the custom, speaking before a public audience in the presence of the colony's governor. These public exercises lasted for three days, to the glory or shame of the students' families. In my time they lasted only a day and were held on March 7, the feast-day of St. Thomas Aquinas. Only members of the college were present. The exercises consisted of a competition involving Latin and Greek declensions, class competitions on the subject of Greek verbs ending in *μι*, recitations of Latin and French poetry, and rhetorical discourse. The winners retired with honour while the ignoramuses were greeted with hoots of laughter. You had to be a good sport.

The *ratio studiorum* gave us a training that would be unthinkable today. We learned a strict code of dress and behaviour. In class, for example, teachers always addressed students as *monsieur*, *mademoiselle*, or *vous* (instead of the familiar form *tu*).

From this hodge-podge of survivals from the Old Régime, certain general traits emerge. They enable me to recognize attitudes in my generation that date from the seventeenth and eighteenth centuries. Society was then based on a hierarchy that must be respected, otherwise its very existence would be compromised. For example, everyone's title had to be acknowledged and shown due respect. The higher your social rank, the more privileges you had, but at the same time—for this was a balanced society—the more you had to give in return. I encountered this concern for hierarchical classification in both elementary and secondary school. We were ranked according to precise marks calculated to a tenth of a point. Much was made of the student who placed first—provided his behaviour was beyond reproach. He wore a gold medal on his lapel showing that he was more worthy of merit than others, for if merit there was, it must be recognized. And since one student came first, there must be one who came last, and this unfortunate was proclaimed as such in public and dubbed "tail of the class," for lack of merit brought scorn.

The professions were subject to the same spirit of classification. My generation considered some professions more noble than others. You were esteemed in proportion to how worthy a profession you had followed, not for the fees you might earn from it. Why did the French-Canadian historians who preceded us deal so little with trade, or when they did, why did they display so little understanding of the subject? For the simple reason that under the Old Régime, as in my own day, a merchant was merely a salesman and his business a *vile* or vulgar operation.

Another indication of this classifying mentality was the way everything, especially authority, came from on high. Authority was automatically invested with *la grâce d'étât,* a state of almost divine omnipotence, to the point where any decision by our pastors and masters was not only unassailable but undeniably for our own good. Only wrongheaded people would criticize authority. In fact there were two capital crimes that merited expulsion: criticism of authority and scandalous behaviour. Authority was exercised by the person in charge. Subordinates had no share in making decisions. Under Governor Vaudreuil, for instance, anyone acting as spokesman for a group with a grievance was considered a mutineer, and soldiers would be sent to arrest him. Under Governor Frontenac, anyone who handed around a petition for signatures supporting some request without first asking permission was committing a crime. It was an unwritten rule that everyone spoke for himself and no one spoke for all. I was familiar with this mentality while in classical college and even in university where, before we formed a teachers' association, we went and asked for the rector's permission like good little children.

This authoritarian stance was tempered with paternalism. Under the Old Régime and in my time, anyone in authority was considered a father. He carried out his responsibilities *en bon père de famille* and was strict but fair, as mythical fathers are supposed to be. This paternalism existed at all levels of society from the highest echelons, whether religious or secular, down to parish or college life. We lived through the long and arbitrary reign of Premier Duplessis. His régime lasted so long because it suited our traditional outlook perfectly.

The man of my generation was therefore born and brought up in an extended version of the Old Régime. Suddenly, without warning, he found himself in another kind of society—a process that took place in the 1960s with Quebec's Quiet Revolution. In 1940, however, when my little backwater was scandalized at the sight of an American priest taking off his cassock to play tennis, who would have foreseen that all cassocks would disappear overnight from our society? Who would have imagined nuns in pants and even miniskirts? Over the last thirty years, the man of my generation has had to adapt to a series of profound changes with lightning rapidity. No generation, it seems to me, has undergone so many shocks since the birth of New France, when the first colonists came to settle the St. Lawrence Valley. We have lived in two worlds—the world of today and the world of the Old Régime. In some measure this explains our actions.

2

A Family is Sold Up

Everyone has his family drama. I experienced mine at the age of five, unaware that it was in fact a drama.

My father, Hermyle Trudel (people said "Émile"), was a carpenter or more precisely a cart-maker in Saint-Narcisse-de-Champlain, then a small village inland from Trois-Rivières. He built sleighs and carts known as four-wheelers. I can see myself as a very young child in his huge workshop, scattered with bits of wood, sawdust, and paint pots. I'm at floor-level, as though not yet able to walk.

We lived in the village on the Rang de la Grand'Ligne—the Great Line Road that ran along the boundary of the old Batiscan seigneurie. The house where I lived until I was four looked like all the others, a square, two-storey building with a pitched roof and a summer kitchen extending out back. On the ground floor to the right of the front door was a parlour. I have no memory of this room, perhaps because I never went into it. We only used it in the summer on rare occasions such as the curé's annual visit. In winter it was used as a cold storage pantry. Behind the parlour, on the same side of the house, was my parents' bedroom. The children probably didn't go into it much either, for my only memory of it is a tin box containing pennies that stood on what seemed to me a very tall chest of drawers. The other half of the ground floor contained the winter kitchen. Was the upstairs divided into bedrooms? In my mind's eye I see no more than this.

My mother Antoinette Cossette was the great-granddaughter of the founder of Saint-Narcisse, and I was the eighth of eleven children, two of whom died before I was born. Eleven wasn't an unusual number in the days when families of twelve or more children were common. It was said that a mother hadn't fulfilled her duty unless she'd had "her dozen." I was born on

May 29, 1917—dying, so I've been told. For a long while I was nothing but a skeleton with a swollen belly laid on a cushion. People remarked that this baby hadn't even the strength to cry. "He's dead," one would say; "No, he's still breathing," another would counter; or "This time it's over," and "*Tiens*, it looks like he's coming to life again!" The baby did indeed come to life again, and for good this time. Since then I haven't passed a single night in hospital.

Despite my frequent efforts to remember a previous existence (I take a great interest in reincarnation), I have only vague memories of my early childhood.

My father's collection of beehives behind the house is fairly clear to me. He would sometimes work there, wearing a large hat with a protective veil over his face. He used a smoker, a kind of bellows filled with smoke to drive off the bees.

I see myself on a sunny day, standing near the kitchen woodbox and therefore the stove. My mother is feeding me mouthfuls of bread dipped in gravy and making sure I don't wander off, for fear I'll dirty the kitchen floor. This is my most distant memory of my mother. Since I could walk but wasn't as tall as the woodbox, I must have been only one or two years old.

And what is my earliest recollection, drawn from the receding folds of memory? I am crawling on the kitchen floor and I can see two big ankle-boots with spurs. I have always thought I saw a World War I cavalryman, but only up to the ankles. I have been told that no soldier ever came to the house. Nevertheless, born in 1917 and crawling, I can still see those cavalry boots.

We left this house in the summer of 1921, when I was four. My only memory of this move is of being in the summer kitchen, of watching the linoleum being lifted, and of the cat, who had to be stopped from running away. Why did we move? A lumber contractor, Jos.-Noé Veillette, had promised my father an important job in the Témiscaming logging camps. Both house and workshop were sold. While waiting to find a permanent home, my parents rented something outside the village, but still on the Rang de la Grand'Ligne. The house was part of a deserted farm. It was two or three *arpents* from the neighbours and resembled the one we'd just left, except that it had no summer kitchen out back. There was room enough for the nine children. On hot, sunny days we ate beneath an arbour in the vegetable patch, near my father's bees. I remember an autumn, a winter, and a summer in this house.

My mother, who hadn't really recovered from the birth of her last child, began to weaken during the winter of 1921-1922. To give her some relief, I was sent to the line road school with my brothers and sisters, a kilometre or two from the house. Being too young at four and a half to follow the regular curriculum, I found myself in what we would now call daycare—or better still, kindergarten. The schoolmistress, who taught everything from the first to the sixth grade, sat me down on her platform and tried to keep me occupied. My only memory of this first school year is of myself sitting on the platform step in front of a nebulous group of "big people" who must have simply been the schoolchildren, ranging from in age from six to twelve.

It was at the end of the following summer, in 1922, that our family drama took place, brought on by my mother's death on September 16 at the age of thirty-nine.

The death of a mother has often been described in literature. The child, however, doesn't understand what is happening or the significance of the event. He sees it, registers it, and forgets it. The adult looks back, seeks, speculates, and dramatizes. What could I, a child of five, comprehend about this death? All I remember is an unusual atmosphere of calm in the house. I see someone coming out of my parents' room, motioning me to stay quiet. Then, on the film of memory, I see again my mother laid out in the parlour. There she lies, on the planks supported by trestles, dressed in her brown lay cowl of the Third Order (a phenomenon then observed in all its strictness), her face covered with a white veil. Someone comes and lifts the veil, looks at the face, and goes away. When it was time for the funeral, the body was placed in a plain wooden coffin and lifted onto a horse-drawn hearse. We followed on foot.

I saw my mother again two years later. The old cemetery where she had been buried, between the church and the road, had become overcrowded. The curé had opened another burial ground outside the village on land given by an uncle of mine, and the bodies had to be exhumed. The man who had become my adoptive father took me to the ceremony. Curious onlookers crowded around when my mother's coffin was opened, making it impossible for me to see. My adoptive father lifted me up as high as he could. "Look, that's your mother," he said. I saw a skull and some bones. People are usually horrified when I tell them about this encounter. I didn't suffer the shock most would expect, however, for I was already familiar with the idea of death and had been taught in school that the body decomposes. For a child everything is simple and is accepted as a matter of course.

Normally, while waiting for their widowed father to remarry, the big sisters would have taken their mother's place and looked after the family. It was at this point that our family drama intervened. Either the Veillette project came to nothing, or possibly my mother's death prevented my father from leaving for Témiscaming, and since he was now without work or a workshop, he wanted to find a job in Montreal. I don't know if he even considered moving there with nine children, the youngest only a year old. Perhaps there was something else that we children weren't told. In any case, the solution was found: liquidate the family, just like a bankrupt business.

Relatives crowded into the house after the funeral service. I seem to see myself wandering through this silent gathering—for there was no playing. Then it was time for the family council, the assembly that acted in the absence or incompetence of a father or mother and that I had heard talked about so often in my childhood, always in a tone of reverential fear. I can't recall faces as such. Of course my father was present and, so I was told, my uncles and aunts, some from distant parishes. And there were us children who had to be placed. We were, in order of age, Théophane, seventeen, Isabelle, fourteen, Conrad, twelve, Ruth, ten, Marceau, nine, Lucille, seven, myself, five, Paule, three, and one-year-old Julienne.

For the most part, as I've been told, there was no difficulty in distributing the children. Théophane was studying for the priesthood at the Trois-Rivières Seminary and Isabelle was about to enter a convent to become a nun, so they only needed a place to stay for the holidays. Grandfather Cossette, who worked a fine farm with his son-in-law Doucet, took them in. Aunt Victoria, Cloutier's wife, had only one boy to help with the farming, so she was given Conrad. Aunt Angélina, married to the carpenter Joseph Cossette, had only an adopted son, so she took Ruth. Uncle Joseph Mongrain was a well-to-do farmer with no boy at all, so he took Marceau, and as his house was large and he prided himself on doing more than anyone else, he took baby Julienne as well and went home to Saint-Stanislas with two extra children in his buggy. Uncle Wilbrod Trudel, a farmer in Sainte-Geneviève-de-Batiscan who got *rentes* from his neighbours like a seigneur, already had four daughters and three sons, including a two-year-old boy. He wanted to contribute to the cause, nevertheless, and so left with Lucille.

The difficulty arose when the moment came to decide the fate of Paule and myself. Until then the adoptions hadn't necessarily been made according to the responsibilities of godmothers or godfathers. It seems that at first, in my case, this status served as the basis for discussion. Since I was the godson of Uncle Ernest Trudel, I should have gone to live with him. He was a merchant in Saint-Roch-de-Mékinac and supplied goods to the logging camps in the Upper St. Maurice Valley. However, this uncle already had five boys as well as a daughter. He therefore wanted a girl. The widow of my Great-uncle Théophile Cossette, Great-aunt Mary Trépanier, had an adopted daughter of twelve and wanted to adopt another girl. They could both sleep in the same room and the younger would use the hand-me-downs of the elder. If Paule went home with Uncle Ernest Trudel, that would leave only myself, a five-year-old boy. Now it happened that there was no spare room in Aunt Mary's house, and moreover, without an older boy to provide hand-me-downs she would have to buy new clothes every year. Uncle Ernest won the day, however, refusing to take his godson and going off with Paule, Aunt Mary's god-daughter. In the end, Aunt Mary agreed somewhat grudgingly to adopt Uncle Ernest's godson.

That same day, without fully understanding what was happening (and perhaps without trying to), I went to live in the village. I don't remember feeling any sadness on leaving. It is adults who have such regrets. My brothers and sisters too set off in their various directions, each going toward a new lot in life. Our father moved to Montreal, the house on the Rang de la Grand'Ligne became deserted once more, and the family of Hermyle Trudel was broken up.

After this I was only to see my father on rare occasions. He visited my Grandfather Trudel at Christmas several times, and there he could meet the children who didn't live too far away. He only came to my new home once, in June 1930, when there was a family party in the village school to celebrate Théophane's entry into the priesthood. This was the first time the children had all been together after the eight-year diaspora, and it was the last. After this I didn't see my father, who had remarried, until I visited Montreal briefly six years later. The following year I attended his funeral.

Because of the differences in their upbringing and careers, the brothers and sisters were to become strangers to one another. I didn't see my brother Conrad, who settled in Windsor, Ontario, near Detroit, for forty-five years. We wrote each other once or twice, and he died not long ago. My brother Marceau and my sisters Lucille and Paule were in Montreal, which I often passed through and where I now live. I saw Paule a good thirty-five or thirty-eight years ago, and Lucille some fifty years ago. Although I was very fond of my brother Marceau, I didn't see him for forty-five years. I always told myself

I would visit him and was even in his neighbourhood, but as we had had such different educations (he was a labourer), I was afraid of overwhelming him with my academic way of speaking and the material advantages of my life. I always put the visit off. Then I learned, a year after the fact, that he had died. He was the most unlucky of us all in the family council's distribution of the children in 1922. He wasn't able to stay with Uncle Mongrain for long, and a neighbour took him in. For a time we were together in Trois-Rivières at the Jardin de l'Enfance. A scout for the Brothers of Saint-Gabriel conscripted him. Marceau had a very troubled juvenate and later took refuge with Aunt Victoria in Saint-Narcisse. Later again, he and Conrad left to find jobs in Montreal where, it seems, he was at last happy.

My relations with my other brothers and sisters ended in the sixties. The oldest, Théophane, a parish priest, tried to bring the family together, but he did not approve of my role in the Mouvement laïque de langue française nor my divorce followed by a civil marriage. However, he was kind enough to mention me in his will. My true sister—my only sister now—is my adopted sister. What about blood being thicker than water, you may ask? A pipe dream, I feel. Take a child out of his environment, give him a different education from his brothers and sisters, and you will find that the family to which he responds with all his being is the one of which he has become a part. His *natural* ties are with the people among whom he has grown up and known the sorrows and joys of childhood, adolescence, and maturity.

As a grown man, I sometimes regret having been cut off from my biological family—but it is an adult regret. As a child, I gradually became attached to my new environment. There I had food, lodging, and a sense of well-being, as though what had happened was just as it should be. When I said "my father," I meant my adoptive father and not the other one, even though the latter was still alive. When people called me an orphan, I thought to myself, "No, I have my father, my mother, and my sister."

And so I entered a new house, the house that was to be my childhood home.

Aunt Mary's house was in the village on the road that led to the Rang des Chutes. It faced the large parish plot used for grazing. Beyond that lay my paternal grandfather's land, so that we had an open view as far as the distant blue line of the Laurentians.

To the left of the house, separated by a lane called "the little road," was Dr. Philippe Baril's place. He was always called Docteur or Monsieur Docteur, and his wife and daughters were Madame Docteur and "les petites Docteurs." The house had a big, grassy back yard that, because of the doctor's children, was to become my habitual playground. Behind this yard, giving onto the lane, lived the butcher Brouillette, my adoptive mother's brother-in-law. He was commonly called *Ti-Gros*, but out of politeness my parents said *Gros*, and I called him "Uncle Gros." For a long time the triangle formed by the butcher's house and store, the doctor's house, and our own marked the boundaries of my activity, and I was forbidden to go further afield. I never went to play with the third neighbour, even though he was my adoptive father's nephew. I always had to be within view of my parents.

Like the two other houses I'd lived in, my new home was a two-storey building with a pitched roof. An open balcony ran along the front and left walls. The half of the ground floor giving onto the lane was used as a winter kitchen—all kitchens were family rooms. The other half contained a spare room where the family never slept. It was kept for visitors and invalids, and was the most carefully arranged room in the house, being more or less in public view. There was also a parlour—another room we hardly ever used. In it was a small set of furniture as prim as a presbytery. On the wall hung unrecognizable portraits of our parents in their younger days, staring down at us from huge, gilded wooden frames. One of the parlour doors opened onto the kitchen, the other directly to the front of the house. This second door was opened only on rare occasions. Everyone except the curé and "strangers," as we called those from outside our parish, used the side door that led into a small summer kitchen, and from there into the winter kitchen. We were always surprised, and I would say apprehensive, when we heard someone knocking on the front parlour door.

Upstairs, on the left side, were the bedrooms of my parents and my sister Clémence. Across the hall from her room was a bathroom the size of a regular bedroom. It had running water (cold only) and contained a sink, a toilet, and a high-rimmed, heavy metal bathtub on feet. The last and fourth room was unfinished. It had no ceiling and rose right up to the pitched roof. We called it "the attic" and used it to store provisions, trunks, and things we no longer used but didn't dare throw out. Among them was a long piece of furniture with a hinged cover called a *farinier*. It had a lid that opened like a school desk and was divided into three sections used for storing flour, sugar, and the dirty linen for Monday's wash.

Behind the house we had a vegetable patch, partly enclosed by a picket fence, partly by a cord of wood.

My adoptive father, Théodore Baril, had just married at the age of fifty-two. Until then he had been a bachelor, travelling all over Canada and doing all sorts of work. He was brought up in a farming family on the Rang Saint-Pierre and went to the line road school until he was twelve. His studies ended after he attended catechism classes prior to his First Communion, a ceremony that took place at about that age. We used the expression *marcher au catéchisme* (literally "walk to catechism") because we had to walk to the village church where the curé held his classes.

My father must have shown much talent at school. He was twice awarded the inspector's prize for having the best marks. The prizes were, in 1880, Faucher de Saint-Maurice's *Promenades dans le golfe Saint-Laurent* (third edition, 1880) and in 1882, Joseph Marmette's *Le tomahawk et l'épée* (1877). These books formed the foundation of his little library, which consisted of perhaps a dozen volumes. After he married my aunt, these were installed in full view on the wall of the parlour, which opened into the kitchen. Next to the curé, the doctor, and the notary, my father had the most books in the village. Apart from the two volumes mentioned above, his library included a copy of Abbé Jorry's *Histoire universelle de l'Église et des papes* (second edition, 1861) autographed by the former curé, Jean-Baptiste Chrétien. I wonder whether this signature denoted permission to keep the book, as was the practice in our classical college, or had the book belonged to the curé and been bought after his death? My father's library also had three books on the 1914-1918 war, including an illustrated album, as well as a *Histoire populaire de Napoléon Ier*, some brochures about establishing settlements, and various pious works. My father read a great deal, but since his reading was limited to the few works he possessed, he reread them constantly. As a child I did the same, always rereading the same things and ready to peruse anything in order to satisfy my need to read.

Following his schoolboy triumphs my father left home to earn his living. He often talked to me about his travels, but a bit at a time, so that I'm unable to establish their chronological order. He was in the Canadian West for a while, especially in Alberta, where he worked on a ranch belonging to the Prince of Wales—the future Edward VIII. He spoke of this ranch with great pride. It must have been near Medicine Hat, a name he often mentioned. He also had a career in the Canadian Pacific Railway. When he retired from the CPR he received a gold watch engraved with his name and a chain and fob to match. He worked as a watchman for the stockpiles of supplies left by logging contractors at various points along the line. He would spend months alone in the upper reaches of the St. Maurice Valley among the bears and moose. It was here that he learned all there was to know of life in the woods—how to get his bearings or forecast the weather, and where to look for a spring. He taught me these things when we went walking in the forest, picking wild berries and fishing. Some of the characteristics of the hero of my novel *Vézine* are based on my father. Perhaps his long sojourns in the woods developed his habit of saying little and sitting for hours on end in his big chair beside the stove or on the porch bench, quietly pensive but never seeming bored.

His longest term of employment (or in any case, the one about which he liked to talk most) was with the Grandes-Piles logging contractor, Jean Crête, nicknamed "king of the St. Maurice Valley." My father was his Man Friday. These years seemed to have been very dear to him. He always spoke of Jean Crête with deep admiration. Crête was one of my father's great men—a list that included Honoré Mercier, Prime Minister R.B. Bennett, Caruso (whom he had heard at an outdoor concert in Montreal), and the curé, Georges-Elisée Panneton.

What had my father amassed during his peregrinations? Everyone said he was rich. To those who made much of his wealth, he would reply mischievously, "Yes, I've got a little," which people interpreted as an admission of affluence. In fact, his savings weren't as great as rumoured. It is true that he sometimes lent money, but he lost a lot in the 1929 Crash because of an incompetent notary. He had many debtors among the local farmers. At the time, investing in a parcel of land was considered the safest bet, but my father was the big loser when the farmers "threw themselves" on the government's farm credit bureau. In any case, my father lived frugally, never drank alcohol (there was never a single bottle of beer in our house), and only smoked the occasional pipe of Rose Quesnel tobacco.

In 1922, when my father was fifty-two, he came back to Saint-Narcisse "to settle" and lived on the income from his savings. For a brief time, to keep busy, he worked as a handyman for his nephew, the merchant Joseph Jacob. He even became a Sun Life insurance agent for a few months. My father was not one to importune others, however, and as he had no car, his clientèle remained very modest. Even so, among his papers I discovered a certificate of honourable mention for his work.

My father's family and Curé Panneton found a match for him in Mary

Trépanier, a widow and occasional seamstress with an adopted daughter of twelve and a good house. This marriage of convenience was decided upon quickly. A dower or widow's portion was agreed upon (how often I was to hear this dower discussed!), and so it was that, eight months later, the newlyweds in their fifties adopted me, a five-year-old.

My adoptive mother's dual personality was a matter of continual astonishment to me. With visitors or while out of the house, she was full of life and loved to tell or listen to amusing anecdotes, always laughing until she cried. Everyone liked her and called her Aunt Mary, whether they were related to her or not. And yet she was a very strict woman. She rose early and never missed early-morning mass (she would get to the church before the verger and wait for the door to be opened) or any other religious ceremony. She felt the Church's teachings should be followed to the letter. On the day of my confirmation (May 31, 1925), when Bishop Cloutier, wearing his gold mitre, preached against "yellow" or sensational journalism, my mother wanted to stop me reading *Le Nouvelliste*, the most anodyne, most innocent of newspapers, in case it was yellow. I narrowly escaped this ban by promising only to read the articles on accidents and robberies! When I was first adopted, my father wanted to take me on his lap one day, but my mother intervened, scandalized. "He's not a baby any more," said she. "He's too big to be lifted up like that. You mustn't give him bad habits." My father gave way to this dictum and put me down. He was a man who'd had no home between the ages of twelve and fifty-two. I've always felt that, if it weren't for my mother, he would have openly bestowed on me all the affection he himself had always missed. As it was, my parents never kissed their child except when exchanging New Year's greetings.

My adoptive mother's strictness was also expressed in her housekeeping. There was a rule for everything. Monday was wash day. She used to get up earlier than usual. By the time she left for the first mass of the day, the washing was already drying on the line. In this spic-and-span house, with its brilliantly waxed linoleum covered with bits of carpet to keep the dirt off, nothing must be out of place. If a corner of a carpet were scuffed up or a rug skewed, I had to set it right. When sitting, I had to hold myself as straight as a ramrod. No slouching was tolerated. Once, at a neighbour's, I saw a child my own age sleeping on the ground in broad daylight. I envied him being able to stretch out just anywhere at any time of day. When I became drowsy I was sent to bed. I played in the house but was never allowed to make any noise. My toys had to be treated very carefully, but when one is having fun things do get broken. How many times have I heard myself scolded for being a little ruffian!

Above all, I was not allowed to interrupt grownup conversations. Being the only child in the family (I looked upon my thirteen-year-old adoptive sister as an adult), I was used to remaining silent. When visitors came, as they often did, they found me "no talker." "He's a shy one," my mother used to explain. I became increasingly shy, silent, and withdrawn, and remained so until the end of my teenage years. This mother, so lively with visitors, resumed her austere manner the moment they left, and I found myself once more with an impatient woman of few words. Naturally she demanded absolute obedience and was fond of saying, "He's got to obey," or "You're going to learn to knuckle under."

I knew—having been told often enough—that she had adopted me out of duty, for lack of a girl, and that my natural father was "heartless." My adoptive father either hid his affection for me or didn't know how to demonstrate it. I should add, however, that all parents of that generation who knew how to bring up their children "properly" avoided demonstrations of affection.

As a result, I felt I was a burden. From the beginning I understood that finding a room for me had upset the established household order. I was less of a burden in summer, when a cot was set up for me in the attic and the door to the neighbouring bathroom left half open (another bother). The mattress of my cot was stuffed with sweet corn leaves that crackled noisily every time I stirred. The attic had no stovepipe running up through it, however, so it couldn't be lived in during the winter. Where would they put me? There was only the bathroom. The bathtub, standing tall on its feet, was hardly ever used. My parents put my mattress in it and that was my bed for three winters in a row, until I left for the orphanage. The fact that the bathtub was beside the toilet was an enormous inconvenience. The rest of the household had to wait until I was asleep to use it, otherwise I was told to turn my face to the wall and not budge. What a nuisance I was!

It was on the corn-leaf mattress in the bathtub that I felt the famous earthquake of February 28, 1925. What really upset me wasn't the actual tremors, which sounded like thunder or a big wind, but the excitement around me. Why was I pulled out of bed? Why were the candles lit and the rosary recited? Then everyone got dressed and went to a neighbour's house in case the danger wasn't over.

Once I had entered boarding school and came home for winter vacations, a less complicated solution was found for me: the kitchen sofa. In the evening it had to be turned into a bed (even when visitors were still there, for I went to bed early), and the blankets had to be taken off next morning, all of which was a further nuisance. This arrangement also meant that I slept alone on the ground floor. My childhood fears began the moment the light of my father's candle disappeared up the stairs. Many a time I would wake up, certain that someone was walking on the porch. My father tried to tell me it was only the bitter cold making the nails pop. But maybe someone was hiding in the closed parlour with its door to the outside? Or in the storeroom beside the parlour? Or in the summer kitchen with the door we could never shut properly in winter? My fears would last until about four in the morning, when my father came downstairs to light the stove. At last I would go back to sleep, happy and comforted by the cheerful crackle of the fire and the flicker of warm light reflected on the floor.

Finally another solution was found for the winter. I was given the end of a corridor, curtained off with a length of calico. I was closer to the others yet alone in this tiny space, and I had my own little world.

From the material point of view I lacked nothing, although unlike my neighbours I had few toys or candy (one mustn't foster "habits," as my mother would say). Nevertheless, I was living in a well-run household where food was always plentiful and good, for my mother was considered an excellent cook. Being the only boy, I never wore hand-me-downs. During the week, I wore my everyday clothes and was happy to run about barefoot, but on Sunday I went to church dressed like a little prince. By all accounts, as my birth family often said, I was living like a bird in a gilded cage.

This state of affairs made me something of a loner. Within my own little island I was content to be my own friend, confidant, and support. I learned very early to be self-sufficient and have remained so. When, in later years, I learned Corneille's lines, "In so great a calamity, what is left? 'I am,' say I, and that is enough," I recognized my childhood state of mind and the inner shell that I had cultivated over the years. But because of this very isolation, what a turmoil was going on inside! What a world of imagination, an endless stream of dreams! I was everywhere and nowhere, inventing all sorts of things out of almost nothing. Standing at the window, turning the white knob of the window latch back and forth, I was a captain at my ship's helm on the high seas, veering left then right, slicing through the waves. Life was wonderful.

I went to the school run by the Daughters of Jesus, whom we called the French sisters because they had come from France twenty years earlier. It stood on the hillside opposite the presbytery garden. At home, my father followed my lessons closely, listening to me recite and even teaching me to count to twelve in English, something that wasn't in the curriculum. To comprehend a little English at that age was something of a miracle, for the other children didn't know a word. Sometimes there would be discussion at home. For example, we said *popa* and *moman* for *papa* and *maman*. I knew how to write the word *maman*, but one day I asserted that this word could also be written as *moment*, which I had seen somewhere in my book but couldn't find again. I was never able to clear up this matter, however, for I had reached the limits of my parents' knowledge.

As my adoptive parents hadn't gone to school after the age of twelve, they spoke as those around them did. At home we said *moé, toé, betot* and *ousquila* (for *moi, toi, bientôt,* and *où est-ce qu'il est?).* In a parish where there wasn't a single English-speaker, no English-language newspaper, and no radio, my French was nonetheless laden with English words. Many articles, tools, and pieces of clothing had English names—for example, *signe* for sink, *bâleur* for boiler (the *bouilloire* or hot water cauldron on the stove), *bombe* for bomb (a small kettle with a spout), *thé-pot* for teapot, and words like *carpet, rug, fleur* (for flour), *wrench, coat, swetteur* (for sweater), *brodclot* (for broadcloth), *les rubbers* (for galoshes), *coffre* for trouser-cuff, as well as *waguine* (for waggon) and *sleigh* (for the French *traineau*), these last two being used on the farm. As children, we used to run pushing a *tire* (for the French *pneu*), go wading in a *calvette* (culvert). Since horses were imported from the West and trained to obey English commands, they were driven in English without our realizing what language we were speaking: "*Back!*" we would say, or "G*uedop!*" (get up or giddyap), which resulted in the verb *guedoper* (the children were always "giddyapping," for example). These horses had English names like Maggy, Tom, or Paddy. But why, I wonder, were so many people's first names given an English pronunciation? My mother signed her name Marie, but everyone called her Mary. Her sister Mélanda was called Melandy. Someone named Hygin Dessureault was called Iguine (for Egan), and there were numerous individuals called Johnny, Nelson, Jeffrey and Meredy.

This English invasion of French in a parish isolated from the English-speaking world is curious. Obviously, I didn't think anything of it at the time. If anyone had said I was speaking half English, half French, I would have been insulted. The only explanation for it that I can think of is the effect of commerce. There were English names on commonly used products and English-only catalogues from the big Toronto stores. Perhaps there were also old social ties with people who had travelled in the Canadian West (there were many in my parish) and others who had emigrated to New England and returned. At one time, people used to laugh a lot at the campaigns mounted by the Société du Bon Parler Français (literally, The Society for Well-Spoken French). Looking back on it, I think there was a dramatic need for such campaigns.

Were we, in fact, still French-speaking? Even our French traditions were going with the wind, so to speak. On Christmas, it was the Anglo-American version of the original German Santa Claus ("Do you still believe in Santa Claus?") who left our surprise gifts. He wasn't yet the consumer-society sort of Santa who visits nowadays, but we were moving away from the traditional Saint Nicholas. The old saint was still fairly popular, however, and was the subject of a song that, alas for me, I had to sing over and over again to show visitors how clever I was:

Saint Nicholas, young scholars' patron saint,
Bring me sweets to fill my tiny basket;
When to school I go, I'll learn my lessons
And be as well-behaved as a little lamb.

It never entered my head that the wonderful Santa Claus who came by my bed on Christmas was simply my Saint Nicholas.

One day during my third year of elementary school, 1924 to 1925, I came home with the inspector's prize, just as my father had twice done forty years earlier. I'd come first among the boys in a competition for reading aloud, and we drew lots to see who was the winner between myself and the first on the girls' side. I was given Joseph Marmette's *Héroïsme et trahison* (1924), one of the fine editions with a red and gold cover put out by Beauchemin. Another Marmette! My first was a work of history that my father had put on his small bookshelf beside the Marmette he'd won in 1882. This event was a topic of discussion between my family and our neighbours for quite a while, and my father made me take the book down from the shelf countless times for visitors to see.

Suddenly, however, the foundations of this new life began to crumble.

Why and in what circumstances this happened, I do not know. Perhaps in addition to being a burden I was a difficult child to manage, or perhaps it was hard for a couple nearly sixty years old to bring up a boy of eight. In any event, in September 1925 I was placed in a Trois-Rivières orphanage, although it was understood that I would come home for summer and winter vacations.

The author sitting on the porch of his adopted family's house,
Saint-Narcisse-de-Champlain, 1923.

3

My Third Family: Boarding School

THIRTY KILOMETRES was a long journey in 1925, when I left Saint-Narcisse for Trois-Rivières. Except for those rare individuals who owned a car, we travelled by bus in summer and in winter took a sleigh to the village, six kilometres away, to catch the train from Les Piles. People very seldom went to the city, and children almost not at all.

This said, it's understandable why my departure caused such a rush of emotion among the members of my family. I myself remained more or less indifferent, not knowing what a city was or what awaited me. As I saw it, I had to take a bus—a long black car that rode high on wooden-spoked wheels and had six or seven seats, each running the width of the vehicle. At either end of the seat was a small door. The only glassed-in space was the windshield. When it rained, canvas blinds were attached to the open areas on each side of the bus. This protected us from bad weather, but we couldn't see a thing. The bus announced its arrival from afar, just like the old stagecoaches with their bugles. Everyone came out on the porch to watch it go by and to identify the passengers, or at least count them. The result would be the topic of conversation for quite some time—even longer if the bus actually stopped. Each time I left, all the people in the neighbourhood came out to watch until the bus turned the corner by the church. I was someone important.

When I first left for the orphanage, my adoptive father came with me. His excuse was that he had a stove plate to be repaired at the foundry in town. I can't remember the moment when he handed me over to the nuns, but I can still picture another scene from the same day perfectly. I was in the courtyard when I was told that someone was waiting for me in the parlour. It was my father who had come back before taking the bus home. He brought me a little bag of candy, something he never spent money on except at

Christmastime. Clutching this little bag (I can still see the candy canes sticking out of it), I went back to the courtyard, climbed to the top of the slide, and there, standing higher than the wooden fence that shut us in like prisoners, I made my acquaintance with the city of Trois-Rivières where I was to be a boarder for thirteen years.

The orphanage was on Rue Saint-François-Xavier, behind the seminary. It was an old wooden building two storeys high with a mansard roof on two sides. It had first been used to lodge the seminary servants, but in 1915 the building had been moved to its new location to be joined to the three-storey brick convent of the Dominican Nuns of the Rosary. The garret above the second floor had been turned into a dormitory for the pupils—about a hundred of us. When I look at old photographs, I can't see how we'd have got out if there had been a fire. The whole thing smelled like an old shanty. The sanitary arrangements were wretched, and there was only one bath for all the pupils. We used to line up, wearing our short linen underpants. One after another, the nun would sit us in the same water, scrub our faces, and yank us out to make room for the next in line. There were no lice in my family, but at the orphanage it was common to see a nun in our recreation hall seated with a newspaper open on her knees and a child leaning over it so she could go through his hair with a fine-tooth comb, looking for lice.

In my novel, published in 1946, I devoted a few pages to the orphanage where I made my hero, Vézine, pass some time. He recalls his childhood:

> It was the dining hall that he remembered best, with its sickening, heavy smell of grease that filled the room and permeated the paintwork. He remembered the pieces of meat criss-crossed by strings of gristle, that tired, grey, boiled beef that appeared on the plates after first being used to make broth. The bits of lean meat had to be torn out one by one. He saw it on his plate once more, like a huge nerve on which a dense, short growth of lean meat had sprouted. Near the table loomed Sister's stern face, her expression demanding that he eat all the bits of meat. The other pupils were out playing. Only Vézine remained in his seat because he wouldn't swallow his serving. "Very well: next Friday there'll be no butter for Tiny Mouth." Oh! That weekly butter, how good it was, cool and hard on the knife, how mouth-watering on good, hot, potatoes, baked in their skins, and what big pieces Sister would give us! . . . He remembered once

more the annual purging. A nun would hold a spoonful of sulphur and molasses up to his mouth, and he would take it in spite of himself, for fear of the cane. It tasted of earth and burned his throat. Another nun gave a candy to those who didn't balk.

I mentioned the cane. In the novel I wrote the following passage (but this time I wasn't masked by the character of Vézine, but by a small fellow-pupil from Saint-Paulin):

> The cane! He could see it clearly because for two years it had loomed menacingly over him—the cane on his knuckles, but mostly the cane on his behind before bed, when he wore only his thin underpants. Sister hit him, and he cried while the others laughed. He shrieked *names* at Sister and she sent him to sleep in the garret. He climbed up, so furious that he forgot to lift the trap door and banged his head hard against it while the whole dormitory broke into gales of laughter. . . . Oh! All those half hours of silent penance he had done, *holding his mouth shut* with his forefinger and thumb!

There are some images of the past that keep recurring. They may not be connected with anything very exceptional, but each time one looks back they reappear, never changing. I have been reproached for the above description (completely accurate, by the way) as being invented out of whole cloth or exaggerated. Long ago I received a letter from Canon Georges Panneton, brother of the writer Ringuet (Philippe Panneton), reminding me of his part in my first communion and even my mother's death, when he was vicar of Saint-Narcisse. Canon Panneton implored me to suppress all these passages in a new edition of my novel. There was a new edition, but no retraction or answer to his letter.

It was under these miserable conditions that I experienced group life—I, the only boy in an adoptive family, who until then had led a reclusive life. I have only bitter memories of this time, but I don't recall having broken down or trying to run away. I continued my solitary existence, a little lost island in a fogbound archipelago. Nevertheless I do remember a curious reaction, despite the institution's depressing régime. On my return from the winter vacation, I found some pupils who hadn't been able to go home, but who had been consoled by presents given by some kindhearted souls. I regretted not having stayed in the orphanage over the holidays and getting such gifts too. One boy in particular had received an old mandolin, and I considered him very lucky.

We had classes, but today I feel that their main purpose was to keep us occupied. The method adopted for reading aloud, for example, was most surprising, even for the time: we were made to read from a Latin psalter. I can't remember getting any intellectual stimulation in the orphanage. Still, I came home in the summer vacation with a prize—and what a prize for a child of nine! It was a hardcover volume bound in red and gold and weighing two kilograms (about five pounds)—783 pages of close print, entitled *Vie de Léon XIII*. It was a life of Pope Leo XIII by Bernard O'Reilly, published in 1903. At least it had the merit of being lavishly illustrated. My first prize at the village school had been a history book; my second was a weighty biography. I became accustomed to reading history and handling "fat bricks" as we call them in French. My father was even more dazzled by this acquisition than I was. The book remained prominently displayed for the benefit of visitors for a long time before taking its place (of large proportions) in the little bookcase. And so, at the age of nine, I read what was for me an enormous tome—and reread it several times, so great was my mania for reading. I didn't remember much about it after each perusal (imagine, papal encyclicals at that age!), but from then on, every time a pope died I knew the ritual formula for recording his demise: *Papa vere mortuum est.*

After the summer holidays of 1926 I went back to the same orphanage, but another change was in store for me—a very lucky one this time. During that autumn someone came to take me to the Jardin de l'Enfance, also in Trois-Rivières. The Dominican nun who helped me pack my suitcase predicted that I'd be rich one day because of my big ears, or so she said. I'm still waiting for my fortune to materialize.

The Jardin was a primary school run by the Daughters of Jesus. I was to spend four marvellous years there, and I quickly fitted into this little world. My brother Marceau was already a pupil (I'm not sure how long he'd been there), but being four years older, he was already one of the big boys. I hardly saw him except when we went to visit our older brother who was a student at the Grand Seminary. Once again, I had slipped through the ties with my biological family.

The Daughters of Jesus came originally from Kermaria in Brittany and had emigrated to Canada in 1903 because of a law prohibiting them from teaching. The following year, they founded their school in an old, prosperous neighbourhood of Trois-Rivières, at the corner of Rue Notre-Dame (now Rue des Ursulines) and Rue des Casernes.

I was soon to learn that the Jardin was at the crossroads of the Trois-Rivières region's history—a subject I would one day explore. To the west of the school the neighbouring post office stood on what was once the site of the 1634 fort, later the barracks, and even later the first seminary, established in 1860. On the northwest side of the Jardin courtyard was an enclosure with a Sacred Heart monument marking the site of the old parish church of 1710, destroyed by fire in 1908. Further along to the east were a few old stone houses dating from the French Régime, among them the Maison de Gannes and the former Recollet monastery with its chapel, now an Anglican church. Here lay the remains of Brother Didace Pelletier, who in my part of the country was appealed to as a saint. We were shown the birthplace near this church of the explorer La Vérendrye. On the same side, opposite the Jardin, there was a tiny park called Place d'Armes with its old French canon. The olden-day Algonkins had camped here when the *bourg* of Trois-Rivières (the section that has become the historic quarter) was surrounded by a palisade. When the Algonkins left, the space became a military parade ground and we schoolchildren used to say that if we dug there we'd find the weapons hidden at the time of the British Conquest. I often day-dreamed as I faced this mysterious park from the school courtyard, gazing beyond the fence and the street.

Part of the Jardin itself was a historic site. Its modern three-storey brick building was attached to a huge old structure that housed the nuns' residence and parlour as well as the pupils' infirmary. We were told it had been the governor's residence under the French Régime. I was fascinated by its thick, bulging walls, its strange roof, and the tiny-paned windows. Its past wasn't as illustrious as rumoured, however. The old building hadn't sheltered governors, but it had indeed been the manor house of the Godefroy de Tonnancour family and of Judge Pierre-Louis Deschenaux. For a time the government had used it as officers' quarters. In 1822 the parish used it as a presbytery, and when Trois-Rivières acquired a bishop in 1852, the old building became the episcopal palace (the celebrated Bishop Laflèche lived here for four years). It later went back to being a presbytery, then in 1904 became the Jardin de l'Enfance for boys.

Several of the nuns in 1926 were still "French from France," or more precisely Bretons who still spoke their Celtic language. Our infirmary sister would have fun scolding us in Breton. Her tone and expression were meant to scare us a little, but her guttural language only made us laugh.

The Jardin was as clean as a whistle. The floors of the halls and rooms shone with wax. In the classroom each pupil had two pieces of material called *patins* (skates) attached to his feet to prevent him from scuffing the floor. In the dining hall we learned to eat according to a strict etiquette. To put a knife in one's mouth would have been a very serious fault. The cutlery had to be placed on the edge of the plate according to a precise protocol, and prizes for decorum rewarded our efforts. The same sense of order and cleanliness reigned in the dormitory. The white beds stood in straight lines, their blankets smoothed until the slightest wrinkle vanished. Our clothes and toilet articles were stored in the chest of drawers according to an immutable principle, and we took an individual bath each week in a well-equipped bathroom. Before bed we had to file by the nun in charge to show her that our necks and ears had been properly washed. If we went out into the town, we had a dress inspection. Our suits had to be clean, buttons shining, socks well pulled up, shoes polished, and in addition to the regulation cap we had to wear kid gloves, even in summer. And woe betide those who slouched as they walked! In any case, our uniform obliged us to move sedately. Over short pants we wore a long jacket of navy blue, fastened from the waist right up to the throat with gold buttons, topped with a black collar and bow tie. Triple rows of gold braid trimmed our cuffs and hard-visored caps, which gave us a rather military air.

As a matter of fact, we were already subjected to militia training. A senior classman from the seminary used to come and teach us gymnastic exercises and military drill. We would spend some of our spring afternoons at the city's riding school to complete our training under a professional officer. He might have been a *maréchal* of France, so impressed were we. Our training goal was the big review in May that took place before officers of the general staff. We didn't carry guns or swords, but over the Jardin uniform we wore a wide leather belt with a diagonal shoulder strap. These two pieces of apparel were enough to fill us with martial feelings—especially me, as each year I was a sergeant or captain, continuing the family tradition as I zealously bellowed out orders in my breaking voice.

All of this—the sense of order, the impeccable dress, the emphasis on decorum—were part of the distinctive behaviour that the nuns wanted to instill in us. A pupil at the Jardin must be recognizable on sight. We hadn't the right to be like others such as the *gars des frères*, the "guys" from the brothers' school who loped along like toughs and swore. This, at least, is what the nuns warned us against and what we ended up believing, rightly or wrongly. However, to the pupils at the neighbouring Académie de La Salle, we were only (supreme insult) *les petits gars des soeurs*—the sisters' little guys. Be that as it may, the Jardin nuns wanted to educate an élite group that would be different and a cut above the rest. According to the mentality of the time, they were only fulfilling their mission.

As in all teaching establishments, there was corporal punishment. Each nun carried a leather strap (*la strap*, as we called it) in the bag worn under the outer layer of her habit. The mother superior, a Frenchified Londoner, preferred to use a narrow little ruler that she applied to the left hand (which for some strange reason made us fear it all the more) on the inside knuckles. Fortunately, I only speak as an onlooker. In this school of *bourgeois* sons, the nuns rarely struck the pupils. I only got the strap once, and this on the occasion of a general thrashing. One evening, when the dormitory supervisor was absent, about twenty of us were having a fine old time horsing around when the nun returned earlier than expected, surprising us *in flagrente delicto*. As she had no way of telling the guilty from the innocent, she decided—once we were all back in bed—that everyone should have one stroke of the strap on the bottom. This ritual proved difficult from the start, one little gentleman refusing to be the first, another protesting that it wasn't his turn. The good sister finally proceeded from bed to bed, lifting the blanket and applying the single stroke over our nightshirts. However, as she advanced, the reactions of the current victims made their predecessors at first smile and then explode in bursts of laughter and comic remarks at the wails of those whose posteriors had never been maltreated in this fashion. Even the nun couldn't keep a straight face, and the final strokes of the strap were applied amid general merriment. From then on, this nun (of whom we were very fond) confined herself to dire threats of punishment that no one, herself included, took seriously.

In my last days at the Jardin, I had become the sisters' little Man Friday. Everyone knows what a sense of importance a pupil feels when singled out for special duties in a boarding school. I used to accompany one or other of the nuns about town, most often the mother superior, or else be sent with a message—to the bishop's palace for instance, or to Kermaria, the motherhouse on the hill. This taught me the ways of polite society, and at the age of twelve I became a man of the world without being aware of it. I was guilty of the occasional lapse because of inattention to my instructions. One day, a friend of the nuns had prepared a particularly succulent dish of shepherd's pie, and I was instructed to fetch it at eleven thirty. I left at the appointed hour and the good sisters waited, their mouths watering piously. Noon came and went, the half hour struck, but no shepherd's pie. At last I returned to the Jardin emptyhanded but pleased at having accomplished my mission.

"But where's the dish that you were supposed to fetch?" asked the desolate nuns, to which I replied, "The Franciscans send you their hearty thanks."

"Little wretch!" they cried. "It wasn't for the Franciscans. That was our dinner!" In the end, they laughed heartily at their involuntary charity.

I often went to be an altar boy at mass in the Ursuline convent, a few minutes' walk from the Jardin. The mass was always so early that, during the school year, it was inevitably dark when I left. For this reason a nun would stand on the sidewalk in front of the Jardin door while an Ursuline nun awaited me at the other end. This Ursuline was an externa or lay sister whom we nicknamed "Sister Brandy Nose," she being far from pretty. Watched over by these two guardian angels, I bravely made the nocturnal trek, although I hastened my steps a little as I passed in front of the old Anglican church, which we had been told was the gate of Hell.

In those days, as I have mentioned, boarding-school pupils stayed over Christmas and went home two or three days later for the holidays. And oh, what a marvel the feast of Christmas was at the Jardin de l'Enfance! We began preparing for it in early November with singing exercises. As the time drew nearer, we had all sorts of little tasks to keep us busy. Among others, we had to write our parents a letter in English, expressing the season's greetings. The English-speaking world's custom of sending Christmas wishes was beginning to spread among French Canadians. Until then, we usually sent New Year's greetings and nothing more. It made sense for us to practise an English custom in the language of the English, and it was also a way of impressing our parents. I don't know why, but instead of going to my adoptive father, this letter had to be sent to my true father, although I no longer had any real contact with him. He can't have got much pleasure from a letter written in English, whereas my adoptive father, who had taught me my first English vocabulary, would have been very proud to receive it.

We also had to prepare the *crèches*. The nuns put these little manger scenes everywhere—in the chapel, in every classroom, and at the ends of corridors. We had to cut out cardboard clogs for our "surprises," just in case the little Jesus (it was not then Père Noël or Father Christmas) happened to pass through the dormitory. It was early to bed for us on Christmas eve, and we awoke to the sound of hand-bells. A mass followed, wonderfully candle-lit, where we sang in harmony. We went down to the dining hall for the *réveillon*, and at each place was fruit, cake, and candy. After this we went back to bed. Next morning we found, under each bed, a little cardboard clog filled with good things to eat, placed there by unknown hands.

The winter holidays followed. I went home to my adoptive parents, whom I kissed on New Year's Day. We didn't practise the tradition of the paternal blessing, since (as I understood it at the time) this was reserved for real, not adoptive fathers. On that day I received a present. My time for toys was short-lived, unlike other children of my age. My parents preferred to give me something useful.

My family consisted of farmers who celebrated the New Year's feast in the old way, by which I mean visiting one another. I didn't stay home for long and soon followed uncles and aunts in a sleigh, sleeping now with one, now with another (we children often slept three or four to a bed). Every night we stayed up late for those long evenings of the good old days, singing, dancing, listening to stories, trying to "make the tables talk." Then came the novelty of radio. Everyone began listening to this marvel, program after program. Gone were the songs sung by this or that cousin; Uncle So-and-So no longer told his scary stories, and the old evenings of fun and laughter vanished. I lost interest and suddenly stopped visiting my relations—as is the case with anything that I find tedious.

During my last three years at the Jardin, my teacher was a Breton nun, Sister Thérèse d'Avila, for whom I had and still have boundless admiration. When I first visited France in 1957, I made a long detour to see her in Quimper. She had aged much, and I had become a university professor, but she remembered the child she had nicknamed "the little philosopher" or, to tease me because of my large head, "my little Boche." Sister Thérèse was a very demanding teacher. Any grammatical fault or sloppy pronunciation was pounced on with horror. She drove us to work under the threat of her ruler and by emulation, using the airplane as a model. She had stretched some strings above the edge of a long blackboard at the back of the classroom. Little cardboard airplanes could slide along these strings, while below them the cities of the world were lined up according to continent. When we had enough good marks to acquire a plane, we started on a world tour, advancing from city to city according to our good marks. If the marks were bad, we stayed in the airport for repairs or even went back two or three stages. The pupil who went around the world had a gold star stuck on his plane, after which he set out again in search of a second star. I was the most enthusiastic and came top of my class. If my enthusiasm flagged the least bit, I got myself going again and set records for the world tour. At the end of the year my plane was covered with gold stars.

I returned home for the summer holidays laden with prizes. Prize-giving was a particularly grand ceremony, sometimes presided over by the bishop, sometimes by a high-ranking superior. I used to think that the hierarchy was measured in terms of physical size. Our teacher was short and fairly thin, our mother superior at the Jardin was taller and portly, and the mother provincial was very tall and very fat. Then one day the mother general of the order came. My word—a veritable tower! These prize-giving occasions were always enlivened by songs, recitations, and theatrical sketches. One year I was a Chinese dancer and sang "Hip! Chop sasa!"—presumably as in Peking. The prize-giving brought together the boarders' relatives, dressed to the nines. Most of them were middle-class people from Trois-Rivières. Countless prizes were displayed on tables beside the platform. Each pupil got one, whether or not he was a success, sometimes for good work in class, sometimes for good behaviour, for appearance, for obeying rules of etiquette, or for religious devotion. Any poor fellow who hadn't distinguished himself in some way (it does happen) received what was loudly proclaimed as a consolation prize. We, merciless children that we were, would burst out laughing each time.

Lucky as always, but a hard worker, I stepped down from the platform several times be awarded large tomes and went up again in full view of the public, but unfortunately no member of my family was there to witness my triumph. While attending the Jardin I was awarded at least eight sizeable, hard-covered, gilt-edged volumes. One, a six hundred page work, actually weighed four and a half kilograms (nearly ten pounds) and measured thirty-four by twenty-five centimetres (thirteen and a quarter by nine and three quarter inches). Its title was *Les deux captifs du Spielberg, Silvio Pellico et Alexandre Andryane*. Unlike the orphanage's scholarly biography of Leo XIII, a work written for the educated adult, this prize contained tales of adventure and war, including Thorel's *La conquête de l'air* (I'd gone around the world often enough to deserve it), Pierre Maël's *Petit Ange*, and works such as *À travers les déserts, Les maréchaux de Napoléon,* and *Perdus dans l'Arctique,* all of them illustrated and fascinating to read. Oh, those beautiful books! How I used to read and reread them during the holidays! We had to enlarge the bookcase. The little Marmette won by my father in 1882 and my other Marmette of 1924 had long lost their place of honour.

In the summers I was clearly not the same boy when I returned to Saint-Narcisse and my little comrades of earlier days. Each year I felt more and more different from them, and my pleasure in seeing them slowly faded—or my awkwardness increased. I had become "a little city gentleman" who was only visiting the country. "Uprooted" would be the word today. Indeed, at the time I felt that I'd been transplanted, but I was used to adapting to circumstances and felt no regret. I was more inclined to draw closer to the adult world (which made people say I was old for my age), and particularly to my adoptive father, whom I was forever following on long berry-picking excursions. As we gathered strawberries in the fields and raspberries in the woods, I would ask him about his past, about the people he'd known, about birds and plants. It was too bad that he could only reply vaguely to questions about these last two subjects. When I asked about the American goldfinch, he told me, "It's called a little yellow bird," never having learned its proper name. More and more, I used to chat with our neighbour, the doctor. Although he wasn't very approachable, he loved being asked scientific questions, especially about astronomy. How many times of an evening would he show me, with a large sweep of his hand, Betelgeuse in the Orion constellation. The doctor taught me to recognize the planets Mars and Venus. About the Aztecs he was very knowledgeable, and there are words like *Chapultepec* and *Tehuantepec* that still ring in my memory. He used to lend me books, for he had more than we did, among others the marvellous *Encyclopédie de la jeunesse* that gave me so many hours of pleasure. Little did I know that one day I would be asked to write the preface to a new edition.

Five years in boarding school had turned me into a far different child from the one that encountered the city for the first time in 1925. Son of a carpenter, then the adopted son of a villager with a small pension, I had spent the last four years with the children of middle-class city dwellers. I had learned their fine manners, I dressed like them, I played with them. And yet I didn't receive the daily treats they got. At our four o'clock snack my fellow-pupils would pull an apple or some chocolate out of their pockets. Sometimes they would visit the parlour and come back with candy and fruit such as I had never seen in my home—pears and peaches, for example. The boy who sat beside me at table had his orange every morning. I wasn't really one of them, and I felt it keenly when I saw what they had and what I had not. I noticed that the nuns spoke deferentially about the families of these fellow pupils, while they knew nothing about mine. In any case, I never had occasion to visit the parlour.

I was poor: there you have it! I had been taken from the orphanage. I never had a penny in my pocket, whereas the others would publicly drop pennies into the money-box kept by one of the nuns for her little South Sea Islanders. At least I could be proud that I, the country orphan, did better than any of them in class. I continued to be content with my own company, living from day to day for my studies. I asked nothing of anyone, neither material things (a nun had shown me how to darn my socks, which I did and still do), nor affection. I was filled with beautiful dreams, and they made me happy.

The author in his boarding school uniform at
Jardin de l'Enfance, 1928.

4

The Road to Becoming a Man of Letters

What governs the path a life takes? What is a vocation? In 1930 at the age of thirteen I decided (or it was decided on my behalf) that the religious life was the one for me. In 1939 I dreamed of a career as a Greek specialist. Six years later, I was teaching Canadian history at a university.

At what moment and in what circumstances did the idea of becoming a Franciscan enter my head—or did the suggestion come from someone else? Becoming a priest was nothing out of the ordinary in Saint-Narcisse-de-Champlain. The village was a "parish of priests," as we used to say, and what we called "children of the parish" were not lacking. Not counting cousins by blood or courtesy, my immediate family had two priests (a paternal and a maternal uncle) and my oldest brother had just been ordained. It was only natural that the exceptionally bright younger brother of thirteen should dedicate himself to the Church. But why to the Franciscan Order?

If the schoolchild that I was—and a former inmate of the Saint-Dominique orphanage—didn't choose the secular clergy, he ought to have first considered becoming a member of the Dominicans. I had lived for over a year with Dominican nuns and had served mass in a hooded white tunic. Perhaps it was because of the unhappy memory of my stay in the orphanage that I never for an instant considered this option. Anyway, I would have had to live near a Dominican juvenate, which wasn't the case.

There was, however, a Franciscan juvenate in Trois-Rivières called Collège Séraphique, well known in the region. Still, a schoolchild needed some pushing. The Franciscans were ever present in Saint-Narcisse in the form of the Third Order founded by St. Francis of Assisi. Its aim was to unite devoted laymen and laywomen by giving them an official religious status. The tertiary was a lay brother or sister governed by the rule of the order, bearing a religious name and wearing a religious habit (reduced, it is true, to a sash worn around the waist next to the skin). A number of tertiaries, including my mother, had themselves buried in the actual dark brown cowl. Both my adopted parents were tertiaries, and because of the Third Order we often saw Franciscans in the parish.

A *frère quêteur* collecting for the Franciscans used to visit Saint-Narcisse. We nicknamed him "the egg brother" because the parish was invited to supply mainly eggs for the order in Trois-Rivières, while neighbouring parishes devoted themselves to other charities. I had an aunt who, at a certain time of year, would say to her husband, "The egg brother is about to come by. Get your boxes ready."

In this sphere of Franciscan influence, one individual fascinated my parents' generation. This was *le Bon Père Frédéric*, or Father Frédéric Ghyvelde, who came to Canada to re-establish the Franciscans here in 1888 and died in 1916 in an odour of sanctity. Prayers were addressed to him; miracles and even apparitions were attributed to him. One such apparition concerned a poor woman and her children, about to die of hunger. The house door opens by itself, an arm holds out a basket of bread, then disappears. When the mother and children run to see who it is, not a trace can be seen in the snow. Good Father Frédéric, no doubt about it!

It is true that while in the Jardin de l'Enfance I carried messages to the Franciscans, but their parlour was a dark old place that smelled of stale cooking oil—not likely to inspire a religious vocation. And anyway, how could I choose between secular and religious life at the age of twelve or thirteen? It is my firm conviction that the impetus for my vocation came from my parents, who were not only very devout, but were members of the Third Order and admirers of Father Frédéric. They may have begun to steer me in this direction early on. Even before I was ten they would often ask me, as visitors looked on, "What do you want to be when you grow up?"

As through reciting a lesson, I'd reply, "I want to be a father."

"Oh, that's fine!"

But just to be a smart-aleck I would add, "Yes, but a father of a family."

I'm also told I wished to become a Franciscan because I liked running around barefoot and wanted to go without shoes and socks all the time. However this may be, I get the distinct feeling that there was more or less persistent pressure on the part of my family. Just think of it: a Franciscan son, what an honour!

Long before I finished the Jardin de l'Enfance, the nuns and my whole family knew I wouldn't being going to the seminary like my classmates, but to "the little fathers," as the students at the Collège Séraphique were called. This was a classical college offering a six-year program in what was called *lettres*, from the initial *eléments latins* year to the final *rhétorique* class. It included a *méthode* class. The program in other colleges was only five years long because it didn't include the method year, except for retraining the weakest students. Method was obligatory at the Franciscan college, however, and the curriculum very taxing. Once students had completed the first segment of the arts baccalauréat at the end of the rhetoric year, candidates would don the cowl and do a year's novitiate at the Sherbrooke monastery. From there they moved on to Quebec City for three years of philosophy in preparation for the second segment of the baccalauréat. Finally, they did four years of theology in Montreal, and this led to the priesthood.

The Collège Séraphique didn't accept just anyone. Vocations were common in those days and the supply of candidates more than ample. The selection process was very demanding. I was accordingly summoned to the college along with some thirty other hopefuls for the entrance examination. I had to uphold the honour of the Jardin de l'Enfance, but all the others had a similar mission, be it only for the honour of the village school. I was among the lucky twelve . . . and ranked first! The event was much talked of in Saint-Narcisse. The following September saw me once again boarding the bus with my suitcases, this time to begin a new life with the Franciscans.

The college stood on Rue Laviolette, just north of the Trois-Rivières Seminary, and was connected with a monastery that served a working-class parish. It was a four-storey brick building with a huge courtyard in the back surrounded by a row of poplars and a high wooden fence. The students, 132 in number, lived a family life unlike any I have ever known. The Franciscans made it their mission to live simply and with joy. The regimen was conducted in an atmosphere of good humour. Unlike other colleges of the time, there was no uniform. At the most, we had to wear a blue suit on Sundays, black shoes, white shirt, and optional bow tie.

Who paid the annual $125 for board, lodging, and laundry? I have never known. It can't have been my adoptive parents, who had just lost a great deal of money in the 1929 Crash, nor my real father, who earned a low wage as a carpenter in Montreal. I had uncles in the secular clergy, but they weren't in the habit of subsidizing religious vocations. When speaking of their income

Marcel Trudel's birth family reunited briefly in 1930 to celebrate his brother Théophane's entry into the priesthood. A party was held in the village school. Shortly after, Trudel entered Collège Séraphique.

among themselves, they used to say, "The bread of the altar should return to the altar." I suppose I benefitted from college scholarships. The major religious orders and communities of religious brothers and sisters had always maintained a large network of benefactors. From this standpoint, my school and college life was a continual flow of good fortune, for I never had the money problems that forced others to look for work during the holidays. Many people helped me without my being aware of it. I hope I have not disappointed them.

Although the college was a juvenate, the religious régime was no more strict than in other classical colleges. It must be remembered that in those days most colleges (which were almost always diocesan seminaries belonging to an episcopal "corporation") imposed a regimen designed to prepare students for the religious life. At the Collège Séraphique, as in other colleges, we had to get up at the sound of a bell, attend mass every morning and all religious services on Sundays, and go to confession often. Our excursions about town were duly supervised, our mail was censored by the authorities, and we were forbidden all newspapers except the occasional *Devoir* or *Action catholique*. We had to have permission for every book we read other than a textbook, smoking was strictly forbidden, and instant expulsion followed any public breach of morality. It was the same throughout the province of Quebec.

True, the Collège Séraphique was more lenient than others in certain respects. We would have been expelled for sneaking a cigarette and, above all, for carrying on a correspondence with a young lady—not because of the offense itself, but because such conduct ran contrary to the vocation we were supposedly following. It was also true that we had to remain in college from September to June without going home for the New Year's celebrations. However, on New Year's Day those with families in Trois-Rivières were allowed to visit them for the paternal blessing. On the same day, in the recreation hall, cigarettes donated by well-wishers were handed out, and we were given as many cigarettes as we could smoke.

We had more devotional exercises to perform than students in other colleges. Apart from the usual routine of mass, communion, and common prayer, we were asked to visit the chapel after each meal. Our daily rosary was longer: what we called "the Franciscan crown" consisted of seventy Ave Marias instead of fifty. Before supper each evening the principal gave us what was termed a spiritual talk, in fact a lecture on various points of religious training. Meals were usually eaten in silence, although we took turns standing on a special podium and reading aloud from a biography or some educational book. Good Friday was spent in total silence. At midday we ate while kneeling, served by the Franciscan fathers wearing their voluminous white aprons. Despite the kneeling we were always very keen about this meal, because the menu included delicious baked beans and we could eat as much as we liked. The discipline, based on encouragement to do right, seemed very gentle to us. It was rather like living in a family where authority was maintained through trust. Often, whether in study hall or during recreation, we were left unsupervised except for a monitor in his final year who could give us permission for various things. Our toilets and showers were never locked and could be used at all times, contrary to the custom in other colleges.

When it came to religious training, however, we were under very close supervision. Like other colleges, ours had a spiritual director for the whole school, but at the Collège Séraphique we also had a personal spiritual director whom we had to meet regularly. When it came to spirituality, you might have expected the college to be a religious hotbed, but that wasn't the case. As a matter of fact, the major orders fear religious zeal as much as lukewarmth, heat and cold being equally dangerous in this respect, and apply the principle *in medio stat virtus*—the virtuous man is a well-balanced individual. I'm naturally a down-to-earth realist (which doesn't prevent me from occasionally dreaming). Mystical frenzy wasn't my thing, and in matters spiritual I tended to be less rather than more enthusiastic. Some of my fellows considered their spiritual advisor as important as their class teacher and would visit him at all hours of the day. I was always satisfied with meeting him for weekly confession. I can't remember having to work out spiritual difficulties. My problems were intellectual and I lived for my studies. For the rest, if I dreamed of becoming a Franciscan priest, I didn't see myself, once past the *Introïbo ad altare Dei,* in the confessional booth directing a flock of pale blue souls nor in a pulpit declaiming to a crowd of churchgoers—and even less did I visualize myself explaining transubstantiation to the peasants of Cochin China. For me, a career in the Franciscan cowl meant teaching Latin, Greek, and literature. I learned my lessons by explaining them (in my imagination) to the other students. I envisaged my future self standing on a platform in front of a roomful of students.

We were trained in Franciscan virtues that could serve us equally well in civilian life: observe economy in all things, be content with little, and do humble tasks yourself. Apart from a lay brother who was in charge of maintenance, we students were responsible for keeping the college clean. We all took turns washing sinks and tubs, sweeping, and dusting, not to mention the meritorious job of cleaning toilets. On fixed dates we washed the windows, walls, and desks. Good Friday, during which we observed a penitential silence, was floor-scrubbing day. These domestic works were conducted under the orders of a student called the *Grand Chevalier*, this being the knighthood of the brush. I held this post for a year. Deep in my corner of the cellar, I watched over the munitions (Old Dutch, rags, and brooms). I put up the duty list, urged on laggards, and inspected the work once it was done. If necessary I made them do it again, but sometimes I found it safer to do it over myself, for I had to answer to the discipline master who dropped by from time to time to see how things were going. He congratulated me on the good job the others were doing, but I also got the blame when it was bad.

The Franciscans wanted to give their future clerics a healthy physical training. They put into practice the principle of *mens sana in corpore sano*, making sure each student took part in sports. Other colleges of that era encouraged sports such as skating, hockey, skiing, catch ball, softball, and fives, but sports were optional and most often only a minority took part, the rest being content to walk about chatting or watching the players, thus preparing themselves to become enthusiastic spectators (but from the depths of an armchair in front of a television set). At my college, anyone who didn't play some sport would have been considered a bad student. Our college gear had to include a pair of skates, for example. All the students belonged to one of the regular clubs, divided into major, intermediate, minor, and even what are now called peewee leagues. Outside the hockey or ball-playing seasons, we engaged in huge collective sports such as the celebrated flag game.

On days when we had a whole holiday, wide-ranging expeditions were organized for anyone who was interested. The Young Naturalists, of which I was one, ventured far along the hillsides gathering specimens. Sometimes the good hikers walked to and from the Forges Saint-Maurice (some thirty kilometres in all), or crossed the St. Lawrence by boat to Saint-Angèle and from there walked to Nicolet to visit the college and back, a return trip of forty kilometres. When I was still a junior, I even saw the big boys skating on the St. Lawrence as far as Sorel. Because of their vow of poverty, the Franciscans had a tradition of walking. We were reminded of the seventeenth-century Recollets who set out for New France by first walking from Paris to their port of embarkation. And then there were those wonderful snowshoe rambles through the swirling snow and the long hikes in the country on the first spring days!

Physical fitness training began in the morning with gymnastics. After rising at five, we all went down to the basement recreation hall where the discipline master put us through a half-hour of Swedish movements. During my working life, especially the stressful years when there wasn't time for sports, I would feel the need to return to this routine of daily calisthenics, doing them first thing on getting out of bed. I don't think I've missed a day for some forty years, and it has become as necessary to me as orange juice and coffee at breakfast.

Emulation enhanced our training. For the annual sports day on May 24 we were split up into various groups, according to our tastes and aptitudes. The gymnasts were the most numerous. There were the Indian club swinging corps (I was the instructor one year), weightlifters working with dumbbells, gymnasts on the parallel bars, Scottish sword dancers performing with two crossed sabres laid on the ground, and even a few tightrope walkers who had learned with infinite patience to manoeuvre on a wire. On May 24, the day we commemorated the hero of New France, Dollard des Ormeaux, each group performed its routine dressed in white trousers and marching to music. By the end of the day every student had taken part in these Olympics.

Nor did we lack for distractions of a more intellectual nature. On Sunday afternoons we listened to recordings and were introduced to the great works of music. We had a concert band. In October 1932 Father Ferdinand Coîteux, then head of the school, founded the band by recruiting students who already played an instrument and getting others started. Despite my dreams, I hadn't yet had any musical training. I was asked to take cornet lessons. Although I would have preferred the flute or clarinet, I agreed enthusiastically, since both instrument and teacher were found for me. There were soon some twenty of us forming an ensemble of piano (the pianist had been playing since the age of five and was considered a prodigy), five violins, four clarinets, trumpet, trombone, two saxophones, a double bass, and a percussion section with a triangle, xylophone, and cymbals. It was the typical small concert band. After months of practice we were good enough to add a pleasant touch to festive meals and theatrical productions as well as supplying the rhythmic background for gymnastic displays. We even played outside the college in one of the city's theatres. The chance to enter the world of music was a culturally enriching experience for me. Later, as a professor of history, I paid greater attention than some of my colleagues to the artistic activities of our early society.

The orchestra members formed a group somewhat apart from the other students, what with our special hours of practice and musical friendships (something another college principal didn't particularly appreciate). I must admit that since there were several of us in the same class, we spent a lot of time surreptitiously copying pages of music or trying our hand at composing while the poor Latin teacher was doing his best to make the rules of syntax palatable.

In each class we had to do elocution exercises that our comrades criticized with gusto. It was good training for public speaking and a lesson in humility. We often had to face a larger audience. Both for our diversion and to accustom us to public performance, the college organized "family evenings" (variety shows, in fact) at which we were invited to recite a fable or a poem, or act a comic or tragic scene. We stayed in college during the winter holidays, and there was a show every evening. Each class presented a program. The seniors were better at staging shows than the juniors, but everyone had his moment of triumph. We were so busy with costumes, rehearsals, and preparations in general that we completely forgot about missing our families.

There were other occasions for exercising our talents, such as the feast day of St. Cecilia, patron saint of musicians, the feast day of the patron saint of the principle or the discipline master, or the visit of the order's provincial superior. As there weren't a great many students in the college, everyone had a chance to tread the boards sooner or later. I was familiar with those terrible "first nights" when we would stand on an improvised stage (three or four big tables arranged end to end for the so-called family evenings) in front of an audience that was all the more critical because everyone would eventually be in the same situation. Our appearances, whether willing or unwilling, were preceded by hours of stage fright. However, when we thought we'd done well, they were followed by a sense of euphoria, as though we'd accomplished something that would go down in the annals of theatrical history.

Alas, although I could recite La Fontaine's fables competently enough, I was a dreadful actor. Like other colleges, we staged great tragedies such as *Cinna* in 1931-32 and *Britannicus* in 1932-33. I didn't take part. In Henri Ghéon's *Trois sagesses du vieux Wang* (plays by Ghéon and Brochet were often performed, as their subject matter corresponded to the Franciscan spirit), the organizers tried to make me act the role of a missionary. I couldn't do the serious voice or express the feeling of proselytizing fervour and had to resign myself to becoming the catechizer Ly Tring Haï. I had fallen from the Peking dancer of my Jardin de l'Enfance days to end my theatrical career as a modest Chinaman.

These forays onto the stage were merely sporadic events in the course of my regular studies. Our curriculum was bursting at the seams and we certainly didn't lack for stimulation. One such stimulus was the library, the most exciting discovery of my teenage years. Imagine: five thousand volumes, just for the asking! Never had I seen so many books in one place—I, who prided myself on having thirty books at home. The library had everything you could ask for; it didn't matter whether you were a junior or senior student. And these books were within arm's reach, for the library was open three or four times a week and we were allowed to take out three books at a time.

As soon as I got to the college I went on a reading binge, devouring all of Léon Ville (you unfortunates know nothing of Léon Ville!) and Paul Féval. So immersed was I that one October evening, when marks were being read aloud, the principal had me stand and proceeded to give me a dressing-down.

"You, sir, were head of your class, but since your arrival you've been trailing near the bottom. It occurred to me to look at the list of books you've taken out of the library. I counted eighty, sir: eighty in six weeks!" Actually this wasn't the true total, for it didn't take into account all the books friends used to exchange while waiting for the next library day. I almost regretted having come first in the entrance exams. I was told to pull myself together and climb back up to the top rung, otherwise the college wouldn't keep such a lazybones. The upshot was that I had to curb my mania for reading and work toward the standard of excellence demanded of me. I moved up slowly and finished the year with marks near the top. In the years that followed I came first in my class. This was the level I had been ranked at, and it was up to me to maintain it. Still, I'd gained access to Ali Baba's cave, and the treasure was a lifetime of reading.

Our study régime was a demanding one. This college followed the old *cursus studiorum* of the Sulpicians, who trained the first Séraphiques of Montreal. In addition to the usual subjects, we began Latin in our first or elements year, Greek in the second, then method in subsequent years, during which our studies in Latin, Greek, and French became increasingly specialized. At the versification level—an aptly titled class—we wrote Latin verse. Those who have never done this can't comprehend how difficult it is to write a single line of Latin verse. To begin with, we had to decide what thought to express, then translate it into Latin, choosing words to fit a set number of long and short syllables, arranged according precise rules. To do this work (or rather this forced labour), we used a fat dictionary known as the *Gradus ad Parnassum* (literally "rising to Parnassus"), which supplied the number of syllables for each word. If we couldn't make our words fit the required pattern, we'd pick another subject and begin again. It took a good student an hour and a half to produce two short lines. But in the end what a pleasure it was to read Virgil! In this as in other subjects, I chose the most difficult projects. I had read Victor Hugo's poem, "Oceano Nox" ("Night on the Atlantic") and decided to translate its forty-eight lines into Latin verse—a considerable challenge.

In the literature class (*belles-lettres* or simply "letters"), we explored the growth of Romanticism, discovering the great French authors of prose and poetry. Here all the intensity of adolescence found its long-awaited outlet. To read Chateaubriand and Lamartine at seventeen! There were many among us who thought far more about becoming poets than Franciscan priests. How often we composed pastiches of these lines from Lamartine's "Le Lac":

Ainsi, toujours poussés vers de nouveaux rivages,
Dans la nuit éternelle emportés sans retour,
Ne pourrons-nous jamais sur l'océan des âges
Jeter l'ancre un seul jour?

(Thus, ever swept toward further shores,
Carried unendingly through th' eternal night,
Can we never, on the ocean of time,
Cast anchor for a single day?)

We would regularly compose an *Adieu à ma plume*, following some disappointment or other; then, our farewell soon forgotten, the pen would begin writing again.

In the rhetoric year we mainly practised discourse, the primary purpose of which, so we were told, was to move our audience. As in other colleges, we weren't taught to *speak* to the audience, but to deliver a speech. Alongside this program, however, rhetoric provided us with a cultural background and in fact was an extension of the previous year's letters course.

The strength of the *cursus studiorum* lay in the library's rich resources, the teachers' excellent preparation (most had gone to university, travelled in Europe, and even in some cases had had work published), and above all in the rigorous demands of the course. We had lengthy assignments in Latin and Greek, never less than twenty-two lines to be done in an hour and a half. During each term we had to translate and construe some two hundred lines of Greek and a little more Latin. We had to do it on our own in a special notebook. It was up to us to find the time in our individual work schedules. We practised extensive memorization by learning about a hundred lines of Latin and some fifty of Greek per term, as well as the poetry and prose of the great French authors. To this we added special projects such as the optional Holy Week competition, which consisted of reciting by heart—and in Latin—the Passion of Christ from one of the Gospels.

The feast of St. Thomas Aquinas on March 7 marked the end of the second term. We spent the entire day in the auditorium engaging in intellectual jousts. Each class took its turn on stage for a public competition. Students in the *éléments latins* class were divided into two teams and did battle with Latin verbs for weapons. Those in the syntax class were armed with examples of Latin grammar, in the method class with Greek grammar, and in the versification class with *iμ* verbs. The letters students took part in a poetry contest, while those in rhetoric displayed their oratorical prowess in debate. Prizes and honourable mentions were handed out in the evening, after which we went to bed to sleep on our laurels or to try to forget our bitter disappointments.

Each term ended with a period of written and oral exams. Oh, those orals! We had to suffer them in front of the whole class and invited teachers. Sometimes orals were even presided over by the study master. For a time this was Father Alcantara Dion, who had a doctorate from Milan University (the very title of "doctor" terrified us). Father Dion was a man of few words and rarely smiled. Indeed, when he did smile we sensed a trap. Presiding over the orals, he would casually open his copy of Livy at random, point to a paragraph, and say, "Translate!" We would immediately start to stammer. If we went down a wrong path he would encourage us to follow it as though it were the right one. We would stumble on from one blunder to another until we had made complete fools of ourselves, at which point he would remark coldly, "Do you realize what you're saying?" After one or two such ordeals we finally managed to rise to the challenge and mastered the art of combat. Thus in education, as in sports, hard training is necessary.

Our marks were read out in public every week, and term marks were announced with great solemnity before the entire teaching staff. All honours were publicly accorded in front of the whole college, and all admonishments too. The student who couldn't keep up was sent home. He was informed of this banishment in public, and proclaimed unfit for classical studies.

I had managed to keep pace with this demanding curriculum as far as the rhetoric level . Since the warning given me at the beginning of my elements year, I'd worked up to first place in my class and had held onto this position ever since. Each year I won the prize for excellence and came first in most subjects, including geography and history, although I didn't feel any special attraction for the latter. I became a Grand Chevalier (which meant I was in charge of college maintenance), head of the Mils gymnastic group, and president of the Young Naturalists and the Duns Scotus Academy. At the end of my letters year I received the school's top prize for good conduct. Finally—and we considered this the pinnacle of achievement and glory—I was named a monitor on entering the rhetoric year. The student who bore this title (Greek *monos* for short) acted as a middleman between the students and those in charge. If the teacher was absent, the monos presided over prayers, gave permission to leave the room, accompanied group outings, and read a pious text for the *Benedicite*.

Another thing that went to my head was my fledgling reputation as an author. During a college arts festival in the 1933-34 school year, I had read a sonnet of my own in public, *Invasion de Rome*. I was a great admirer of José Maria de Hérédia, and my fourteen lines were a brilliant (but involuntary) pastiche of his sonnets. I chose the same learned and powerful words, the same military hardware with the resounding fall of the last line. At this period I had written a five-act tragedy in alexandrine metre called *Nisus et Euryale,* based on a subject from Virgil. At eighteen, here was I, who had dreamed of being published one day, getting my first taste of the joys of authorship. All forty-eight lines of a poem I had pompously called "Magister adest et vocat te" ("The Master is come and calleth for thee") appeared in print. Of course this was a set subject; the *Annuaire* would never have published romantic reveries such as the one I had written on the death of my mother. My sermonizing alexandrines, with all the literary tricks that one soaks up at the age of eighteen, ended with this pathetic peroration:

Come to Gethsemane, climb unto Calvary
'Tis there thou shalt see into thy father's heart,
And give up hope then, if thou canst!

I was in print, and my one dream was to write a book.

Then came a day in my rhetoric year when my small universe was once again rocked. On December 8, 1935, during a public reading of term marks, I was sent down from college. Why?

The preceding year Father Léopold Boiteau had been named to succeed Father Coîteux, who had presided over us like a good father loath to scold. Father Boiteau, a tall, red-faced, narrow-featured man, practised austerity and was continually striving for whatever was "the most perfect." Judging that too much tolerance had been shown students whose Franciscan vocation was less than sure, he proceeded to purge the college. In September 1934 he refused to readmit one third of the students! In June 1934 there were twenty-four of us in my group, but by September there were only nine of us left to form the letters class. The purge had eliminated my toughest competitors in the race for first place (with the mercilessness of that age, I was glad of it). Not only that; it had also wiped out nearly the entire orchestra, which there was no mention of reorganizing under the new régime. By September 1935 we were down to six students for our rhetoric year.

A lack of sympathy had grown up between the college principal and myself that I imagine explains some of my blunders. Perhaps, having accumulated so many local honours, I had become like those whom Jove renders ridiculous when he wants to rid himself of them. However this may be, it was my duty as monitor to read a text from Holy Scripture or *The Imitation of Christ* before the noon meal. I took great care to choose a picturesque passage that related to some facet of everyday life. Unconsciously, I tried to amuse my audience rather than edify it. The new principal failed to appreciate my efforts and, rightly or wrongly, felt I had deliberately mocked him. He never breathed a word of this to me, but left me plenty of rope with which to hang myself.

I compounded my sins by causing a scandal in the Duns Scotus Academy, of which I was then president. The father who acted as moderator had made a decision that displeased me. Confident that without me everything would collapse, I handed him my resignation. To my great surprise, it was accepted, and someone competent was immediately found to fill my shoes. For the first time I learned that no one is irreplaceable and that resigning—however theatrical a gesture—is a pointless act. A few years later, I made a point of noting and trying to follow Benjamin Franklin's maxim: "I shall never ask, never refuse, nor ever resign an office."

My correspondence also got me into trouble. We wrote to our families once a month or more if necessary, but we had to hand in our letters unsealed, and the principal was entitled to read them. To amuse my correspondents, I willingly joked about this and that with a touch or more of sarcasm, as I still do. I wrote in complete confidence, never thinking for an instant that a college principal could find time to examine my letters.

I was unexpectedly warned by my spiritual director that there was talk of expelling me, even in the middle of the school year. The college council was to meet, and as the Franciscan provincial superior was passing through, I was encouraged to see him so as to present my version. This interview took place at the eleventh hour. The next day the marks were read in public. In the great study hall, with the teaching staff arrayed on the platform, I was asked to stand up. I, a monitor, invariably first in my class, holder of the grand prize for good conduct, learned my fate: for having done this, for having done that, for having behaved in such a way on a given occasion, I was to be sent away from the college for being a *mauvais esprit*—that is, critical and inclined to disobey. The expulsion took effect that very day.

There was nothing left for me to do but pack my bags. All contact with my fellow students was forbidden as of that moment. I did, however, have the nerve to return to the college a few weeks later and ask to meet three or four of my comrades in the parlour. To my amazement, they came to chat with me for a few moments. The principal was away and a master had felt it would be all right to tolerate our meeting. The principal soon heard about it and sent a very sharp letter to the seminary where I was studying, forbidding me to visit the college at any time in the future.

And so my apprenticeship for the Franciscan life came to an end on that early December day in 1935. I was eighteen and a half. My fall from grace was trumpeted abroad as loudly as my past successes. The circumstances surrounding my departure left me bitter for a long time. The five marvellous years spent at that college had benefitted my physical and moral well-being as much as my intellectual development. I had been very happy devoting enormous energy to fascinating tasks, and I had known a great many joys of mind and spirit. Then, without warning, like the *deus ex machina* of a tragedy, the principal declared me unfit and banned me from what had been my life. No one even cared to find out whether, seven months short of completing my baccalauréat, I could finish my letters course and at least get my *premier diplôme*. The college only cared about getting rid of a black sheep. I shouldn't have been so surprised. For five years I had witnessed such expulsions implemented with lightning speed at any moment of the school year.

My expulsion wasn't only the work of the principal. The decision was taken by the college council. Nevertheless, for a long time I laid the blame at his door. I felt he had intentionally *not* warned me, allowing me to dig my own grave as though afraid he might be forced to keep me otherwise. Perhaps it was only my imagination. Years later, when my work as an intellectual and a historian had brought me many laurels, I finally admitted that the principal had done the right thing. If there had been no expulsion, would I have stuck to my Franciscan vocation? Or would I have returned to secular life after wasted years, like so many I knew who have remained forever at odds with life?

When I think back on all this, I'm reminded of the optimistic philosophy of *Candide*: "All is for the best in the best of all possible worlds."

The author (front row, third from right) entered the Franciscan Collège Séraphique at age thirteen, to train for the priesthood.

5

Is Paris Worth a Mass?

I HAD ONLY TO WAIT for what the morrow would bring. For the moment, I was guaranteed at least a month's holiday. Given my eagerness to study, my record of repeated successes, and the imminence of the first-level baccalauréat exams, my family clearly saw that I mustn't remain idle for long.

I registered at the Trois-Rivières Seminary and entered the rhetoric class on January 8, 1936. But who was to pay the annual boarding fee of $230? This I never knew, just as I have never known who paid my earlier fees. Perhaps I received a seminary scholarship, funded by the legacies of old curés. Perhaps help came from my two priest uncles, one of whom was reputedly well off. In any case, the family naturally saw in me a future secular priest, although I hadn't yet pledged myself to such a vocation.

The seminary, a diocesan college belonging to the episcopal corporation, but which Bishop Comptois continually referred to in public as "my seminary," stood on Rue Laviolette next to the Collège Séraphique. An immense building of dressed stone had been recently constructed. It consisted of a basement and four storeys crowned by an impressive dome. At each end was a wing, with a basement and three storeys, also of dressed stone. The seminary was constructed to the most modern standards and almost entirely of highly durable materials. It had high, wide windows and was equipped with the latest in furnishings and sanitary arrangements. The kitchen generally and its stoves were the best available. A vast gymnasium had even been fitted up, something rare in other classical colleges. The rear of the central pavilion was connected to the old chapel that had survived the 1929 fire, a building in the Gothic style housing enormous organ pipes. On the south side of this complex, between Laviolette and Saint-François-Xavier, lay a large garden enjoyed by the teaching fathers. On the north side, between the same streets and as far as Rue Saint-Maurice (which separated the seminary from the Franciscan college) lay the immense, tree-lined schoolyard, a few giant elms shading the centre.

At the seminary I rediscovered my classmates from the Jardin de l'Enfance, but the members of my 1929-30 class were already doing their first year of philosophy. As the letters course in my Franciscan college had taken an extra year, I found myself among slightly younger comrades in my new rhetoric class and quickly formed a new group of friends.

Seminary students were no longer drawn from the almost exclusively professional and business backgrounds of the Jardin de l'Enfance pupils. The sons of the Trois-Rivières middle class who aspired to the liberal professions or the priesthood always attended the seminary, but there were others from a wide variety of backgrounds, some from rural elementary schools and working class neighbourhoods in the city. These were sons of farmers and wage-earners for whom a priestly career was already more or less decided upon. The clergy itself was drawn in large part from the countryside. Seminary priests were distinctly rural both in language and manner, and refined behaviour wasn't always their strong point.

I had come from a Franciscan juvenate where one would have expected a stricter, more meticulous regimen, and now here I was, entering a college run by secular priests whose rule was far less liberal. We had to wear a strange, outmoded uniform that looked like a cassock—a long black jacket in the shape of a greatcoat, called a *surtout*, the function of which was not only to disguise the shape of our lower trunk and thighs but also to cover our knees, although these were already hidden by our trousers. The knees tended to reappear as we grew. One day someone informed me that my uniform was too short. This coat had the added feature of being tied at the waist with a green wool sash, knotted on the left so that the ends fell over one hip. A tie and a black cap with a hard visor completed the uniform. Wearing a fedora, referred to as a *chapeau de monsieur*, was forbidden. Any student caught wearing such a hat in town instead of the regulation cap would have been punished. Even on hot days we had to wear the full uniform, cap included, in the playground. The only exception allowed was for students taking part in official matches between the major clubs, and the only acceptable substitute was a hockey or *balle-au-camp* (our baseball) outfit, so that in fact we were still wearing a uniform. Inside the college we weren't allowed to take off the long coat, wool sash, and tie until bedtime. On extraordinary occasions such

Marcel Trudel (third from right, front row) began studying at the Séminaire de Trois-Rivières in January 1936.

as June heatwaves, some priests in their infinite goodness permitted students to take off their coats—a red-letter day for us!

The rule about smoking was no less surprising. Cigarettes were strictly forbidden, but—and this is astounding—we were allowed to smoke not only pipes, but cigars! The latter, a luxury article, wasn't at all popular, but we sometimes smoked cigarettes on the sly by concealing them in a well-hollowed-out wooden cigar supplied with the necessary vents. As with cigars, pipes were not always what they seemed and didn't always burn just pipe tobacco. We sometimes broke cigarettes in two and stuck them into the bowls of our pipes, giving ourselves the illusion of indulging in forbidden fruit—a sometimes bitter-sweet illusion, especially if the cigarette smell reached the nose of our supervisor, who was never far away. No more pipe-smoking for the guilty party for many a day!

Pipe-smoking (for upper-classmen only) was a common activity. Each midday after lunch the smokers retired to a corner of the courtyard reserved for them, called the pipe corner. We had the right to stand there smoking for fifteen minutes. Sometimes we got the right to smoke after the evening meal, but it was a favour asked of the principal to mark a special occasion such as a major feast day, the birthday of an abbé or even one of our comrades, someone's success, or a group effort to clear the skating rink. We used to put our imaginations to work, and one of us would be delegated to ask the principal for a pipe session—the principal himself being at that moment in the priests' smoking room. One day, we couldn't think of a presentable excuse for smoking. I had become a smoker myself at this period, my friends being smokers, and boasted that I would get permission to smoke a pipe for the simple reason that we had no reason. My comrades took me at my word, and off to the principal I went with my tongue-in-cheek request. The good man granted us our pipe session because in his heart of hearts he thought me rather absurd, and my friends gave me a warm welcome.

What surprised me most at the seminary—and remember I was coming from a religious school to a college where students were destined for all kinds of professions—was the regimen concerning toilets and confessional booths, two places that evoked the fear of sin. Unlike the Collège Séraphique, the toilets at the seminary were always locked. The only person authorized to unlock them was a priest who came to open the door at the beginning of the recreation period. This same priest stood at the door throughout the allotted time until finally calling out his habitual, "Sign your papers," as though we were in class. We had to hurry up, otherwise he would go from one cubicle to another, chivvying laggards. Once everyone was out, he locked the door behind him.

Outside these specific opening hours we had to ask the supervisor for the key. He made sure that only one student at a time used the toilet. This was a fairly embarrassing proceeding if we happened to be in the study hall. A toilet cubicle had been constructed at one end of this immense room, against the wall facing the students. It was always kept locked. If you felt an urgent need you went up to the supervising priest's platform on one side of the hall, asked for the key, then walked to the front and unlocked the cubicle door with a loud click. You stayed inside for as long as need be; the sound of the toilet flushing announced your imminent reappearance. You duly emerged, locked the door, walked down the hall to hand back the key, and upon returning from this expedition tumbled into your seat. After a certain hour students would begin trailing up to the supervisor and on to the cubicle—usually the same boys. We knew, for example, that one boy would routinely begin his daily perambulation at twenty past eleven. Thus were morals maintained.

Morality was also preserved by supervising attendance at confession. At the seminary I discovered the confession voucher. Students weren't trusted to practise the sacrament of penitence voluntarily. We had to hand in two confession vouchers every month. The student signed his name on a slip of paper, rolled it up tightly, and slid it through the grillwork in the confession booth. The confessor would hand this voucher to the principle, who would enter one more confession to the student's credit, or ask a trusted student to keep the tally. If your two vouchers weren't handed in by the end of the month, you got a black mark in piety and your monthly holiday might be docked. This system was under considerable fire when I entered the seminary in 1936. Boys would slide two slips of paper through the grillwork instead of one. The confessor didn't notice a thing or else turned a blind eye to this ruse. A boy going to his third confession in a month would write the name of a less fervent comrade on the voucher. The trusted student who tallied the confession vouchers could be bribed. If you chose a confessor known to scorn the voucher system, you could simply say to him in the confession booth, "Monsieur l'abbé, I don't want to confess," and leave him a voucher or two. The authorities could sleep in peace, secure in the knowledge that the students went to confession.

At the Collège Séraphique we had gymnastics every morning, but all that ended at the seminary. We went straight from dormitory to study hall and waited there until it was time for chapel and the obligatory mass, after which we went to the dining hall. As for games, there was no question of forcing us to play, alas! We were left to ourselves on this score. Sports were played, however, and on a grand scale, but they were spectator sports, where members of very small group played hockey or our version of baseball before an immobile audience made up of fellow-students. The college's major sports clubs left no room for others. A group from our year finally made a small skating rink on our own initiative. Here we played hockey using a puck but not the traditional rules. I played hard and usually took defense. It was the man I was chasing, not the puck.

Inside the school a huge gymnasium had been installed in the basement, but in all my time there it never contained a single piece of equipment. It was used as a cloakroom by players in the major clubs as well as for band rehearsals. Senior students had the privilege of a corner to themselves where they could hang out, chat, and play cards.

Given the circumstances, small groups formed in the courtyard, talking as they walked. We called them "the peripateticians" (no big word could scare us). These groups always consisted of the same friends: the "little fathers" (from the Collège Séraphique), the "Shawins" (from Shawinigan), and the "band guys." I had my group, made up of musicians, avid readers, and poets. We dreamed of an intellectual career, and for us recreation was the pursuit of works of the mind. We considered ourselves a nucleus of culture amid an indifferent mass.

When I arrived at the seminary I noticed that its letters course was very inferior to what I was accustomed to. Admittedly, we had forty students in our rhetoric course compared to just six at the Collège Séraphique. In any case, none of the teachers, who were all abbés (that is, members of the secular clergy), had progressed beyond the baccalauréat level and none had gone on to specialize in the subject they were teaching. They were there by virtue of the *grâce d'état*—the grace and favour of the religious powers. None of them had spent any length of time in the great capitals of the human mind and spirit. Our Latin teacher had visited Europe, but only as a tourist, and it was told of him that, seeing the abundance of art everywhere, he had remarked admiringly in his broad Québécois, "Des estâtues, y en â jusque sus les piquas de clôtures!" ("There are statues all over, even on the fence posts!") *Si non è vero* . . . it may have been a joke, but it captured his language perfectly. This was the teacher who told our class, in the midst of a campaign for speaking good French, "Our ancestors said 'moé pis toé' (moi puis toi), and we're going to keep right on saying 'moé pis toé.'" He used to translate Latin texts for us word for word, as though we were beginners, losing himself in the long Ciceronian periods. We never had time to get very far in the subject.

The highest praise we could find for the Greek teacher was that he knew his Ragon grammar by heart. With much huffing and puffing he could barely construe a few lines of Thucydides, but when it came to grammar he would refer us to Ragon from memory in the following fashion: "See remark number three of rule 255, or the fourth in article 322," leaving the class open-mouthed. Of Greek culture, art, and all the humanism that animated the ancient world for centuries and nurtured Western society, there was no question. The teacher was there to prepare us for our baccalauréat exam next June, and that was that! His first name was Auguste (we called him Gus), and he was given the task of producing the annual play, despite his laborious manner of speaking. Because he was fat, with a huge paunch that served as a sounding box for his double-bass voice, he was asked each year (but only on this annual occasion) to preach the All Souls' Day sermon. Speaking from the high pulpit beneath the chapel's soaring vault, he became the veritable Judgment Day trumpet.

Our English course used the same exam-oriented approach. We were being prepared for "the bac." Our teacher was a spruce young abbé whose main qualification for teaching the subject was a stint in New England performing some ministry or other. He carried himself with a jaunty air and was the very picture of the abbé who soon becomes a military chaplain sporting a trim officer's uniform, swagger stick tucked under his arm. Of English literature he imparted nothing.

Our French teacher, who also taught Canadian history, was no better prepared. Two abbés by the name of Tessier, apparently cousins, were on staff at the time. One, a very tall, kindly, and somewhat effeminate man was nicknamed "Grand-Tess," while the other, very short and stocky, with a brusque and scornful of manner, was dubbed "Ti-Tess." This was Albert Tessier, our study master, known for his writings on regional history and responsible for a great awakening in his milieu. Grand-Tess was in charge of preparing us for the French baccalauréat exam, in which we had five hours to write either an analysis of a classical author or a discourse on Canadian history, as we chose.

Yes, a discourse—for Canadian history was taught in our rhetoric class to prepare us for the essay we would have to write, without notes or reference works, based only on what we had learned or could invent. History was not a subject for research, but for emotion. The best work was the one that struck the most responsive chord. We wrote by heart and with heart, and were therefore bound to portray the past in all its beauty and glory, complete with heroes, missionaries, and grand schemes, all told in a high-flown style. Later, as a fledgling career historian, I had to combat this deep-rooted system. In 1949, at the beginning of my first work of Canadian history (*Louis XVI, le Congrès américain, et le Canada, 1774-1789*), I shocked many readers by writing this sentence: "History, in French Canada, has always been comfortably ensconced in the rhetoric department."

The year of my first bac exam, Laval University set the fur trade as the history essay subject. By the time I entered the seminary in January, Grand-Tess had apparently been drumming the topic into the students since September, and he kept right on doing it. He would come to class, his long arms loaded with every book that had a chapter on the fur trade. But of documentation to show, read, or discuss, there was none! And the worthy abbé railed repeatedly against the use of brandy. We came away feeling he must take us for recovering alcoholics.

In the Franciscan college we were encouraged to memorize as many passages from great literature as possible, whether in French, English, or Latin. At the seminary the art of memorization formed no part of the program. And yet what pure pleasure it was to recite to oneself texts that became inner music, such as this Villon ballad:

Brother humans, who live after us . . .

or the sonnet to Hélène:

When you are very old, at evening in the candlelight . . .

or this passage from one of Madame de Sévigné's letters:

Do you know what it is to ted hay? I must tell you that tedding hay is the most enjoyable thing in the world . . .

or this passage from Chateaubriand:

So saying, I strode along, my face aflame, the wind whistling in my hair . . .

or Verlaine:

The long sobs / Of violins / In autumn

or Francis Jammes:

There are days when the soul is sad. It droops . . .

or Mallarmé:

This virgin, this exhilarating, this beautiful day . . .

or even these first lines from one of Virgil's eclogues:

Tityre, tu, patulae recubans sub tegmine fagi, / Silvestrum tenui musam meditaris avena. (You, Tityrus, 'neath a broad beech-canopy reclining, on the slender oat rehearse your silvan ditties.)

These and how many more passages came and went through memory.

At the seminary I decided to keep up the habit of learning things by heart, ever conscious of the need to enrich my mind. It brought me a minor triumph in which I saved the honour (or so one believes at that age) of French Canada in the presence of a *Français de France*. We saw very few Frenchmen in those days. This one went from college to college, declaiming poetry with an artistry that charmed us. During his visit, the students were taken to the assembly hall to hear him. At the end of the performance he issued a challenge. "Quote me a line from any classical piece, and I will recite the next line!" Someone in the hall responded with, "À moi, comte, deux mots" (A word or two, Count," from *Le Cid*. The Frenchman easily continued with, "Parle. Ôte-moi d'un doute. Connais-tu bien don Diègue?" ("Speak. Enlighten me. Do you know Don Diego well?") Another offered a quote in the same easy vein: "Que vouliez-vous qu'il fit contre trois?" ("What could he do against three?") As before, the response was quick: "Qu'il mourût, ou qu'un beau désespoir alors le secourût." ("He might have died or been saved by a fine despair.")

While the audience clapped, a line of poetry popped into my head that I had unwittingly quoted in my poem "Magister adest." I stood up and recited, "Devine si tu peux et choisis si tu l'oses." ("Guess if you can and choose if you dare.")

The Frenchman thought hard, but in vain. The next line just wouldn't come. To save face he said, "Tell me what play the line is from."

"From Corneille's *Héraclius*," I replied, citing a play that is something of a rarity.

The Frenchman tried to cover himself adroitly by finding fault with me. "So sir, reader of *Héraclius*, can you give me the next line?"

I took care not to admit my ignorance. "Sir, you were the one who issued the challenge." How I savoured the applause that followed!

Our rhetoric class lacked a good library. The seminary had been known for its fine library before the fire of 1929. Everything was lost, to be replaced by a hodge-podge of donations from various quarters. The library, reconstituted in this hit or miss fashion, was now a poor one. Each class had a cupboard of books gathered for specific needs, but in rhetoric we could find little more than the authors needed for our Canadian history essay. The only solution was to build one's own library by buying secondhand books or the little Larousse classics. With my meagre pocket money I put together a good collection of books that I devotedly lugged along through all my various moves.

Accustomed to a demanding curriculum and a hard-fought battle for first place, and trained to read Greek and Latin authors almost fluently, I was in the top rank when I arrived at the seminary and well ahead of the usual first-ranking student. From then on, my goal was to be a good ten points ahead of the student who placed second. This competitive approach wasn't exactly encouraged. One abbé made no bones about repeatedly saying, "First in class, last in life." I swore to myself that I'd prove him wrong.

In any case, life was going along just fine. I sat at the back of the class, busy with other things while the teacher floundered through his analyses. I read, wrote verse, helped a friend with his Greek translation for the day, and continued these leisure activities in the study hall, having sprinted through the few short lines of our translation assignment in fifteen or twenty minutes.

We had to ask permission to read in the study hall, as though reading weren't an intellectual activity. After putting my exercise book on the corner of my desk where it was easily seen, I would hold up the book I wanted to read and wait until the supervisor gave me the nod. Initially he was very surprised to see me raising my hand at the beginning of the study period. He would stand up, and while the others looked on with derision, would step down from the platform with a reproving frown and walk over to my seat, at which point I would show him the fair copy of my completed translation.

I finished my rhetoric year with the usual prize for excellence. My awards included first prizes in French and Greek literature. In Canadian history I received a mere honourable mention. As a subject this wasn't very important to me. I really applied myself when it came to the first-level baccalauréat exams (called *bac de Rhéto* or *bac de Lettres*), netting 82.1 percent. I was a tenth of a point short of being first among all the candidates for Laval University. This lessened my triumph, but I knew that if I achieved an overall average of 80 percent in the two baccalauréat sections (familiarly called "Rhéto" and "Philo"), I would be awarded a year's free university tuition. This 80 percent was my goal from then on.

The seminary was better equipped for my subsequent two philosophy years. The teachers were university graduates. Most had doctorates in theology, a discipline then very close to philosophy, and in fact we were taught that philosophy was the servant of theology. Even the mathematics teacher had a theology doctorate. This was no drawback, for he was well-versed in his field and knew how to stimulate our interest. The chemistry and physics teachers were equally well qualified. Day after day we discovered the laws of nature under their tutelage. We enjoyed these two subjects all the more for having access to huge, well-equipped laboratories. We were a small group of friends working in the context of the Young Naturalists' Club, and on holidays we were allowed to have the precious key to the labs, with the inevitable admonition to be sensible. I'm amazed the seminary was still standing after all our unsupervised experiments.

We had two excellent philosophy teachers. Abbé Albert Bordeleau was the epitome of the stimulating teacher, a skilled dialectician who never allowed us to fall asleep and spurned all our objections with a flick of the wrist. He appeared to be enjoyably occupied in explaining a textbook to us all year long. For metaphysics and ethics in our second year we had Abbé Jules Gélinas, a more austere but intellectually refined man and so open-minded that he was barred from acting as a spiritual director for students.

We still studied philosophy from the three-volume Latin textbook written by Abbé Stanislas Lortie. The teacher would give most of his analysis in French for the salvation of those who hadn't yet taken to Latin. He would often question us in Latin, mostly for his own amusement. The stronger students replied in kind. "Dominus Trudel," he would say, "dic mihi quid sit auctoritas." And Dominus Trudel would reply, sticking as closely as possible, word for word, to the textbook. We were allowed to write essays in the language of our choice. As Latin was easy for me, especially in philosophy, I found it simpler (as did some of my fellow students) to do my homework in that language. The vocabulary and turns of phrase were supplied directly by the textbook, with the result that an essay was soon done and had a particularly scholarly air about it. I have in front of me one of these assignments from my first year of Philo, entitled *De identitate intellectus et objecti in cognitione*, and in the margin is the name of the author, *Marcellus Trudel*. I began with a brief statement: "*Cognitio nobis verum est mysterium*," and went on to develop the subject over five pages. The teacher wrote the following comment: "*Bene! satis completa; habes verum sensum theseos.*"

Clowning with fedoras (aged 18-19), at the Trois-Rivières Seminary.
Trudel's first day there was January 18, 1936.
(The author is on the left.)

With Clémence, Trudel's adopted sister, prior to beginning his second year at the Trois-Rivières Seminary.

We were taught Thomist philosophy exclusively. The great Canadian pontiff of this philosophy was still the celebrated Monseigneur L.-A. Pâquet, whom I glimpsed when he was ninety-three in the seclusion of his room at the Quebec Seminary. Thomist philosophy was certainly an admirable tool for demonstrating the mechanics of knowledge and it supplied a useful framework for thought, but its major drawback was that it blocked access to any other system. Everything that didn't come from St. Thomas Aquinas was to be rejected. In Christianizing Aristotle, he had formulated a system of thought that no one after him could supplant. Cartesian philosophy was presented to us as childish. It was debunked in one short page, the core of the rebuttal being contained in a three-line syllogism.

This Thomist interdiction could be accidentally circumvented, however. Among the little Larousse classics that I had bought were a few small works on philosophy. As usual, when we were marching in file through the corridors (as we always did), I pulled out of my pocket a French translation of Locke's *Essay Concerning Human Understanding*. I was walking along, my feet on the ground but my head in the clouds, when the supervisor (who happened to be my philosophy teacher that day) came over to see what could be so absorbing for one of his students. I proudly showed him my Locke. He was visibly taken aback. "But Monsieur," he exclaimed, "this philosopher is on the Index!"

"On the Index? You must be mistaken, Monsieur l'abbé. I have the principal's stamp on the cover." He looked. Yes, the stamp was indeed there. When I had presented my stack of books to the principal for the stamp of approval required for everything except textbooks, Locke hadn't meant much to him and the good abbé had signed. My teacher was generous and let me off with a warning without confiscating my Locke.

Many of the arguments put forward in our textbook were outmoded and bore no relation to developments over time. Nevertheless they remained on the curriculum because they were part of the system. Our textbook accordingly rejected the idea of free schooling, asserting that it destroyed the family. How could this be? The answer was simple: free schooling would deprive the father of the noble satisfaction of raising his family by the sweat of his brow and thereby remove the crown of paternal authority. The final blow was the incontrovertible argument that anything free was worthless! Our textbook also rejected the idea of obligatory schooling and non-denominational schools. Freedom of religion and of the press, it stated, were absurd in themselves and at the very most could be merely tolerated. Moreover, the duties of a wife (listen well, you feminists) consisted of *exhibere marito reverentiam et obedientiam, domestica negotia curare, educandae proli operam navare*, in other words, showing respect and obedience to one's husband, managing household affairs, and devoting oneself to the upbringing and training of children. In a nutshell, it was what our ancestors had learned in the eighteenth century in Monseigneur de Saint-Vallier's *Catéchisme*. If you want to understand anything about the behaviour of the public men of my generation or even (because my generation has begun to react) of preceding generations (I'm thinking especially of a man like Maurice Duplessis, or many of our bishops and curés), you must go back to these textbooks of Thomist philosophy from which they learned their line of conduct.

The two years of Philo that concluded my schooldays began very badly. After my triumph in Rhéto came a mediocre Philo I. No more literature, no more Greek, nothing but philosophy (in the most technical of courses), mathematics, and chemistry. Those who were strong in letters weren't always good at sciences. As we moved from Rhéto to Philo, the class rankings changed radically. I'd never been much interested in mathematics and hadn't touched the subject since entering *éléments latins* at the junior high school level. Mathematics was an important feature of the philosophy course. Philosophy interested me as a means of forming one's reasoning powers, but nothing more. I liked the natural sciences and was enthusiastic about chemistry. If I had made as much effort in other subjects as I did in this, perhaps I would have kept my first-place marks, but my zeros in math inevitably sunk me. My only prize at the end of the year was an award for . . . patriotism! I had scoffed at consolation prizes in the Jardin de l'Enfance, but now it was my turn. The patriotism prize drew derisive hoots from the audience. Still, when it came to the chemistry exam, which counted in the total for the next baccalauréat level (and I was aiming at 80 percent to win the university scholarship), I got the mark I had dreamed of with something over, just in case: 19.2 out of 20.

How would I do in the Philo II finals, with its philosophy, mathematics, and physics? This ultimate year presented a tough challenge. I decided to give it my all. Algebra and logarithms were a closed book to me, but I would just have to start from zero and master them. From the beginning of the final year I studied my textbook, beginning on the first page and promising myself not to turn to the second until I'd understood every line perfectly. And so it went: from line to line, page to page, I worked at understanding what had always left me indifferent. This draconian approach didn't keep me from my Greek authors, however, and I was in the process of translating a minor work, Lucian's *The Cock,* into French.

For the June finals we had to do a general review of all subjects so as to master them. Courses therefore stopped in May, and we were left pretty well to our own devices for this pre-baccalauréat phase. Prudent as always, I decided to do the revision three times: a first, starting in January, very slowly and thoroughly, a faster-paced second revision, and the third at lightning speed. I drew up a daily timetable listing the number of pages to be reviewed, and followed it strictly from January to mid-June. This schedule for each day and hour still left me some leisure, and as the review speeded up I had even more free time. The other students who had waited until May to get down to work were feeling the increasing pressure. As my free time expanded I got out my Greek authors, like someone with nothing better to do.

"Are you crazy? What about your bac?" my comrades asked.

"It's okay, I'm finishing up my second revision."

In the final three or four days, while the others were making a supreme effort and complaining of lack of time, I had arranged for a period of complete relaxation, all textbooks closed, so as to come to the exams with my brain well-rested.

My method worked. For this final section of the baccalauréat, I, the previous year's weakling, got surprisingly good marks—over 80 percent. Taken together, the two baccalauréat sections gave me a *bachelier ès arts* with 82.4 percent, *summa cum laude.* I was the only one in my year to receive this accolade. The year's free tuition in the faculty of my choice at Laval was mine.

During these three years at the seminary I had taken part in a number of extracurricular activities. One was the St. Thomas Aquinas Academy, a college study and discussion group. For the entry competition I submitted a hundred or so lines of my tragedy, *Nisus et Euryale*. This shower of alexandrines placed me well in front of the others, but the Bossuet chair awarded for it wasn't really appropriate. Within a few months I proudly took the president's chair. I also experienced the dangers of authorship for the first time. Another candidate wanted to follow my recipe for getting into the academy. He got hold of my tragedy and lifted pages from it, representing them as his own. The fraud was discovered and the candidate rejected. Today this man is a respected canon.

I joined the Cercle Dollard, which trained us for public debate. As in other areas, I was an aggressive debater, giving no quarter to my opponents. I had to have the last word and if need be it could be brutal. How I've changed since my untamed youth!

The band was another of my activities. The leader was J.-G. Turcotte, a well-known musician. Although I looked back wistfully on my happy hours with the Collège Séraphique's orchestra, at least I was continuing my musical training.

I joined the Young Naturalists' group, which included dissection as part of the program. I specialized in raising white rats, also referred to as white mice. A corner in the basement of the Grand Seminary was assigned me for my cages and food. Every day I went down to look after my mice. I used to take one or two out of the cage and let them run over my shoulders and down my sleeves. This was my inspiration for the passage in my novel *Vézine,* in which my hero also raised white mice in his old house.

> There were little rats, completely white, that were sometimes mistaken for mice. They carried their food to their mouths with their paws, licked their fur after a meal, and were as well-behaved as dolls. They all had friendly faces—even the large male who used his cone-shaped head to block the nest entrance at the end of the cage.
>
> Vézine lifted the wire panel on one side of the cage. Luce thought the little rodents were about to run away and was afraid, but the animals stayed put and looked at the visitors, their little muzzles quivering. Run away? But where to? They were at home in this wooden box. They'd been born in a nest of wood shavings in the box, and there they'd learned to scamper about without getting dirty, eat neatly, and clean themselves. They were the masters and mistresses of their dwelling. . . . He took the female in the hollow of his hand. . . . Suddenly, noticing the opening of his sleeve at the cuff, she dove inside. His rippling sleeve revealed her laborious progress to the tip of his shoulder. Vézine felt inside his jacket and gathered up the little tunneller at the end of her run. He put her on top of his head, where she clung on with her tail to keep from falling.

Like Vézine, I too had a favourite female rat. I was very fond of her, but one day while I was away a fellow student came looking for something to dissect. My rat being used to people, she went up to him and he took her away. My enthusiasm for raising animals fell by several notches.

Unlike some of the other students, I took no part in politics. These students were already involved in municipal or even provincial and federal parties. Even so, I had a passive involvement. In 1936, I attended the large banquet organized by the Union Nationale Party to celebrate the rise to power of Maurice Duplessis. Don't look for my face in photographs of the head table at this celebration—a feast that, with a brief hiatus, was to last a quarter of a century. I and other seminary students were merely waiting on tables. The banquet took place in the large students' dining room, echoing with the hubbub of animated conversation and victory speeches. Next day, all the waiters filed through the bursar's office where he handed each of us a dollar tip on behalf of Maurice Duplessis. One dollar was quite a handsome sum in 1936 and it provided me with pocket money for some time. I deduced from this that the Union Nationale had a sizeable war chest and that politics could net more money than perusing Demosthenes.

Patriotic activity interested me more than politics. In those days nationalism's driving force was the Church, soon to be replaced by the Union Nationale. The seminaries took on the mission of being schools of patriotism (our school motto was *Religioni et Patriae*—Faith and Fatherland). They were constantly kindling the spark of nationalism among their students. The principal laboratory of this nationalism was the practice of discourse in our rhetoric classes with arguments drawn from history. Its manifestation *par excellence* was the celebration of Dollard Day on May 24, substituted for the Victoria Day holiday. The 1931 Statute of Westminster that enshrined Canada's independence from Great Britain was very recent, and we all—or almost all—had a more specific dream of independence. We'd never heard the slogan, *Québec libre,* and in any case the name Quebec for what was generally known as the Province of Quebec wasn't in current use. We talked of an independent Laurentia. What student of those days has not drafted a constitution for this republic?

I founded my own movement and, being a mere student, thought it absolutely splendid. Imperialism was the enemy. Our activity consisted of printing threatening slogans in a stamp-sized format. The only one I remember is "Death to imperialism!" We found comrades with the courage to stick these everywhere—on shop windows, lamp posts, and the backs of tram seats—and imagined the Mounties on our heels, although we certainly can't be blamed for the demise of the British Empire. At least, thanks to this heroic campaign, I was awarded a prize for patriotism at the end of my Philo 1 year.

Curiously enough, our nationalistic practices had no connection with contemporary movements, in particular the activities of Jeune-Canada. From the standpoint of ideas our city of Trois-Rivières was an enclave where Abbé Albert Tessier preached the religion of regionalism. Only a Catholic Action movement could break through the barriers of this isolation, and with great difficulty, since each bishop wanted to keep total control of everything that moved in his diocese. These were the years when Catholic youth movements were much in vogue—Jeunesse étudiante catholique (J.É.C., young Catholic students), Jeunesse ouvrière catholique (J.O.C., young Catholic workers), and Jeunesse agricole catholique (J.A.C., young Catholic farmers). The J.É.C. was beginning to invade the classical colleges. Like the others, its goal was to win young people and the world for Christ, a universal aim that frightened no one. But how could we possibly feel the need to win the youth of the colleges for Christ? Didn't we live under almost the same regimen as the major religious orders? We went to mass every day, said frequent prayers, and were taught even the most secular of subjects by priests. Win over this youth for Christ? What was going on, anyway? Was there an unconscious feeling that the all-pervasive Catholicism of our lives was already little more than a facade that might collapse? Like everyone else, as a student I didn't foresee any change in society. I was simply amazed (as were plenty of others) that a society where everything was governed by the Church needed to be reconquered for Christ.

Joining the J.É.C. became the thing to do. There was a badge, a beret, and an attempt to find a new way of discussing religion. My group of friends were against it. I myself looked on any form of regimentation with horror. I was furious at certain fellow students who joined the group, knowing they couldn't have cared less about winning over anything for Christ. It was merely a means of getting in their teachers' good books. I was among the dissidents. The seminary authorities were much disturbed by the battle that was dividing the class, and they put an end to it with a compromise: all students would join the movement without being required to fulfil the formal requirements. We became "Jécistes" in name only. I even agreed to work on the J.É.C. newsletter. If other students had joined just to curry favour with their superiors, why shouldn't I take advantage of it to satisfy my passion for publishing?

My approach to social activism was the same. A temperance campaign was being mounted by Abbé Henri Moreau, professor of chemistry and the college's spiritual director (a plurality of benefices sanctioned by his superiors).

He called on my imagination to illustrate his talks, which in fact needed considerable livening up. My good friend Albert Bergeron and I wrote comic sketches designed to amuse everyone while getting the anti-alcoholic message across, and I was the actor.

As in the Collège Séraphique, I continued to write a great deal for pleasure. After the publication of my poem in 1935, I felt the need to write about something—anything, provided it was published. In May 1936, a month before my final baccalauréat exams, I published an article in the J.É.C. newspaper entitled, "L'as des jécistes" ("The J.É.C. Ace"). The ace in question was Jesus in the Temple, "the little carpenter guy." Like ourselves in college, he was a beardless but wise debater confronting the scoffers who mocked his ideals.

In that same month I published another article in *Le Bien Public* of Trois-Rivières entitled, "Agriculture, carrière ouverte au bacheliers" ("Farming, a career open to graduates"). The following week it was "Comment établir les bacheliers sur la terre" ("How to start graduates farming"). This was the era of the back-to-the-land movement, seen as a way out of the Great Depression. At the same time we students were eagerly searching for new openings for graduates outside the Church. Graduation was fast approaching. After that we either had to take holy orders or train to become lawyers, notaries, or doctors. There were almost no other choices in the secular field.

The first agronomists ran into stiff opposition from traditional habitant farmers, but we were beginning to be convinced that agriculture should no longer be merely a matter of having a sturdy arm. It required method, knowledge, and good management. The term "industrial" wasn't yet used in relation to farming. If a classical college graduate came from a rural background and couldn't go on to university, then he could help revitalize our agriculture. I felt it was a mistake to believe that farming was, as I put it, "independent of the intellectual and moral training that made a man complete." Greek might be as useless in a clover field as in a notary's office, but wasn't the aim of the classical course "none other than to produce a mental outlook?"

In September 1937 I submitted a story about the Rebellion of 1837-38 to a contest in the *Le J.É.C.* I called it "Une nuit de 1837." The story won first prize, offered by Abbé Lionel Groulx. This was my first encounter with Groulx, although very indirect, since I wasn't required to meet him. At the time I admired him less for his history than for his stimulating work with young people.

While still in college, I published another poem in the May 1938 issue of *Le J.É.C.* called "Logarithmes." *Le Nouvelliste* reprinted it ten years later under the title "De moins l'infini à plus l'infini" ("From the less infinite to the more infinite"). Using the style of a sonnet by José Maria de Hérédia and a strictly mathematical vocabulary, I wanted to parody the poets of my day who loaded their poems with abstract words to give their work profundity. Avant-garde critics fell into the trap and saw a "message" in what was merely a spoof by a knowledgeable school-boy:

> From sine to sine, from circles to radii,
> My vector calibrated my rational beings;
> Saturating my concepts with cubes and prisms,
> I probed the binomial and the bone of syllogisms.
> The hexagon and the point, those owls of the brain,
> Hoot in the abstract where the angle's a cave.
> And my dream marks out an infinite straight line
> Of nebulous segments, senseless staves . . .
>
> Weary of developing the trapezoid funereal
> Where the straw-stuffed mind cleaves to the parallel,
> I foreswore the sliding gauge and base eternal
>
> To go, for x time, beyond the ideal,
> Much farther from things distant than the void in total,
> To ponder, face to face, an isosceles triangle.

What amounted to the final curtain of the family drama of 1922 had fallen in September 1937, when my natural father died suddenly in Montreal. He had lived there since my mother's death, working as a carpenter at the Saint-Jean-de-Dieu Hospital. He had married a widow with grown children in 1936, an event that caused indignation among some of my sisters, even though he'd been separated from his family for fourteen years. A few months after this marriage I'd been taken to see him in Montreal. It was my first trip to the city. I took the ritual tramway ride to St. Joseph's Oratory, but without my father, who had to stay at home. I had been brought up far away and hadn't seen him since my oldest brother's ordination in 1930. I found myself face to face with a stranger and couldn't help thinking about the home we'd had in the village, the big shop, the garden with its bees and the big fields behind it. Now this father was living in east-end Montreal in an old house on Amherst, near St. Catherine Street. The house was flush with the sidewalk, had no back yard, and was beset by the infernal din of trams racketing right by his door. Today when I look out of my condominium in Longueuil I often gaze across the St. Lawrence at the cluster of poor dwellings that form the neighbourhood of small wage-earners where he lived, and I say to myself that some people have a pretty wretched fate.

The classic family scene took place at my father's graveside. It had been agreed that he would be buried in the plot belonging to his second wife. The funeral procession therefore went to the Côte-des-Neiges Cemetery. Papers were signed at the office and we proceeded into the graveyard. However, instead of heading for the section containing family plots, the hearse moved toward the potter's field where paupers were buried.

My older siblings were shocked and angry. There had been some underhand business. The second wife didn't want him in her plot, yet refused to have him buried in our family plot in Saint-Narcisse-de-Champlain. A decision was immediately taken: he would be buried in our plot—but the papers had to be revoked. An enterprising brother-in-law went to the Superior Court and got a judge's order on the same day. We left the cemetery with our father's body, and he was buried in the Trudel plot. Possibly because of his remarriage or for other reasons (I took no part in the family council), he wasn't buried in the Cossette plot with his first wife.

My father's burial was also a reunion for my brothers and sisters. We hadn't been together like this for seven years. In any case, once children have set up for themselves in different places, families usually get together only for weddings or funerals and enjoy themselves equally at both.

On June 15, 1938, I left the seminary. I was twenty-one, and my classical studies were over. All through that final year and even the preceding year I had thought about my future career. To help us choose, the college authorities had provided numerous resources, both useful and useless, but mainly of a religious nature. Promoters called "recruiting fathers" from various religious communities visited us often. We were assembled in the lecture hall each time to hear what they had to say. Religious communities that resorted to this kind of advertising weren't the most distinguished, nor did their promoters always spring from Jove's brow. The major orders didn't need to drum up business in this way since they never lacked for applicants.

There was no drumming at all on the lay side. Most students who didn't go in for the priesthood became lawyers, notaries, or doctors. There was a hierarchy in these lay careers, however. Doctors were considered almost as laudable as priests. Lawyers were still presented to us in all seriousness as the defenders of widows and orphans. Accordingly, medicine and law were classed with the priesthood as quasi-religious callings. There were few other lay careers on offer. Apart from the traditional liberal professions, training was newly available for chemists (Laval University's School of Chemistry had just opened), actuaries, sociologists, and economists. However, those who opted for these new career openings were considered marginal, and we were convinced they wouldn't go far in life. One of my fellow students decided to study ichthyology. We guffawed at the idea of studying fish, and in fact he only lasted for two months.

In the spring the much-talked-of "graduates' retreat" was held in the Grand Seminary. For three days (days of devotion, obviously, allowing the Holy Ghost to manifest itself), we listened to sermons and talks that focussed as much on the noble goals of a career "in the service of God and the Nation" as on Man's ultimate end—for the word vocation meant answering God's call to serve in a predestined field.

Our mentors continued to preach the message that God was calling us to a particular place in life, and if that place was the priesthood, refusal meant damnation. And how would we know whether God wanted us for the priesthood? By meditating, by listening to an inner voice that would be made manifest in the self-communion of the retreat. Some of us couldn't sleep. One of my friends, who had already come forward as a candidate for the White Fathers but had become hesitant, received a threatening letter from the recruiting father: save souls in Africa or be damned. Some seminary priests tried to advance a new theory, according to which the call to the priesthood was heard only at the moment of ordination for the sub-deaconate, and uniquely through the voice of the bishop. When that worthy pronounced the words inviting the candidate to step forward, the young man remained free to accept or refuse. In my day, adherents of this theory weren't allowed to be involved with the students' spiritual direction.

My dream as a Franciscan student at the Collège Séraphique was to teach, and especially to teach classical literature. Since coming to the seminary I had kept this dream of a teaching career, knowing that it provided the necessary free time for anyone wanting to write and publish in the field of literature.

In 1938 there were no lay people teaching in the colleges familiar to me—the Collège Séraphique, the Trois-Rivières Seminary, and the seminaries of Nicolet and Joliette. The only lay teacher was the traditional music instructor who appeared on the scene two or three times a week. With rare exceptions in Quebec City and Montreal, lay people didn't teach in classical colleges, which belonged either to the diocesan clergy or to religious orders. These had a large supply of possible candidates and made a point of encouraging the brightest students to specialize. If no specialist was forthcoming they simply appointed someone, whether or not he had the desire or the ability to teach. He received the *grâce d'état*, a blessing from on high that for many years served as an excuse for incompetence in Quebec society. A girl who dreamed of a teaching career as anything higher than a rural school mistress had to become a nun. My situation was in fact the same. I wanted to teach classical literature, attend university in Paris, visit Greece—and to do this I would have to take holy orders. However, since I had absolutely no mystical urge (and I wasn't the only one to take a realistic view), I opted for the secular clergy.

I entered the Trois-Rivières Grand Seminary in September 1938, along with five of my classmates. The recruitment was pretty small that year. The diocesan clergy in the province was accustomed to having many more applicants. Most (four-fifths) of the Nicolet Seminary graduates chose the Grand Seminary, but this was already the exception. A drop in recruitment was evident almost everywhere. Blinded by their century-old triumphalist outlook, the religious powers clung to the conviction that this was a minor, short-lived crisis. They kept on building magnificent grand seminaries such as those in Trois-Rivières and Quebec City, as well as costly novitiates like the one in Joliette. But the grand seminaries and novitiates were soon empty. The provincial government rescued their buildings, buying them for use as a university (the brand new Grand Seminary of Trois-Rivières became part of the University of Quebec) or, like the Quebec Grand Seminary, as a repository for the provincial archives.

The Grand Seminary where I began my religious studies lay behind my classical college and overlooked the Rue Saint-François-Xavier, which meant it faced the Saint-Dominique Orphanage where I had once lived for over a year. I found myself confronting the gloomy memories of my first days in Trois-Rivières. The Grand Seminary building was an antiquated brick structure four storeys high, nicknamed "the butterbox" because of its square shape. It had been used as a dormitory for classical college students before the college was rebuilt in 1929. The old building was renovated for young priests-to-be, and one or two of the upper floors were kept as closed retreats for college students.

Grand seminarists now go through their studies without further contact with classical college students. Until fairly recently, however, they donned their cassocks and acted as supervisors and teachers while following their theology courses as best they could. Eventually, however, higher standards were introduced that guaranteed future priests a minimum of regular training. When I entered the Grand Seminary, the bishop had just decided to make the first year a propaedeutic or preparatory class, which meant that we took a third year of philosophy (after our two years in classical college), with sociology, Church history, Hebrew, and elocution tacked on. As the curriculum had been set up at the last minute, not all the teaching tools were ready and the choice of teachers smacked of haste. Accustomed to a heavy work load, I immediately got the feeling that our preceptors didn't quite know how to fill this preparatory year for theology.

In any case, the director of our studies (a canon whose only distinction was to pass for a saint) wasn't one of the Church's brighter lights—his culture being limited to his devotions. He was responsible for teaching us nevertheless, and we were obliged to have an ironclad faith in the merciful intercession of the *grâce d'état*. An atmosphere of perpetual boredom reigned in the butterbox. The days dragged by in this intellectual and artistic vacuum, just as in certain rural presbyteries that I had to visit later in life when doing historical fieldwork.

Our elocution course epitomized the entire system. Guided by a good abbé who might never before have spoken in front of a large audience, we had to write a sermon for the common man on such fascinating topics as the grace of the Holy Ghost, dividing it rigorously into the exordium (the oratorical introduction), followed by two points and a peroration. If we didn't, the common man wouldn't understand a thing and grace would pass him by. We then had to learn the sermon by heart and deliver it without notes of any kind. In a word, this was a contrived sermon modelled on those of an earlier age. It amounted to spouting vain eloquence that would pass over the heads of the ordinary churchgoer—the type of sermon that the Church had revelled in for so long—instead of actually talking to the gathering, saying simple things, and looking the audience straight in the eye. And I used to dream of teaching!

I soon returned to my literary authors, especially the Greeks. I had brought my entire personal library with me and had it neatly shelved. The director found it decidedly unecclesiastical and insisted that I round it out with mystical works. He forbade us to lock our doors, claiming to have the right to enter without knocking to see what we were up to. The game of covert reading began again, to the detriment of philosophy. As the Grand Seminary had no library, I became friendly with the librarian of my classical college (booklovers soon recognize one another) and had all the books I wanted. During the few months I spent in that butterbox I borrowed some sixty volumes (I still have the list) on the widest possible range of subjects. I took out whatever interested me—books that developed the mind, biographies, Church history (including the seven fat Rohrbacher tomes), and, above all, literary works. It was here that I discovered the splendours of *The Divine Comedy* and the dazzling pages of the Bible.

The more I read on my own account, the less I felt in harmony with my surroundings. I saw myself there as a useless individual whom people would only respect as a man of the cloth. I had hoped to become a professor of literature by donning the cassock, a lengthy and roundabout proceeding. I had made a mistake and would be better off trying for a lay career, even if there still seemed to be no opening in the field of letters. I would find a way of getting a *licence ès lettres* in Paris, as some of my Franciscan teachers had done. I thought of them because no one at the seminary had yet earned a degree in literature. From there, I thought I would push on to a doctorate—but how lofty this goal seemed! Yet why shouldn't I become a university professor some day? Dreams are grand at twenty-one, but is not success in life the very realization of such dreams?

Early in 1939 I ended my ecclesiastic career. It didn't last long. I was merely a pre-theology student and hadn't received even the most humble of minor orders—not even the tonsure. And I went home.

6

The Charm of Sophocles and Balzac

WERE MY PARENTS upset to see me giving up a career and a uniform that would guarantee me prestige? If so, they didn't show it. There was a compensating factor: I was going to register at the university—I would still be someone.

This wouldn't happen until the autumn, however. I had months to wait and a financial problem to face. My first year of courses would be free because my baccalauréat marks were in the eighty percent range, but I still had to pay room and board. I knew my parents couldn't help. For the first time in my life, I had to deal with the problem of where to find the money. For a while I thought about looking for work as a journalist, since I liked to write. Then I decided I would rather fall back on doing radio sketches—dialogues portraying village life. My outline for the project was accepted by Station CHLN of Trois-Rivières, which commissioned thirty fifteen-minute sketches at a dollar each! Thirty dollars was enough to pay for my lodging in Quebec City for three months or feed me for more than four. I could conceive, draft, and polish a sketch a day for a dollar. Compared to a university professor, who began with an average of five dollars a day, my situation wasn't so desperate, as long as the heavenly manna of CHLN continued to fall.

I did my sketches in thirty days—some 300 pages entitled *Life in Saint-Saphro*. I received a fine cheque for thirty dollars, the first money earned by my pen! Then, like all playwrights, I was on tenterhooks. I expected my work to be performed soon, and for a long time I fretted and fidgeted about it. Alas, nothing came of it. My sketches never reached the air waves. Today I say, "Thank God!" Still, they weren't useless, for they served as the basis for scenes in my novel *Vézine*, where village gossips make and unmake reputations.

Marcel Trudel, 1939.
Photo by Hervé Cossette

While working on these sketches, I gradually began thinking about a more ambitious project. Instead of doing my *license ès lettres* in Quebec, why not go to Paris? I dreamed about this for several weeks, then made up my mind: I would look for the necessary scholarships. Abbé Albert Tessier, our study master at the seminary, was considered to be on excellent terms with his fellow citizen of Trois-Rivières, Maurice Duplessis, premier of the province. I wrote the abbé and he replied immediately. "Work on your provincial assembly member. That's the way to do it. He'll no doubt ask you for references, and that's where we come in." I wrote our member and he answered with a letter that was officially encouraging. The process looked rather involved, however, and I hadn't much time left. A more expeditious way of unearthing funds was needed.

A paternal uncle, Monseigneur Hormisdas Trudel, was curé of the Trois-Rivières cathedral, which meant that the premier was one of his flock and practically a neighbour. Moreover, my uncle's courtesy cousin, Auréa Cloutier, was the premier's private secretary without whose blessing no favour came from on high. I didn't know this uncle at all well, as he had always kept his distance from his family, not liking to be solicited for favours. He sought the tranquil life and devoted himself wholly to his pastoral tasks. His only leisure activity was reading; he almost never took a holiday and didn't even own a radio. It was only in his late old age that he agreed to have one beside his bed. When he discovered the hockey broadcasts, he was as happy as a child.

I laid my plans before him and he was immediately enthusiastic. Just think of it, a *licencié ès lettres* in the family, and a Paris graduate to boot! "I'm seeing Monsieur Duplessis tomorrow," he said. "I'll speak to him about it." The next day, the premier responded by saying, "Your nephew will get a $2000 grant, and I'll have the first half sent to him right away." So it was that in the early summer of 1939 I received a cheque for one thousand dollars and booked my room at the Cité Universitaire in Paris.

My grant was a large one. True, my academic record was excellent, but the premier had seen no proof of that. I came by my grant through patronage. At the time there was no other way, no organization responsible for evaluating candidates and choosing them according to predetermined criteria. If you wanted a grant, you arranged to get the most powerful patronage possible. It was the established system and the only workable one, whatever its advantages and disadvantages. The lucky ones came away with the advantages.

My imminent departure for Paris caused a sensation in my little village.

No lay person had ever left it to pursue studies in France. My parents were proud of me and would make me talk of Paris in front of visitors as though I had just arrived from the French capital. Advice flowed in on all sides. A priest warned me about the immorality of the great city, although I don't think he'd really heard anything about it, apart from the Folies-Bergères. "The newspapers," said he (I never knew which papers), "deliberately hide the subject of death. There's nothing in them to remind Man of his End."

Then the heavens fell, not only for the world at large, but for me personally. On September 3, 1939, I was in Trois-Rivières to apply for a passport. Going into a store, I heard on the radio that war had been declared. My first reaction was to leave for France anyway, but my uncle made it clear that my only option was to register at Laval University. When I got home I snatched up a book and began reading in an effort to forget.

Another thunderbolt was to descend on me in short order. The Duplessis government was voted out of office and I couldn't depend on getting the second half of my grant. Someone said to me, "Go to the parliament buildings before Duplessis hands over power. You might just get the other thousand." I went reluctantly. The lobbies were filled with people who had also come to make one last attempt. I hadn't the courage to wait.

All the same, my summer fund-raising activities had solved my financial problem. Since my first year's fees were waived, I'd have enough for my *license* tuition if I budgeted my thousand-dollar grant properly. In those days you could rent a good room for ten dollars a month, and meals (spartan but sufficient) for twenty-five cents each at Yong's Chinese restaurant on the Rue Saint-Jean. I often went there to meet fellow students in letters and other faculties such as social sciences. They, like me, were deemed to have no future. Instead of taking the tram, I walked. Actually, I only took it once in two years (it was expensive at ten cents a trip). I husbanded my pocket money and still remember lending twenty-five cents to a buddy who never paid me back, the infidel. As it turned out, I was only twenty dollars short of the amount needed for the entire two years of the *licence*.

The summer of 1939 prior to entering Laval's faculty of letters had indeed been a busy one. My radio sketches had brought in enough pocket money to last a long time, and I had succeeded in getting funding for my university studies. I had also shared in the life of my small village. During the Saint-Jean-Baptiste celebrations, for example, I had paraded through the parish in military uniform. I carried no rifle (five minutes had sufficed to turn us into soldiers), but was the group's bugler. We marched into the church for high mass and I sounded the call at the moment of dedication. That summer I also read voraciously—mainly Shakespeare.

Since I was now committed to a lay career, I could call on girls—*aller voir les filles* as we used to say. My friends and I went the rounds, turning up uninvited at evening wedding parties or attending wakes—those nights when friends and relations sat vigil with the body, then relaxed with an always lively *réveillon*. During a wedding party on the Rang Saint-Pierre, I noticed a very young blonde, quiet and well-brought-up. She was sitting along the wall with the other wallflowers, as we called them, waiting to be asked to dance. I went over to her. We chatted, danced, and agreed to see each other again. Her name was Colombe, which means "dove."

During the few weeks that our "love" lasted, I didn't manage to get to know Colombe very well. In traditional households—and along the roads they were certainly traditional—calling on a girl followed an ironclad procedure. Visiting was only allowed on "at home" evenings, in other words on Sunday and Thursday. If you knocked on the door on a Wednesday or Friday, you were apt to find your ladylove in work clothes, her hair uncombed and her face innocent of makeup. In any case, the parents would have put a stop to such goings-on without further ado, because if your intentions were honourable, you wouldn't visit your girlfriend at just any old time or on any old day. Parents chaperoned these visits strictly, a duty that the curé was constantly reminding them to perform in his sermons. If they did not, the most dreadful punishment could befall them, including the disgrace of having a daughter "in the family way."

In the home of one girl whom I visited once or twice, there was a square opening in the parlour wall resembling the wicket in a confession booth. This opening was at head level, facing the armchairs. At any moment the scrutinizing countenance of the girl's mother could appear, and suitors with wandering hands were living dangerously. At Colombe's home things were even more strictly chaperoned. As soon as I entered, I noticed in the parlour, on my left, two rocking chairs placed in the middle of the room. They were side by side, but with a large space between them. Facing these chairs, in the doorway to the kitchen, I could see another rocking chair. Once the lovers were seated, the mother sat down in her chair with her knitting and the evening of seemly courting began. All three of us rocked to the same rhythm. When the conversation lapsed, the mother would intervene to get it going again. At the end of the evening, Colombe would see me to the door, but not onto the porch—escaping surveillance wasn't allowed. We kissed, a mere brush of the lips. If the girl said, "Au revoir," she would be expecting you on the next at home evening. If she didn't, you could consider yourself on the receiving end of a polite brush-off.

My zeal soon turned to indifference. One day I was fascinated by the turquoise-green skirt of a neighbourhood brunette. Yvette was her name, and we weren't subjected to any chaperons in her home. The parlour was some distance from the kitchen, and there was no peephole in the wall and no sentinel facing the sofa.

In October 1939 I had to leave for Laval University. The faculty of letters, founded in 1937 and still called École Normale Supérieure (Section Lettres), was in Old Quebec at the foot of the Rue Sainte-Famille, separated from the law faculty by a *porte cochère*.

There weren't many students. Most of them were lay priests or men following a religious career and for whom teaching in classical colleges was reserved. There were also two monks. They were the first brothers to register in this faculty. Nuns hadn't yet entered this man's world. Since 1920, out of fifty-five graduates of the *licence ès lettres* program, only fifteen were laypeople. In my year there were three of us laymen at the same time, something never before seen. As for girls, only one had graduated from the program so far. The faculty also allowed people to audit lectures. Most were girls or women who came for cultural enrichment or, as some spiteful tongues said, to find a husband. In any case, I remember the daughter of the editor of *L'Action catholique*, a girl who would one day marry a man from the Gaspé who was in social sciences—one René Lévesque.

The letters faculty prepared students to teach language and literature by awarding a *licence ès lettres* after two years. This degree was half way between the baccalauréat and the doctorate. It was based on the *licence* at the Sorbonne (but different, in that course attendance was obligatory), and it was made up of four "post-secondary certificates" preferably in French, Latin, Greek, and a fourth chosen by the student.

History and geography did not yet figure in this program. During my two *licence* years, from 1939 to 1941, you couldn't prepare yourself for a professional career in history, either at Laval or other French-language teaching institutions in Quebec. History was used as a subject for discourse in the rhetoric year in classical colleges, as I mentioned earlier. In the Laval education certificate program, Abbé Albert Tessier devoted several hours to the subject of teaching Canadian history at the university level. From time to time, history courses were offered to the general public. These were lectures attended by the same sort of audience that would go to a concert. In Quebec City during the nineteenth century, Abbé J.-B.-A. Ferland gave similar lectures, as did Thomas Chapais in the early twentieth century. In my time as a student, Abbé Arthur Maheux gave public courses, while in Montreal Abbé Lionel Groulx was doing the same. All these men were speaking of a history based on eloquence (as can easily be seen when rereading Ferland, Chapais, and Groulx), or on political or nationalist platforms.

No one I knew thought of having a career as a historian. I myself dreamed of becoming a Greek specialist and a novelist. I was careful to include the Greek certificate in my curriculum. To this I added the obligatory French certificate, as well as Latin (a temporary choice; I soon switched to English), and Spanish.

As a fourth certificate in the *licence* program, Spanish ranked fairly low, being the equivalent of the "little sciences" in classical college. The subject was taught by a charming Quebec lady—a very able teacher, but she seemed to have learned her entire store of Spanish while travelling with her doctor husband. We were only taught the spoken language. At no time did any professor discuss the history of the language or its literature. Why would you study Spanish in Quebec City, anyway? The Spanish-speaking upper middle class of Latin American was barred from going to France because of the war, and so they made their way to Quebec instead. A Spanish craze swept the city, and all the best people made a point of living, thinking, eating, and dancing in Spanish. With the prospect of such a promising future, the university threw together a Spanish studies program. As a result, I could attend a course given by a woman for the first time since my childhood. I found myself in the almost exclusive company of the ladies of Quebec City, some of whom knitted in class, and I couldn't help thinking of the French Revolution's famous *tricoteuses*.

Within the *licence ès lettres* program, the education certificate was somewhat scorned. My old study master Alcantra Dion was in charge, and I was told that his course focused far more on elementary school teaching than high school education. Then as now I instinctively distrusted wide-ranging theoretical courses, having seen so many education graduates who turned out to be very mediocre teachers.

The serious certificates—the real university courses—were French, Latin, Greek, and English. The first three, especially, terrified us because they were so demanding. We were warned in first year that "the *licence* will no longer be easy," as though it had been easy before! Our instructors gave us a hefty amount of required reading, and there were other demands in addition to the regular course load. We were likely to be examined on almost anything in the orals, for example. In Greek and English classes the professors gave us lists of authors to be read, pencil in hand, and we had to produce résumés of these readings with commentary.

I had dreamed of gaining access to the fountainheads of culture. Well, here I was! I was already a great reader, but in the two years of the *licence*, despite the demands of the program, I read the great works of French and English literature of the seventeenth, eighteenth, and nineteenth centuries, as well as all the major and many of the minor works of Greek literature. All this reading included many novels, poems, plays, and works on the history of literature. In terms of history as a subject I read only the Greek historians (Herodotus, Thucydides, and Xenophon), but nothing about the history of France or Canada.

We could use a special library on the faculty premises, as well as the general library owned jointly by Laval University and the Quebec Seminary. It contained 300,000 volumes. In earlier times the thought of the Collège Séraphique's 5,000 volumes had made me positively dizzy. But now I had discovered a Klondike! There were still important works missing, however. Contemporary authors hadn't been around long enough to be in the library, and many editions of complete works had seen better days—indeed, many of them were anything but complete, because the papal Index imposed a policy of weeding out unacceptable works. The general library had its "hell," a small locked room where forbidden books were shelved. They weren't bought by the Seminary, but probably came from donated collections. The librarian—the grammarian Abbé Aubert—had the key. If you wanted to take out one of these books, you had to get written permission from the bishop or his vicar general. As the latter was our dean, Monseigneur Camille Roy, we could get him to give us a special dispensation if we could prove that we absolutely had to read the book in question for our studies. No professor on the faculty had yet dared assign a work banned by the Index.

The marks we got bore witness to the exacting demands of the *licence*. To pass the final exams, our marks had to be at least ten out of twenty. We were warned not to expect to get a ten in first year, otherwise we might think we were ready to graduate. First-year marks were kept low. I was used to getting sixteen or eighteen out of twenty, but for my initial French essay I received a measly five, plus the professor's comment: "An essay is not a pack of facetious asides." He encouraged me, all the same: "With your resources, you can do a lot better." In the margin of my next paper he wrote, "Generally promising," but I still netted only a five. The second year I reached ten, then twelve and even fourteen: I was free to consider myself a genius. It was the same in Greek, and although I flattered myself on being able to read the text in the original, my first translation earned me five out of twenty. In English, my first assignment got a miserable two out of twenty. Apparently my English had more than a whiff of Shakespeare. I needed to get up to date. Thus, with a snap of the whip, our teachers convinced us that we were destined for hard labour. Some professors took every opportunity to remark, with polite derision, "If you don't want to work, take law!"

We never saw the dean, Monseigneur Roy, around the faculty, although he was then considered the sovereign judge of French-Canadian literature. He wore three hats: that of vicar-general of the diocese, superior of the Quebec Seminary, and rector of Laval University. Nevertheless, we had to visit him individually at least once a year. He was typical of the prelates of his day—a man with immensely dignified bearing and a seigneurial manner. He would rest his right hand on his red sash, and was courteous, paternalistic, conscious of his great merit, but with a horror of opposition. In addition to his other functions, he occupied the Canadian literature chair at Laval, but called on the services of a Quebec Seminary abbé to stand in for him.

This abbé was Émile Bégin, red-faced, pot-bellied, and—as everyone knew—literary critic for the *Revue de l'Université Laval*. But although this fact was public knowledge, he persisted in signing his articles with pseudonyms of all kinds. As revealed in his private journal, which he handed out left and right during his lifetime, he would later become a passionate admirer of Elvis Presley. He wrote to him, even wangled a meeting, and carefully noted what colour tie Elvis wore during this conclave of the great. Like many priests, he had a horror of women. When speaking of the nuns who did the house-work in the seminary, he referred to "the feminine domesticity," an expression that fully encapsulated his contempt.

Bégin's course in Canadian literature barely reached the classical college level. He contented himself with going over the obligatory textbook written by Monseigneur Roy. There was never any critical evaluation of sources of Canadian literature, nothing on the social problems it explored, and no examination of its origins or development. His personal contribution consisted of spiteful remarks about any work not written by a graduate of the Quebec Seminary, especially if the author came from a seminary represented by someone in the classroom. We were in the habit of predicting his next victim. Sensing that the professor was preparing his barb, we had the leisure to see it in flight and would be roaring with laughter when it struck its target. In short, his course was a breeze.

The oral exam in literature took place in Monseigneur Roy's office. We were alone, but there was nothing terrifying about this final exercise in the presence of the supreme authority of both the faculty of letters and the university. Monseigneur Roy received us graciously and gave us his full attention. All we had to do was say something nice about his *Manuel de littérature canadienne* or mention how deeply affected we'd been by some passage of this or that French-Canadian author, and we would leave with an excellent mark. One fellow student, Abbé Hermann Plante (who later produced a Canadian history textbook), ignored the need for diplomacy and during the oral told Monseigneur Roy in no uncertain terms what he thought of his *Manuel*. The prelate told the abbé equally bluntly what he thought of the candidate, and Abbé Plante found himself repeating the course the following September.

Our French literature professor, Auguste Viatte, was excellent, being very devoted to his students and possessed of an extremely lively teaching style, due to his nervous energy. He used to arrive for the class with a quick, short step, spectacles perched on the tip of his nose (which forced him to walk with his head tilted backward). Under each arm he carried an old briefcase stuffed with books. He would dump them out and stack them precariously on his desk, shoving them about until they all tumbled onto the floor. Once seated, he kept crossing and uncrossing his legs. In moments of great tension, having crossed the right leg over the left, he would try to twist his foot under the left calf in an apparent attempt to wind one leg entirely around the other. One day, while performing this contortion, he suddenly wanted to stand up to write on the blackboard. Alas, he found he couldn't unwind his legs! He burst out laughing and had to free the straying foot by hand.

Each week, two students were assigned to prepare a spoken analysis of various texts. On the day, Monsieur Viatte used to take out a quarter and toss it, heads or tails, to see who would begin. However, he was so nervous with each toss that the coin inevitably rolled under our feet—and of course we made sure that finding it was as prolonged and complicated as possible.

Professor Viatte's well-documented courses were an intellectual feast. However, since he came from Fribourg University in Switzerland, he was looked down on by French colleagues who had gone through universities in France. And when he sided with General de Gaulle in 1940, he was considered beneath notice by another colleague, Jean Lechevalier, a staunch Pétainist.

This Jean Lechevalier, a Latin professor whose courses I took for a few weeks, is legendary. Tall and slender, with a small head at the end of a long neck, Lechevalier had served in the French army and retained the measured step and methodical approach of the military, as well as a strong sense of duty and remembrance. I offered him a cigarette one day, and he replied politely, "Thank you very much. I haven't smoked since 5:10 a.m., November 11, 1918."

I, the connoisseur, countered, "That's to say since the armistice."

"Not exactly the armistice," he replied. "That day at 5:10 a.m. was the exact moment when the German delegates signed the ceasefire that led to the armistice. Didn't you know?"

Lechevalier has remained famous for the extremely rigid but formative method to which he subjected generations of students. In the first class of the year he assigned each student a seat, something no other professor did. If, the next day, someone by chance sat somewhere else, an endless interrogation began as to why this student had changed his seat.

"Monsieur was too far from the window, perhaps? Or the radiator was in his way? Or perhaps his desk is defective? Or does monsieur not hear well enough?" In vain the student replied that he had sat somewhere else without thinking, "Comme ça." Lechevalier persisted in his exhaustive hypotheses, for he could not conceive of anyone changing seats without some deep motive.

During this first class he would proceed to identify each student and ask where he came from. For this purpose he had fixed a tidewater date: the preceding first of June. "Monsieur," he would ask us one by one, "where were you on the first of June 1939?"

One of us would reply with an English accent, "The University of Ottawa."

Lechevalier would cock an ear. "Pardon me. Did you say *Harvar*?"

"No, sir. Not Harvard; Ottawa."

"Good. I'll correct that right away."

When my turn came I wanted to say I'd had been on the point of leaving for Paris, and that . . . that. . . .

"Where were you on the first of June," he repeated doggedly.

I took the plunge. "At Saint-Narcisse-de-Champlain, sir."

"Ah!" came the reply. "But I haven't encountered that classical college yet."

In this inaugural class we were treated to the ritual distribution of Gaffiot dictionaries, the only Latin dictionary authorized by Professor Lechevalier. He would begin by putting on his desk a stack of the volumes tied with thick string. "Monsieur, do you own a Gaffiot?" he would ask a student. If the student said no, Lechevalier unbuttoned his jacket and reached into the pocket of his waistcoat for a pencil stub, so short he could just grasp it between thumb and forefinger. He ticked off the student's name, replaced the pencil in his waistcoat pocket, buttoned his jacket, stood up, and reached for a Gaffiot. Stepping down from the platform, he walked over to the student and handed him the dictionary, saying, "Here, monsieur, is your Gaffiot." The ritual began again: a second student would be interrogated, the jacket unbuttoned, the pencil searched for at the bottom of the waistcoat pocket, the name ticked, the pencil restored to its pocket, the jacket rebuttoned, then the professor would rise, descend from the platform, and hand over the dictionary saying, "Here, monsieur is your Gaffiot." And so it went, until the list was finished. In this perfectly ordered system, there was no crowding around the desk. Every sale was unfailingly recorded, and there was no danger of two copies of Gaffiot going to the same student.

Lechevalier noted those present by calling out names, and if a student failed to reply would ask in a distressed tone, "Monsieur Cormier isn't there? Has anyone seen Monsieur Cormier? Can any of you tell me if Monsieur Cormier is sick?" This interrogation would be underway in the first few minutes of class when suddenly the door would open and my classmate Cormier would stroll calmly to his seat. "Ah! Monsieur Cormier is here. We were about to begin without him."

The era of the photocopy hadn't yet arrived, and stencil machines (apparently one should say *baudruche* in French, although we used to say *appareil à stencil*) were rather primitive. Lechevalier was therefore in the habit, then customary, of dictating the text for us to translate into Latin. One day he was slowly dictating a long excerpt from Chateaubriand, carefully noting every punctuation sign. When he was finished, he thought it more prudent (an error could so quickly creep in) to make sure everyone had understood the text properly.

"Monsieur Trudel, would you kindly reread this text aloud for the benefit of all the students?"

Intimidated neophyte that I was, I assumed my best voice and, articulating with great care, read the long passage from Chateaubriand. Lechevalier allowed me to finish without intervening, as it would have been impolite to interrupt.

"Very good. Now, monsieur, would you kindly read it again more slowly, giving the commas, semicolons, colons, and periods each time." While the more initiated, who knew his method, looked on smirking, I had to begin again, making sure to say "comma . . . comma . . . semicolon," at each occurrence.

We were subjected to the same demanding method in our assignments, which we sometimes had to do at the faculty under Lechevalier's eye. He divided our work time in two. During the first part, we worked on the draft and consulted our dictionaries; during the second, we prepared the final copy. One day, when I was in the last phase and wanting to be precise, I stopped to check a word in the dictionary. The professor buttoned up his jacket, rose, stepped down from the platform, and walked over to my seat. There he stopped.

"Allow me to ask, monsieur, whether you are working on the draft or your final copy?"

"The final copy, sir, but I wanted—"

"In that case, I beg your pardon, monsieur, but if you are working on the final copy, you are therefore in the second phase and are not permitted to consult Gaffiot."

I had to close my dictionary. Lechevalier returned to the platform, stood in front of his chair, then sat down, unbuttoning his jacket as he did so.

He was a dreaded marker. A compliment from him was considered a piece of extraordinary good luck. One day a classmate got a very high mark for a translation. Unable to believe his eyes, he glanced at the professor's comment in the margin: "A well-translated word." This was the equivalent of "excellent translation." We were even more apprehensive about the oral exam. As I had dropped his course, I feared the worst, because the jury for the oral Greek exam consisted of the Greek and Latin professors. We had half an hour to analyze a text in front of this jury. If we could fill the entire time, the judges wouldn't be able to ask any questions. We therefore had to work hard to fill these thirty minutes. When my turn came, I found, alas, that I had one or two minutes left. My Greek professor politely left it to his Latin colleague to speak.

"Monsieur," asked Lechevalier, "what do you call the sign that you see over the second word on line four?"

I had taken a short introductory course on Greek accents, but the little sign in question meant nothing to me. "It's an *esprit doux*, sir," said I, taking a stab at it.

"No, monsieur, you're wrong. It's a coronis," said he, supplying the scholarly term used in English and French.

I might well look dumbfounded. This was the first time I had heard this word pronounced in my two years at university.

Lechevalier was triumphant. "You don't seem to know what a coronis is! Well, I shall profit from this examination to explain it to you." While he gave me the lesson, I said to myself, "That's it. I've flunked." But he was generous and I had a good mark. He'd realized that our Greek professor had neglected this point, and the impromptu lecture was more for his colleague's benefit that mine.

The dean had put Lechevalier in charge of the faculty library. It was kept in impeccable but not always comprehensible order, according to a system that he explained at length at the start of the academic year. Being a former French army officer, he had invented categories that were pure figments of the imagination, a bit like longitudes and latitudes, among which we had to find our way. It was a moment of great drama when a colleague got permission from the secretary-general of the university to add a table to the library—to add, not remove. All Lechevalier's ideas of learned classification were overthrown. He went to the secretary-general and asked him to reverse his decision. The secretary-general sent him packing. Lechevalier went to the rector, who sent the plaintiff back to square one. At this point, he felt he could no longer carry out his functions and resigned with dignity.

Whatever this professor's oddities may have been, during my short stay in his class I learned that to accomplish anything worthwhile you have to develop highly disciplined habits and adopt a rigorous method of thought and execution, as well as an abiding concern for accuracy. I haven't always been faithful to this precept, but I've made a great effort to do so.

The Greek professor, Maurice Lebel, didn't have Lechevalier's erudition or scholarly discipline. He had done brilliantly in his classical college and graduated at a much younger age than his fellow students. He had studied in England (which was why he was also professor of advanced English) and France, and had travelled widely in Europe. When he became a Greek teacher, he first worked at giving this language some popularity in classical colleges. His book, *L'Enseignement et l'étude du grec,* is evidence of this, but he didn't carry through with it. He spread himself thin among various disciplines, losing himself in writing that served neither these subjects nor Greek culture.

For my dream of becoming a Greek scholar I owe Lebel a great deal. My first year of Greek with him was spellbinding. He brought me down to earth and made me discover ancient Greek literature, art, and civilization as I had never seen them. Through him, Greece came alive for me. I felt he had literally walked through Attica, the Peloponesus, and the Greek Isles. His courses on teaching Greek in classical colleges were full of practical advice, coming from a man who had experienced the method he preached. The second year was disappointing. I was expecting work in detail and depth, but he kept to the level of the preceding year, perhaps because first year students were following the course at the same time. In any case, although he gave us a taste for Greek culture, he was unable to rise to the scholarly level. He should have been of the same stature as his colleague in Latin. The great Canadian Hellenist that we awaited did not appear.

During these years of *licence ès lettres* I had reduced my social life to the strict minimum, as much out of concern for making my scholarship money last as for the demands of my studies. I set foot once or twice in the students' union on Rue Couillard, but for me it was a pure waste of time. I was completely uninterested in all extra-curricular student activities, convinced (as I am still) that a student can be most useful to society by studying.

When I first arrived in Quebec City I took lodgings on the Rue Sainte-Geneviève, just above the Citadel cannon, which used to make me jump at the stroke of noon each day. However, as I had registered for the English certificate, I was advised to find room and board in an English-speaking household. Even then there weren't too many left in Quebec City, but I happened on the Carbrays, third-generation Irish Canadians. The first Carbray, carried to Canada on the wave of nineteenth-century immigration, spoke almost nothing but Gaelic. His son spoke Gaelic and English, while one of his grandsons spoke only English and the other lived completely in French. The family was a perfect example of assimilation. In this half English, half French milieu, I made very little progress in spoken English, but it was here that I met Anne-Marie, who was to be my wife for twenty-six years.

During the 1939-1940 winter vacation, I caused a sensation in Saint-Narcisse-de-Champlain by bringing home a student from Siam (or Thailand as we would say today) for Christmas. Unable to go to France because of the war, Chalung Pungtragul had registered in the letters course in Quebec City at the same time as his compatriot, Chintana Nagavajara. They were the first two Asiatics to study at Laval. Chalung, a Buddhist who'd come straight from Bangkok, was still suffering from culture shock when I invited him home in December with the idea of showing him something other than the city and hotel life.

What a surprise for my little hamlet! The first "Chinaman" to appear there, and a flesh-and-blood pagan to boot—one of the people about whom missionaries on furlough used to tell so many tall tales. He came from the antipodes, from the other side of the globe where people, it was thought, must walk upside down like flies on a ceiling. For the first time in his life he lived in the Canadian countryside, and in a house heated by a wood stove where everything he ate was a novelty. Despite his limited vocabulary, Chalung had long conversations with my father, who had read a great deal about "the old countries." The doctor, who subscribed to *National Geographic Magazine*, amazed our guest by describing the course of the long Mekong River.

In our house there was the traditional spittoon which had its appointed place beside the stove. In Siam a spittoon was a mark of prestige. The king of Siam had himself pictured beside two spittoons, one on top of the other. To offer the spittoon to someone was a gesture of utmost politeness. Like those of his generation, my father used the spittoon. This act was heralded by a loud and lengthy gargling noise as my father cleared his throat. The first time Chalung heard this warning he rushed over to the spittoon, grabbed it with both hands, then deferentially placed it at the level of my father's chin. At first this took my father's breath away. The gargling stopped. But as Chalung was still waiting respectfully, my father finally spat, and Chalung carried the spittoon back to its place, having done his duty. Some time later my father again began clearing his throat and Chalung rushed forward once more. So assiduous was he that after a few days my father managed to restrain himself and spat no more—at least during Chalung's visit.

Being a Buddhist, Chalung had never visited a church or witnessed Roman Catholic ceremonies. I took him to midnight mass. The curé knew we were coming and had reserved a prayer bench for us in the front of the central aisle, near the altar rail, as though we were important visitors of consequence. As usual, the organist pulled out all the stops, and there was the singing, the crèche, and the procession of children disguised as Israelites. Chalung came out of church bedazzled.

My 1940 summer vacation lasted four months. As there were no exams at the end of the first year, I went home in early May. This would be my last long vacation, since I would begin professional life the following summer. I decided to make these holidays memorable and to relax completely before the taxing last year in letters. I closed my books—all of them—for four months.

I began to lead an outdoor life, going on forest rambles, camping, and doing useful community work. As much for myself as for others, I took over the upkeep of the tennis court. We young people in the village used to congregate there each evening. Pierre Grondin, the future cardiologist, was one, and Normandin, the vicar, was another. Like me, he was a former student of the Collège Séraphique. With their help, I transformed the neglected piece of ground that had once been the old cemetery beside the church. We laid out paths, planted trees, and sowed grass seed. As we worked, a tibia or a skull would sometimes emerge from the earth, left behind after the graves were moved in 1923. Ah, the "to be or not to be" of Hamlet!

My most treasured memory of the summer of 1940, lived apart from all wartime worries, is the creation of something like a summer camp with my younger comrades. In my village, crisscrossed by small streams, the children had only their yards or the streets to play in, much like city children. But five or six kilometres away the Batiscan River ran through forest land that Shawinigan Water & Power had abandoned to nature's care for over half a century. This area was commonly known as Murphy's Falls. I used to go there to swim, pick raspberries, and spend lazy hours in the woods and along the rapids, fishing for river mullet that I would cook over a campfire. It was my secret paradise. Sometimes the Trois-Rivières scouts would camp in this landscape of hillsides, falls, and big, flat boulders that jutted out into the Batiscan River.

I wanted the children to benefit from these surroundings. Almost every week, after going the rounds of the local merchants to cover the cost of transport, I would gather a large group of youngsters, each provided with a picnic lunch. I drove them in a truck to Murphy's Falls, and there I handed out the day's chores, saw to their safety (they were less than twelve in age,

Trudel at Murphy Falls, 1939.
Courtesy of Pauline and Léo-Paul Jacob.

some barely four or five years old), got games going in the woods, organized the meals, and built the evening campfire. The fireside gathering required preparation, and I asked the young campers to sing, tell a story, or ham it up in front of the others. At the end of the campfire evening, I drove them all home, making sure each mother had her young ones back. The next week we did it again. Parents or children raced to reserve a place in this "daycare" phenomenon. I came home dead-tired but happy at passing on my father's gift—the love of forest life. What has become of those little campers of fifty years go? One is a senior civil servant in Ottawa, the other heads a major business corporation. Among those budding little men of 1940 I remember one especially: the future historian, Jean Hamelin.

In June 1941 my *licence ès lettres* studies were finished, my highest mark being in Greek. I'd achieved one part of my adolescent dream. There remained another, longer and more hazardous: the doctorate. Normally, since I was hoping for a career as a Greek specialist, I should have focused exclusively on this subject after completing my *licence*. But Europe was closed to us because of the war. I could see no openings for a doctorate in Greek, or for one in French literature, so I settled for French-Canadian literature.

Throughout my *licence*, the literature professor had harped on the theme of God, country, and family, this being in his view the leitmotif of French-Canadian authors. He discreetly passed over *La Lanterne* by Arthur Buies. Being naturally inclined to take the opposite view from what I was taught, I wondered how, in an age when French was an international language and Voltaire its most brilliant exponent, our eighteenth- and nineteenth-century literature could have escaped his influence. I turned this question over and over in my mind, and it soon became a challenge, a bet with myself to demonstrate that this Canadian literature had also been influenced by the spirit of Voltaire.

But how was I to make this a doctoral subject at Laval University? There was no lack of obstacles in 1941. It was barely seven years since the province of Quebec had been the scene of Church censure imposed on Jean-Charles Harvey, editor-in-chief of the liberal newspaper *Le Soleil*. He had published a novel, *Les demi-civilisés*, in which he gently mocked our devotional habits. Cardinal Villeneuve put his book on the Index, and *Le Soleil*, despite being an organ of the Liberal Party, fired its editor-in-chief. Harvey then applied for the vacant post of librarian to the provincial legislature. Premier Taschereau, leader of the provincial Liberals, rejected the application and named a colonel of very limited intellectual powers to the post. Harvey finally found a job somewhere as a minor clerk in the provincial civil service. This was the era when the forces of the Church wielded the utmost influence in Quebec's public affairs. The Catholic press was aggressive and uncompromising, and so-called "liberal" newspapers followed the same path to avoid losing circulation. Was I, in Quebec City, going to put forward the thesis that our literature had drawn sustenance from Voltaire?

I consulted Monseigneur Hormisdas Trudel, the uncle who had encouraged me in my studies. The subject of my thesis amused him greatly, for he himself was of a liberal bent. Members of his family had been condemned by the curé at election time. He encouraged me to persevere. The dean of the faculty, Monseigneur Roy, agreed after much hesitation and strongly advised prudence. The faculty was careful to provide not only support but supervision. Professor Viatte was chosen as my thesis director, but while most candidates were only given one director, I was assigned a second—Abbé Bégin, Monseigneur Roy's understudy in the Canadian literature course mentioned earlier. He was to follow me closely, defending the orthodox view, making me delete various passages or add assorted apologies. I would have to prove myself a tractable pupil.

As the dean was also the vicar-general, he gave me a year's permission to read those works on the Index needed for my thesis. I also had to have access to Voltaire's complete works. The only available volumes were under lock and key in the library's "hell." The librarian was willing to lend me three volumes at a time, which he would send by mail. However, to work effectively, I needed to have all the works before me at the same time, and for a lengthy period. I found an accomplice, assistant librarian Antonio Drolet, a man of great breadth of spirit. Without saying a word to his superior, he put the entire works of Voltaire in a large box and had it sent to me for an unlimited time. It was not the latest or most scholarly edition, but I had no choice. This didn't solve all my problems, though. Upon leaving the diocese of Quebec (for I would be living in Rigaud, near Montreal), my permission to read works on the Index became invalid. I needed a dispensation from the bishop of Valleyfield, Monseigneur Langlois. I got it, but at the cost of a long sermon on the perils of my subject and the dangerous development of the youth of our century.

Primo vivere. Before beginning my thesis, I had to make sure of my livelihood—this in 1941 at the age of twenty-four. Quebec classical colleges didn't hire lay teachers in those days. The Quebec Seminary only began to do so in 1942, and the Trois-Rivières Seminary followed suit much later, preferring to supplement secular priests by monks. The thinking then was that a classical college must be really desperate to hire a monk. In the Montreal region, several laymen were already employed as teachers. In any case, I was offered three posts in 1941: teaching French in Prince Edward Island, doing the same in Trinidad, and teaching Greek and Latin at the Collège Bourget in Rigaud, run by the Clercs de Saint-Viateur. The best salaries were to be had outside Canada, but I gave priority to my love of Greek and my doctoral research and opted for Rigaud.

I spent four wonderful, well-filled years at the Collège Bourget. There I taught Greek and Latin, prepared my thesis, wrote a novel, published articles, and experienced marriage and the birth of my first two children.

It wasn't the Klondike, but I wasn't running after big salaries (there weren't any in the teaching profession). I wanted to do what I loved and I had enough for my needs. In my first year I earned $750, in addition to my room and board in the college with the religious staff. With careful managing this could last. The difficulties came with the second year. Having decided to get married, I couldn't live in the college. It was agreed that I would get $900 dollars a year, to be raised to $1000 in the fourth year. Under these circumstances, my "leisure" budget was meagre indeed, and as a priority came well behind my research needs. I had rented a house with a large garden from the Sisters of Sainte-Anne. I bought the wood for heating it (eighteen cords a winter) and split it myself. As did my father in the country on winter nights, I got up at about three or four in the morning to relight the stoves. My rent was twenty dollars a month, but cost me no more than half that amount, since I had taken in a boarder for ten.

Casual earnings were rare. One opportunity did present itself—the cause of my only bad memory of Rigaud and typical of the asperity of certain churchmen. The normal school run by the Clercs de Saint-Viateur, also in Rigaud, needed someone to teach a Latin course for the brothers who were studying for the baccalauréat. I was asked to give a two-hour course on Sundays (my day off) for a total of $350. This would add a good third to my annual salary. The college superior, one Father Martineau, was scandalized. "Monsieur," said he, "for $900 a year, you should devote all your time to the college. All!" He wouldn't hear of any excuses—the mediocre salary, my heavy teaching load, a pregnant wife—it was no good. "That's your problem, monsieur, not mine," said he. I appealed to the Provincial of the order and obtained the *nihil obstat*, but I had little taste for the social policy of an ardent defender of encyclicals. In addition, if funds were lacking I could call on my uncle, the vicar general, who was always interested in the success of my doctoral studies. He kept up with my small discoveries and gave me sums of money at various times to add to my salary.

In all my years of teaching, the first was the most difficult and had the heaviest load, yet it was the most exhilarating. I taught the versification year, dealing with thirty-six pupils whose voices were just beginning to break. Some were still just kids, some were becoming teenagers, and some considered themselves men. In other words, a class in crisis. The study master, Father Eucher Lefebvre (a dynamic little man whose manner was equally brisk with teaching staff and students, but whose competence I admired) had warned me that this was the most difficult class because of the troublemakers. "I'll manage them by catching their interest," said I, rising to the challenge. He smiled at my optimism.

I began by establishing discipline. The marks were read each morning. The range for good conduct varied from six (excellent) downward, to four (bad), and four with a question mark (borderline between four and three). Three was a catastrophe, since the wayward student lost his weekly holiday.

I didn't beat about the bush. "I'm not here to be a policeman, but to help you with your studies," I told the class. "I'm not going to bother you with nitpicking points of discipline. If you have something to say to your neighbour, say it. That's all right. But if someone bothers me, watch out: I'll bother him right back. I won't waste time deciding whether it's a five, a four, or a four-question-mark. It'll be a three. If the person doesn't mend his ways, neither will I. He'll get a three the next week and another three after that. It's all the same to me!"

I recognized the ringleaders right away and chose the hardest case as an example. During the first week he acted up, but not once did I reproach him. He may have thought he was getting away with it, but on the following Monday the study master called out a three after his name. The boy lost his holiday, but his behaviour changed hardly at all. To all appearances, I remained indifferent. The next Monday he earned another three. That put an end to his disruptions. Another student wanted to test his mettle against mine, but a couple of threes in succession put him in his place. From then on, without ever raising my voice (which is a sign of weakness), I had no discipline problems. Peace reigned—not the armed peace of the Warsaw Pact, but a serene atmosphere. I put up with lots of things—a boy saying a word to his neighbour or giving me a comical answer. On our afternoons off I would take my students for hikes on the Rigaud mountain, something other teachers didn't do. The boys felt more at ease with a lay teacher, telling me about their problems and sometimes about the shenanigans they'd been up to. Even so, I took care not to give them too much slack.

Admittedly, the students made up for their good behaviour by heckling other teachers. One in particular was Pierre Deltour, a Belgian mathematics teacher and a layman like myself. He was a plump man, very knowledgeable, but often with his head in the clouds, a failing that led to mishaps. One day he sent a shoe to be repaired. It came back shining with black polish. Our friend Deltour, paying no attention to paltry vestimentary details, arrived in class with one black, gleaming shoe and the other grey with ancient dust. The class was bedlam for the entire hour. Another time, deigning at last to lose his temper, he spoke to one of the offenders while standing on the platform and tried to stamp his foot with masterful vigour. Alas, the mathematician hadn't measured his gesture accurately. His foot hit thin air and he collapsed in front of his class. Another time, reading a detention list sent by the study master, the Belgian didn't realize that the first name on the sheet belonged to the class teacher. He announced emphatically "Detentions for the following names: Monsieur Marcel Trudel!" He was unable to continue.

With my discipline problem solved, I worked at capturing the students' interest and stimulating their quest for knowledge and culture. I went beyond the text book, reading them choice excerpts from French, Latin, and Greek literature. For example, using some of the best translations, I gave them a few good jokes from Aristophanes and fine passages from *Antigone*, Virgil's *Eclogues,* and Villon's poems. When dealing with a passage from Xenophon that they'd translated with excruciating effort, I took time not only to show them a fine literary translation, but to explain what the text was really about. Here were the Greeks of the Army of the Ten Thousand setting off for the first time in their lives across snowy wastes, inventing wooden spectacles to protect their eyes from the glare. Taking this situation as the starting point, I asked them to make comparisons with our own winter problems. They looked for answers, and we discussed them.

I had to give new life to Latin and Greek, these so-called dead languages, and show what these ancient civilizations meant to us in terms of language, literature, art, and philosophic outlook. In order to lighten the drudgery of looking in a dictionary, I gave the pupils ordinary words and expressions to learn by heart every day, in an attempt to get them to read the literature at sight. For this purpose I prepared two mimeographed notebooks, one a Latin vocabulary designed specially for Julius Caesar's *De Bello Gallico*, and the other a Greek vocabulary for reading Xenophon. At least one expression from these lists stuck in my students' minds at the end of the year—an expression adopted as the class motto: *Aciem fer*, "Don't give up!"

The Versification curriculum included *μι* ("mi") verbs, the traditional bugbear of students of ancient Greek. Having established good discipline, I used to send two-thirds of the class to the two large blackboards. I would ask questions as the students broke up the chalk to write their answers, while those still seated called out corrections. It became a sort of jousting match where honour was at stake. Anyone walking down the hall outside the room at that moment would have concluded that my class was in chaos.

I kept my students constantly on the go. Each morning I dictated a short test, after which I would leave my desk and collect their written answers. They watched me closely. If I stepped back onto the platform with the sheets, the work would be corrected and the marks would count. If I walked toward the wastepaper basket, the lazy ones were saved. The class never knew ahead of time what would or would not count.

I made an effort to teach them the precision of French vocabulary. In leisure moments I had listed in my *Larousse*, under some general word, the special vocabulary attached to it. Under "ear," for example, I had listed auricle, concha, and lobe; under "fat," the words suet, adipose, lipoid, grease, lard, and oil. Each day, I served up four or five and had the students recite them. From time to time they had to write short compositions using this vocabulary. One day I received a description of myself: "We know a man who is short, a little bandy-legged, with wide shoulders and a slightly ovate belly." This, I admit, makes for a rather contrived style (something I was criticized for in my novel *Vézine*), but perhaps the somewhat laboured manner is preferable to poverty of language.

For compositions, I thought up more lively topics than those traditionally offered in textbooks. If my pupils had just come back from a hike to the Elephant Grotto on Mount Oscar, I would give them the following scenario: "You've gone off by yourself to the grotto. You're lying down when you spy enemy Indian canoes. You feel you must run to warn your people, like

Madeleine de Verchères or Laura Secord. You try to get up, but someone hits you on the head with a tomahawk. You wake up: the discipline master has found you and is shaking you." Another scenario went like this: "You're out fishing. You fall asleep and dream you've turned into a fish. One of your mullet friends snaps at a fine worm and suddenly disappears. You're hungry, so you also swallow a worm. A hook sticks in your mouth . You wake up with a toothache." One student wrote naïvely, "I meet a pretty mullet and flick my tail at her." My teenaged students howled with laughter at this. I used to keep a little notebook handy and jot down everything that seemed like promising material for a future novel. In this way, I had a ready supply of amusing topics, scary stories, or detective adventures to suggest. I would read the best compositions in class, and the students would critique them, correcting the vocabulary and simplifying the sentences.

My passion for birds dates from this first year of teaching. One pupil, Louis Genest, was a fervent young naturalist (he became the well-known founder and director of Camp Port-au-Saumon). He gave me a swallow-house that he'd made according to the exacting standards of these birds, who are very particular about their lodging. I put the swallow-house by my window. Around mid-May, a couple of tree swallows made their nest in it. Later, I wrote in *Vézine*:

> The marvellous, slender tree swallow, when perching, holds its chest high and stands on its delicate legs like a proud little dandy, its breast blazing white, its back glinting steel-blue. The little black eyes gleam in its dark-capped head, and the point of its triangular beak is as sharp as a blade.

I used to kneel at my open window watching the swallow descend in a wide circle, a feather in its beak. It would land on the perch at the opening to the birdhouse, look left and right, then pop through the hole. Out it would come again to look for another feather and return without paying me the slightest heed. I was the friend of these high-flying birds.

This swallow-house followed me in my various moves, delighting and amazing my young children. Ever since, in May and June when mating birds sing and before the foliage hides them, I try to identify sparrows, cedar waxwings, goldfinches, and the abundant variety of warblers. One morning at the end of May, lying in a tent before dawn, I heard the most fantastic concert of my life. Thousands of birds were singing at once, and their voices rose in a shrill continuo, seeming very near yet far away. It seemed as though I were inside a beehive and the multitude of high notes had joined in the same soaring strain. How many times have I held a warbler that had stunned itself by bumping into the windows of my house in Charlevoix! I would put the bird in the hollow of my hand, warming and soothing it, then, as soon as it began to chirp, the sign of its reawakening, I would gently toss it into the air like an offering to the sun.

Life in Rigaud included the joys of the theatre. The Rigaud college, like the one in Joliette that was also run by the Clercs de Saint-Viateur, was known for its lavish stage shows under the direction of Father Antonin Lamarche, a man with a great theatrical sense. In the spring of 1942 the college produced Claudel's *L'Annonce faite à Marie*. The scenery was like something out of a fairy story, and the character of Violaine delightfully played (by a boy, obviously, a handsome youth being chosen). The next year, the show was devoted to Beethoven, in particular his *Pastoral* and *Eroica* symphonies. In 1944 it was *Le Bourgeois Gentilhomme*, with the ballet sequences directed by a professional. In 1945 we had Mozart, but the Beethoven production has remained one of the great joys of my life. Since then, whenever life is troubled for me, I play Beethoven's *Ninth*, that glorious and heartening symphony.

I had been seeing Anne-Marie throughout my years of *licence* studies. It was practically impossible for me to leave Rigaud, so a weekly correspondence took the place of the traditional courting. My lodging was in the "monks" wing, with a cleric on my left and another on my right. I woke in the morning to the sound of the monastery bell and the rousing wake-up call "*Benedicamus Domino*," as the crier passed down the hall. Deprived of affection in my childhood, I was eager to set up my own home and give my children what I had missed. At the end of December 1941, without any great to-do, we became engaged with plans to marry the following summer.

My adoptive parents were happy. My worthy uncle, the vicar-general, frowned at first when he learned that the bride-to-be had no secondary education. "Once the emotion of the first years has passed," he assured me, "it will become difficult to get along." I knew a number of young women in the liberal professions, but either I felt they were out of my reach because of my low income, or I couldn't stand their preoccupations, which I thought frivolous, and the rather superficial side of their behaviour.

My fiancée corresponded to my idea of a certain kind of milieu as I then

Back for the summer. Relaxing on the chaise longue, 1942.

saw it. Glowing with health, natural and affectionate, she was also thrifty and perfectly trained in the traditional tasks of women. She had grown up on a self-sufficient farm—one where a penny found was a penny saved. Almost everything was made at home: bread, soap, rope, furniture, blankets, clothing (there was always something on the loom), socks, and children's shoes.

Anne-Marie had lived for a while in a new settlement in the Abitibi region, keeping house for her brothers who had moved there. She was familiar with the log cabin in the first clearings, gardening among the tree stumps, kneading dough, and doing without a doctor, as well as lonely winters and dogsleds. Added to all this experience was a tragedy. Her fiancé, an adventurous man who, like the chance comer in Germaine Guèvremont's *Le Survenant,* hunted for furs on Indian land. He had been found drowned in rather mysterious circumstances. It was this life experience that, in my eyes, made up for the lack of diplomas.

Our marriage took place in the Lower St. Lawrence parish of Saint-Damase-des-Aulnaies in July 1942. We honeymooned in Kamouraska, over the objections of my in-laws who wanted to keep the newlyweds with them for a week-long wedding celebration. As we were leaving, right after the brief midday meal, my father-in-law said to us, looking disappointed, "You're going to leave us all by ourselves." He drove us to the little Elgin station in his buggy. At the end of a week he picked us up at the same spot, and the wedding festivities—*les soirées de noces*—began.

I discovered the world of the Lower St. Lawrence, something completely new to me. Although I'd studied in Quebec City, I knew nothing about the countryside downriver from the Île d'Orléans. I was used to the Trois-Rivières region, but now I would discover a land of high mountains as well as the great river and its islands. People here called the St. Lawrence "the sea," and indeed it was, with its waves, its long-reaching tides, salt water, eel fisheries, and everything that the seigneur of Saint-Jean-Port-Joli, Philippe Aubert de Gaspé, had extolled in *Les Anciens Canadiens* and his *Mémoires.* I heard a different speech, too: a *chaudronne* for *un petit chaudron* (a small kettle or vat), a *fontaine* for a well with no lip, *quetoches* for breasts ("Elle a de belles quetoches"). It was a way of speaking that referred amply to the points of the compass, as though one was at sea. My father-in-law would say to his wife, "Turn your horse to the south." I was told, "You'll find it in the nor'east *(nordet)* or sou'west *(suroit)* room." And people rolled their *r*s with such gusto that you'd think they were trying to outdo each other.

Saint-Damase-des-Aulnaies possessed a curé such as I'd never encountered. In my first visit to the presbytery (for you didn't become part of a parish without first going to see the curé), he asked me to come in, knowing I was a teacher. "You don't teach English, at least?" he inquired. In the pulpit he preached lengthy sermons, speaking his mind on everything, even politics. This was the year of conscription, and his verger had been taken from him. He'd had to replace him with a woman (what the *habitants* then referred to as *une bedoche*). For this turn of events the curé harboured a distinct grudge against the provincial premier, Adélard Godbout. The premier had nothing to do with it, but the curé openly wished for his defeat. His New Year's Day sermon contained the following outburst against the premier: "Le grand Dollard est mort au Long-Sault; le petit Délard va faire le petit saut!"—a play on words making it clear that the premier's political life was destined to be brief. He would denounce this or that without any concern for the most elementary discretion. In his little village, a cluster of houses where everybody knew each other, he remarked from the pulpit, "In the village there's a woman with five daughters. Five whores! Six counting the mother!" His neighbour, the curé of Saint-Jean-Port-Joli, was no less trenchant. At the beginning of every summer he thundered against *ces demoiselles* who were going to appear on the beaches in bathing suits, announcing, "My brothers, the beach cows will soon be among us."

In addition to all these discoveries, I came upon a subject of history that was to fascinate me. This was the famous temperance preacher Charles Chiniquy, who ended by becoming a Protestant and mounting an unremitting campaign against the Catholic Church. I had vaguely heard talk of him in my childhood, and behind this strange name (the Chiniquys were of Basque origin) I saw a kind of bogeyman who came to scare children in the evening. "Go to bed, the bogeyman's coming," people would say. A "Chiniquist" church with a view of the St. Lawrence stood on a mountain, one or two kilometres from my wife's home. The people who lived in this out-of-the-way corner were cross with the bishop for building the parish church so far from them and had "gone over" to the Protestants. Chiniquy, now a Presbyterian minister, had built them a church.

Until his death in 1899, Chiniquy used to come to this church from his country house in Sainte-Louise to carry out his pastoral duties. His son-in-law, the Reverend Chodat, succeeded him. As late as 1942 a few families were still Chiniquists, but the number of the faithful was diminishing. The young men wanted to marry, but in order to find a wife they had to convert to Catholicism. One of these conversions moved the curé to give a touching sermon on the piety of the sheep who returns to the fold. The young man was actually put forward as a model of virtue. Three months after the marriage, the wife gave birth to two bouncing twins! When another Chiniquist converted in order to marry, the curé confined his remarks to a simple word of welcome.

My father-in-law told me he'd seen Chiniquy. He was already influenced by the legend of Chiniquy amusing himself by "blessing" the bread in the baker's carts in full view of everyone, and he swore to me that, as a punishment for his apostasy, Chiniquy's thumbs and index fingers were completely twisted (these were the fingers consecrated during ordination). "It was probably arthritis," I remarked. My father-in-law was somewhat annoyed at me for casting doubt on what he'd seen with his own eyes. In any case, the Chiniquy affair fascinated me, and I hoped to find the leisure one day to write a book on the subject.

I hadn't published anything since my classical college days, being busy completing my *licence*. I still dreamed of publication, and my profession gave me the opportunity. In March 1942, in the revue *L'enseignement secondaire au Canada*, I described my method of analyzing a Latin text, using a passage from *De Bello Gallico* as an example. The next month, in the same journal, I published *Explication d'un thème latin.* I contributed to the journal again with *Correction d'un thème latin* and *Technique de la version.* Each time I dealt with methods used with my pupils and I proudly considered myself the classics specialist in the versification year. Then, warming to a subject that I found far more interesting, I sent the same journal an article on *La crise du vocabulaire.* This essay put forward the premise that the expression of thought depends on our words: the more we know, the better we are able to express our ideas with ease and elegance. I suggested using "three old methods": the study of Greek and Latin roots, translation of classical authors (which forced students to research a specific vocabulary, and going through the dictionary (a method I practised daily). I had also begun to contribute to *Culture,* a journal published by the Franciscans, and had been trying my hand at book reviews. And in 1942 I began my novel, *Vézine*, for if I dreamed of being a Greek specialist, I also wanted to be a novelist.

Fulltime teaching (fifteen class hours a week, in addition to correcting homework), articles, starting a novel—these all went along with writing my doctoral thesis. The four years in Rigaud were focused on the precious degree.

During the school year, I had the complete works of Voltaire to hand, plus a rich collection of nineteenth-century Canadiana in the Collège Bourget library (a very dusty old place in those days). I spent my summer vacations under dormers of the Quebec Seminary where all the newspapers of French Canada, from 1764 to our own day, were kept. Despite the heat of the sun beating on the metal roof and the dust in these huge attics, where I was easily the first person to work in half a century, I went through all the publications, one by one, up to 1900. I had long since acquired the habit of reading massive amounts of text, and I can flatter myself with having read (if only skimming sometimes) everything published in French Canada—books, newspapers, and magazines—from the time of the British Conquest to the beginning of the twentieth century.

With my thesis completed, mimeographed, and sent to the examining jury, my long-dreamed-of goal was within reach. On May 3, 1945, five days after the birth of my second child, I was summoned to Laval University to defend my thesis, or more precisely two theses, as the regulations required. The main dissertation dealt with Voltaire's influence on French-Canadian literature. The second consisted of five propositions for consideration: 1–that the history of French-Canadian literature before 1900 deals with attempts to create a literature; 2–the important dates in our literary history; 3–the fragmentary nature of our literature; 4–that our literary relationship with France had never been interrupted; 5–the debate over the dismissal of New France as "quelques arpents de neige" or "a few acres of snow."

A thesis defense was a very solemn occasion in those days. It took place in the Grand Salon of the Quebec Seminary, a room hung with immense oil paintings. Here the five examiners, wearing ermine-trimmed academic gowns, took their places on one side of a large table, facing the candidate who also wore a gown but no ermine. This was an event announced in the newspapers, and members of the public were seated around the room. The candidate explained his principal thesis for twenty minutes. Each examiner, including my thesis director, then spoke at length, attempting to catch the candidate out and, as was often the case, trying to blow his own horn for the benefit of the audience. We then went on to the propositions put forward in the second thesis. In his response the candidate played the same game of blowing his own horn—and indeed it was a game, because a candidate who was permitted to defend his thesis was already accepted. The jury retired to deliberate, a matter of taking a small break, and returned to hand down the sentence with great ceremony. I was declared a doctor *summa cum laude* and invited to put on the ermine-trimmed gown.

This *rara avis* of the doctoral world (for doctors *ès lettres* were extremely rare in Quebec and looked down on by Ph.Ds) had his photograph and a biographical article in the newspapers, for it was indeed considered news in those days. In my little village, each time a young man was ordained, his family gave him a huge party. His many relatives came, along with numerous other guests, and a banquet with speeches and presents was the order of the day. Alas, there was nothing of this sort for my doctorate, not even a cocktail party! The gown was not as worthy as the cassock.

According to the rule, the thesis had to be published and sold in a bookstore. I couldn't have asked for better, since I always wrote with a view to publication. Éditions Fides had accepted my manuscript early on, but it didn't have the wherewithal to publish the work at its own expense, and in those days there was no assistance from the public purse for book publishing. My uncle, the grand vicar, came to my rescue yet again. He was as pleased by my doctorate as I was. "Have it printed," he said, "and send me the bill."

A run of a thousand copies was printed, and my dissertation appeared in two volumes in the fall of 1945. These were the good old days when newspapers made much of authors on page one or page three. There for all to see was your photograph and a biographical article. The appearance of a book was an important event and the press immediately informed the public. In fact, there wasn't much competition, as only a few books were published annually. Graced with an intriguing title, a Prix David upon publication, and a boost from public controversy, the work quickly became a best-seller. These days it's almost impossible to find. It sold for $3.50 in 1945. Recently, I was offered a copy for $150. I had to refuse, even though I had no copies of my own left.

The Collège Bourget's Greek teacher could now hang out his shingle as a literary historian. It was a first step toward a career as a historian and a university professor. In fact, in that autumn of 1945, I was to be invited by Laval University to become a member of its teaching staff.

Since 1943 I had been giving courses at Laval, but summer courses only, within the special program for teaching French to English-speakers. We were not considered university professors, however. The summer courses, founded by Monseigneur Alphonse-Marie Parent, were run by a para-university organization that recruited university professors, college teachers, and even

Marcel Trudel holding a copy of his just-published first book,
L'Influence de Voltaire. Rigaud, Quebec 1945.

students, according to the level of courses offered. The summer courses were self-financing, thanks to a certain amount of volunteerism on our part, for we never knew in advance what we'd earn by the end of the six weeks. It all depended on how much was left over after expenses. For the first summer I only received $75 for grammar and conversation courses, a bit of casual income that helped me a little in my research. In the summer of 1945 (I had just received my doctorate), I had to give a fifteen-hour course on Balzac, with several hours of literary analysis, and this time I was paid $200—more than I'd ever earned in a month and a half! Was the prophecy of the Dominican nun in the orphanage about to come true?

The Balzac course had its painfully anxious moments. To my stupefaction, among my students I discovered a Balzac specialist named Brucia Dedinsky. She had a doctorate from Chicago for her thesis on the *Comédie humaine* and had worked in France on Balzac's actual manuscripts, whereas my course was based on the few rare copies of Balzac that could be found in the university library. One morning she handed me a copy of her thesis with the dedication, "In all humility." But it was I who, in my heart of hearts, was overcome with humility. Luckily my course dealt with Balzac's descriptive method. I somehow managed to hide my incompetence, and my Balzac specialist had me named a life member of the Balzac Society of America.

These summer courses put me in touch with a very interesting range of people. The teachers had a chance to demonstrate their abilities to the university faculty, and we met adult students who'd come from English Canada and the United States to learn French. It gave us teaching experience and obliged us to speak the best French all the time—a point on which the powers that be were most insistent. Another particular advantage was the fact that we encountered a mentality very different from that of French Canada. It had a great impact at the time, although it would hardly be significant nowadays. I remember how shocked I felt at the behaviour of American nuns—sports-loving, supple-bodied, freed from the old-fashioned corset, with breasts that moved beneath their wide berthas (goodness, were nuns women?), and who looked men in the eye when they spoke to them. I was equally shocked by what we considered the sloppy dress of American students. They came to courses without ties and sometimes even without jackets! Unheard of!

The teaching staff enjoyed meeting at meals and exchanging amusing anecdotes, such as the one about a nun who, instead of reading aloud, "Son épouse dont il regrettait les petits soins" ("His wife, whose little attentions he missed") bravely said, "Son épouse dont il regrettait les petits seins" ("His wife, whose little breasts he missed"). Then there was the one about the female student who, before responding in a drama exercise, put her foot forward, held out a hand, but was unable to utter a word. "Dites-le, dites-le!" the teacher insisted. At last the student took another step forward, lifted her hand once more, and declaimed loudly, "Le!"

Paul Hébert, Pierre Boucher, François Cloutier, Jean-Noël Tremblay, and others of our group began a long career by enjoying ourselves hugely.

In the fall of 1945 my career was to take an unexpected turn. The Greek teacher was about to become a specialist in the history of Canada.

The Laval faculty of letters was getting ready to add history to the university curriculum, and I was offered the job of teaching Canadian history. I was tempted to hesitate, since I was getting so much pleasure from teaching Greek and Latin to pupils whose intellectual development I could follow during the year. I accepted the post quickly, however, for three reasons. The salary was $2000, twice what I earned in Rigaud, teaching at the university would bring me prestige (I was told, "You'll be the successor of Ferland and Chapais"), and I had a taste for history. Even though I had always given priority to classics and the novel, I was an avid reader of history and fond of great reconstructions of the past.

Before occupying the newly-established chair of Canadian history, I needed further training. I hadn't worked in this discipline since my days in the rhetoric class at college—which says something about what a fledgling I was. Beyond our borders the study of history had evolved both in its methods and focus, and I needed to bring myself up to date. In 1945 university life in France hadn't got back into its stride, and I was advised to go to Harvard, on the understanding that I would spend a year or two in Paris afterward.

I belong to the generation that, because of the war, was obliged to attend American universities in order to specialize—Guy Frégault in Chicago and myself in Boston, along with other French Canadians who studied philosophy, social sciences, political science, and economics. On an evening in December 1946 we got together to celebrate the fifteenth anniversary of Canadian independence (obtained in 1931 with the Statute of Westminster, although this is largely forgotten). There was among us a student of remarkable personality who immediately became the centre of our group: Pierre Elliott Trudeau.

Harvard was already bursting at the seams with returned soldiers, and I couldn't register as a regular student in the history option. I was told (and I think it was a polite refusal), "You already have a doctorate, therefore the university can't give you a Ph.D." I therefore became an *auditeur libre*, but I was given a very special status, that of visiting professor, with an office in the Widener Library and the use of all the services.

I discovered the power of American universities. The Collège Séraphique's five thousand volumes had dazzled me. Laval's three hundred thousand tomes had seemed like a pinnacle of civilization. Here at Harvard, in the library built in memory of a *Titanic* victim, there were five *million* books! The Widener had a wealth of collections of all kinds, not only American and British works, but French as well. In French literature, for example, I could look at not only one complete edition of Balzac, but all his editions, and it was the same for the various periods of our literature. I came to the chastening realization that the French literature section in Boston was far superior to what we had in Quebec.

At the same time I discovered the richness of the American heritage. In Quebec, because of our national anthem's original French words "Ton histoire est une épopée" ("Your history is an epic") we had come to believe that we French-Canadians were the only people on the continent who cared about cultivating history and preserving the heritage of the past. I became aware that in this field the Americans far outdistanced us. I was certainly captivated by the Quebec City of yesteryear, but this largely involved the last half of the nineteenth century, a period that no one cared much about in 1945. In New England, where architectural groupings had been preserved—Harvard itself, for example—there was a collective reverence for the dead of past centuries. I found eighteenth-century graveyards in many places that were as well-maintained as parks and decorated with flags as a reminder of the artisans of the American Revolution. Old Boston with its permanently-anchored eighteenth-century frigate in the harbour (not to mention old Philadelphia) had far greater charm than the old city of Quebec.

In New England I also encountered the Puritan simplicity of the Congregationalist church. Everything was white. There were no pictures, no statues, and at the front of the church there was just a lectern standing between the American and state flags. I knew of the Puritans' work, but I had never thought of comparing it to Quebec. If Quebec was rigidly moralistic and led by its clergy (hadn't Premier Godbout asked Cardinal Villeneuve's consent before giving women the vote?), and if this Quebec was intolerant toward other religions, I realized that the same stern discipline existed in Boston. There was even a kind of "hell" in the Widener Library. It had nothing to do with the papal Index, of course, but it was a hell all the same. *Life* magazine had published the photograph of a birth that aroused the indignation of pious New Englanders. The daring issue was banned in the entire state of Massachusetts and put under lock and key at Harvard. As with Quebec during the Old Régime, a decision by the clergy became a decision by the state. I could henceforth explain to my students that New France wasn't alone in its *rigorisme* (not to be confused with Jansenism). The period was one of strict moral codes, whether in New England, among the Quakers of Pennsylvania, or in France itself.

In Boston I got to know the small Franco-American community. Before this I had only heard of it through the propaganda in the review, *La Survivance française en Amérique*, today more simply called *Vie française.* Given the eloquence devoted to annual celebrations in this journal, I had thought that Franco-Americans were "the torch-bearers of French civilization" in the United States. In fact, apart from members of the clergy (mainly French Canadians who had recently emigrated) and a few isolated laypeople, I only saw people of modest means speaking a poor sort of French—small shopkeepers like the Syrians, Lebanese, or Greeks in Montreal at that time. In Lowell, reputedly an important centre of French culture, I looked for "the French survival," but found mainly the powerful Portuguese minority, which occupied the forefront. I met Acadians who spoke to each other in English in my presence. It was among the upper echelons of Boston society that I heard French—good French, that is. This confirmed my thinking about the future of French in Canada. Outside Quebec, it was the cultivated English-speakers who would mainly insure the survival of the French language.

What I saw was an anglicized Franco-American society, both in language and outlook. I observed family life. For the grandparents, Quebec was *chez nous*, the place from which they had come, driven to the States to find work in the cotton mills or the brickyards. They still had brothers and sisters in Quebec and went back to see them in "the old house" from time to time, drawn by emotional needs. These people were still French Canadians, but they were in their sixties or seventies and hoped to end their days in Quebec.

The children sometimes went to Quebec. They were amused by the farms where their parents were born and carried back pleasant memories of their visit with uncles and aunts, but they were content to go home to the States, the land of their past and future. They had married there, and their children no longer spoke French. For this third generation, Quebec was a place of folklore, charming to visit, like Mexico, Spain, or Italy. Sometimes they would choose French as a second language in school, in preference to Spanish or German. The Franco-American world was about to draw its last breath. When I returned from Harvard, I dared to say I had met the last generation of Franco-Americans, an opinion for which I was considered an adversary of French survival.

My main task at Harvard was to prepare myself to teach Canadian history. I was beginning from scratch, and my two years as "visiting professor" were years of hard labour. However, I did reserve one entire day each week (a custom that greatly shocked a colleague who came to join me in Boston) to wander about the historic places in the area, visiting the old frigate *Constitution* and the Boston Museum of Fine Art or strolling along the seashore. Sometimes, trusting to luck, I would get on a bus that took me to some delightful corner of New England—north, west, or toward Cape Cod.

To become up-to-date (for 1945) and to learn the state-of-the-art method in history and what subjects historians were focusing on, I read quantities of American, British, French, Spanish, Italian, and German works by people like Hart, Barnes, Croce, Lebon, Sée, d'Aron, and others. I prepared teaching tools by establishing a bibliographical card index on American and Canadian history and making an inventory of the best advanced textbooks.

Since I was at Harvard, I chose as my main focus of study the relations between Canada and the United States, beginning with colonial relations. I soon came to the Revolutionary period. At the Widener, in addition to the vast archival holdings such as the Force collection and the *Journals of the Continental Congress*, I had access to the complete works (and in critical editions) of the great Revolutionary authors—John and Samuel Adams, Benjamin Franklin, George Washington, Thomas Paine, and Thomas Jefferson—as well as volumes containing correspondence, diaries, and speeches. I began to get the glimmer of a book. It would be a work of Canadian history this time. What became of Canada in this war between the British colonies and their mother country? Did the United States want to annex it to distance the threat of Great Britain? Did Britain want to keep its Canadian possessions at any price? Was France interested in recovering its colony or did it prefer to leave it as a permanent excuse for discord between Britain and the United States, thus forcing the new republic to maintain its alliance with France?

Despite all these other concerns, I continued to expand my knowledge of French literature. In Canada I had been unable to find copies of some of the major authors, but during my two years at Harvard I read over a hundred works, including those of Zola, whose enduring *Rougon-Macquart* cycle makes him the great historian of nineteenth-century French society.

During this time I was putting the final touches on my novel *Vézine*, and in March 1946 it was ready. It began as a retelling of a Christmas story written some years earlier. The main protagonist was then Jaquette-à-Simon, the legendary idiot of Saint-Narcisse-de-Champlain who had been given to the devil by his father in his cradle. From then on he had never been able to wear trousers, despite the bishop's attempted exorcisms. As soon as someone helped him into them, the trousers would be torn to shreds. With this story as a starting point, I gradually developed the plot for a novel. Vézine, a poor bachelor living on the margins of village society falls in love with the little daughter of a businessman. As a means of introducing gossiping women (the wicked genies of the village), I grafted onto this an adaptation of the sketches I'd written for radio. According to the plot outline, my tale about Jaquette-à-Simon became the last chapter of the book. As I went along, however, I realized that this tale served no purpose in the novel and I dropped it. Only a brief paragraph remains in the final version. The novel is really the account, written when I was twenty-nine, of my youthful dreams, my village life, my forest rambles, and also a tale of love, a secret love for a girl much younger than myself. The manuscript was accepted by Fides and published in October 1946 in a run of three thousand copies. A new pocket edition of five thousand appeared in 1962.

Vézine was my last truly literary work, written at a time when I wanted to be both a Hellenist and a novelist. In the spring of 1947 Laval University hastily recalled me to Quebec to begin teaching Canadian history in September. Hurry, hurry, we're starting! Forget the delightful hours of the study years at Harvard, forget about going to Paris for further training! Time to begin your career: *adieu,* Sophocles and Balzac, *bonjour* Garneau, Chapais, and Groulx!

7

Fighting for the New History

My sudden return to Quebec City meant that I first needed to settle some family concerns. I had to find a place to live for a family with three children, including Marc, who had just been born. At this juncture my Uncle Hormisdas Trudel, proud that his nephew was teaching at the university, provided the wherewithal to buy a newly-built house in Sillery. The Rue du Coulonge was then the last street in this suburb, running beside a pasture belonging to the nuns of the Notre-Dame Congregation. Each morning cows came mooing in front of my house, and not too far away the geese ranged freely. I found the country in the city, much as I had done in Rigaud. It wasn't long before the cows disappeared. A boulevard was extended through the field, houses were built, and the natural frontier between Sillery and Sainte-Foy quickly disappeared.

My elderly adoptive mother—whose face had become ever more dear to me as age mellowed her features and as I became more deeply aware of how much I owed her—had become paralysed. My sister Clémence cared for her with great solicitude, but she died on September 6. Clémence had to join her husband in Montreal, so we agreed that I in turn would look after my father. He had to break up his home. My father made me a gift *inter vivos*, what used to be called "giving oneself," as it was practised in earlier times. This act took place before a notary. Wishing to be amusing, the notary in question said to my father after the signing, "So, *père*, you have nothing now. There's only death to look forward to."

My father had in fact aged a great deal during these last years. His woodland treks were a thing of the past. Unable to move about much, he sat in his rocking chair by the stove or on the bench on the front porch in summer. Passers-by envied him. "You're lucky, Father Thador, you spend the time sitting down!" For that generation, work or exercise meant wearing out your body. It was better to spare yourself. The ideal end to a career was to be able to sit still at long last. My father's body had thickened and become stiff with such a sedentary régime. The trembling in his hands from Parkinson's disease increased steadily, and he had to be fed like an infant. He could no longer read, but he continued to follow my career with amazement. A doctor *ès lettres* didn't mean very much to him, since I obviously wasn't caring for sick people. As to what it meant to be a professor in a university, he was equally at sea, but he admired me just the same, confident that I had reached a very high echelon of society.

He followed me to Quebec City without, I think, feeling too much out of his element, for he had been a great traveller in his day. My wife looked after his with as much care as she would have given her own father. I was swept up in the the torrent of a burgeoning career and couldn't give him all the attention that, it seems to me, I would have today. He didn't live with me for very long. With old couples who have lived close to one another, the survivor joins the dead partner in fairly short order. On March 15, 1948, he very quietly died—"slipped away," I should say, as this metaphor so aptly describes the fading of breath, the slowing of the heartbeat, and the gradual dimming of the eyes. I lit a candle near him during his last moments. When it became clear that he had died, I blew out the flame, and a shadow fell over an entire past.

There comes a time when a sort of whirlpool appears, suddenly dragging a whole generation into its depths. Uncle Hormisdas, who had retired at seventy-five, died four years later. To him I owed my literature studies, my title of doctor, my first book, and my house. To paraphrase an affectionate cliché, he had been more than a father to me. Those who had made me what I had become would no longer be there to witness the harvest.

This harvest was my university career. It is important to remind readers at this point what Laval was like when I began teaching there. Located in Old Quebec, it was founded by the Quebec Seminary in 1852 and soon had four faculties (medicine, law, theology, and arts). A century later, it was still run by the founding institution. The seminary superior, whatever his competence, automatically became the university rector. The twelve seminary directors were members of the university board and had the same voting rights as the deans of the four original faculties. The vice-rector and secretary-general were, and had always been, abbés attached to the seminary. Where did the seminary end and the university begin? New faculties appeared later (letters, science, philosophy, social sciences, and agriculture), but as the charter didn't provide for them, the deans of these new faculties had no vote on the governing board. If, for example, the dean of science wanted to propose a measure for his faculty, he had to ask a seminary abbé to act for him and wait for the others, who were mainly members of the seminary, to adopt or reject his proposal. The cherry on the cake, so to speak, was the fact that each professor went in person to the seminary bursar to retrieve his monthly pay cheque.

The university profited from this system. It was almost entirely financed by the seminary. Every salary and every material expense (little as it might be) came to us from the seminary. The annual budget? Such a thing was unknown during my first years of teaching there. If, as director of the history institute or secretary of the faculty of letters, I needed ordinary articles such as a piece of furniture or index cards, I would buy them myself and send the bill to the bursar. If I wanted to hire a professor, I mentioned the matter to Monseigneur Alphonse-Marie Parent (at times secretary-general, at others rector). "Very well," he would reply, "Have him come. I'll arrange it." Then one day the rumour ran through the university that we would be required to estimate our expenses and be held to these figures. General panic ensued. Was the university about to become a matter of dollars and cents?

Thus did budgets come to Laval—and it was high time. By supporting the university, the seminary was exhausting its resources. Its seigneurial forests between the Montmorency River and Baie Saint-Paul were bringing in less and less revenue. Laval had to find other sources of funding. The 1952 centenary marked the beginning of the actual separation, in legal terms, of the university from the seminary, but for a good many years to come the university rector still had to be the seminary superior.

The close relationship between the two institutions was commemorated each December 8 with a banquet luncheon in which the seminary hosted the university staff. Invitations became increasingly selective as the number of professors grew. This banquet took place in the priests' vast refectory and was the occasion for receiving the province's premier, Maurice Duplessis. Each year his mood would be closely watched, since the funding needed for university development came from him alone, depending on his whim. The luncheons during the tenure of Rector Vandry, well known for his public servility toward Duplessis, were the most notable. After an enthusiastic speech in praise of the premier, Monseigneur Vandry would announce the university's projects. Duplessis would then speak, extolling the rector's clarity of vision and referring him to St. Joseph, through whose intercession one had to pass to reach the premier. ("*Ite ad Joseph!*" he'd say. "We're good friends; he'll tell me what to do.") There followed a lengthy talk about how subsidies must be deserved. In years when the premier's mood was sombre, he would give vent to bitter criticism of "bad teachers who are undermining society's foundations."

This mention of bad teachers was mainly aimed at Georges-Henri Lévesque, the Dominican dean of social sciences whose faculty was virtually placed on the Index not only by Duplessis, but also, alas, by many of his fellow clergy. As far as Father Lévesque's opponents were concerned, anything that deviated in the slightest from traditional society was dubbed leftist. I'm thinking in particular of the dreadful pamphlet, "L'infiltration gauchiste au Canada français" by right-wing historian Robert Rumilly, a Frenchman who settled in Quebec in 1928 to escape leftist France. Leftist, you say? Nothing very diabolical about that. But under Duplessis, leftist meant communist. If you strayed from the traditional outlook, you were a communist and therefore excommunicated. It was no laughing matter in the 1950s. I knew a first-rate history professor whom we couldn't hire for the institute because, as a student, he'd been curious about the communist conception of history.

Duplessis was very willing to help the university, "guardian of our religion, our laws, and our rights," but he was determined to have Father Lévesque's head. If not, there'd be no subsidies for the social sciences and consequently no salary for the professors.

The premier had Lévesque's head, and in the most legal manner. The university board decided to apply a rule that prevented a dean from remaining in office for more than two terms. Father Lévesque happened to be in this situation. "It's really too bad, Very Reverend Father, but the rules, you know—" He was replaced by the most anonymous of professors. Duplessis could rest easy and shower grants on the university.

Those in power profited from the occasion to eliminate Gonsalve Poulin, a Franciscan and one of Father Lévesque's close associates. He was a man of consummate culture who taught me at the Collège Séraphique, and the very best among academics. Duplessis was the self-appointed protector of Franciscans in his home town of Trois-Rivières, and assumed a domination similar to that of the French governor over the Recollets in New France. The premier found that the Franciscans were the most enthusiastic preachers against communism. But a Franciscan at the side of Father Lévesque?

Intolerable! Apparently Duplessis said, "So Father Poulin wants to take up the cause of the workers against established authority? Very well, we'll send him to the workers!" And Father Poulin, a career university professor, was removed from the faculty of social sciences by his superior and appointed curé of a working-class parish in Trois-Rivières. He was lucky not to be sent to Haiti or Japan, like some others who owe their missionary vocation to Duplessis.

And what did we professors have to say about these underhand schemes that crushed all expression of intellectual freedom? Not a thing. We lived under an authoritarian régime. Our classical college education had taught us that everything came from on high, especially authority, and that only wrong-headed people criticized authority. Such criticism was one of the two capital crimes (the other being shocking behaviour) that led to expulsion.

Laval was run by the priests of the Quebec Seminary, and was therefore subject to the greatest orthodoxy (you know: "Ye are the salt of the earth, but if the salt have lost his savour . . . it is thenceforth good for nothing.") In addition to its civil charter signed by Queen Victoria, Laval had a papal charter of which it was very proud. Not every university had such a distinction from the Vatican. As a consequence, we as professors in one of the Pope's institutions were obliged to be "popephiles." The university's annual reopening was celebrated by a mass dedicated to the Holy Ghost. In gown and mortarboard, we would troop down the middle of the street from the seminary to the basilica. At the end of the mass another parade commenced. Each professor walked up into the chancel and knelt before the archbishop while swearing on a copy of the Holy Bible, open at the Gospel, not to teach any of the errors denounced by Pope Pius IX in his *Syllabus* of 1864. In a papal institution, you're on the side of the Pope!

It was to this atmosphere of orthodoxy that I came in 1947. As a new professor I had to take my first official step by paying my respects to the dean of the Faculty of Letters.

Monseigneur Camille Roy had died in 1943. The current dean was Maurice Laliberté, a large, plump canon of the Quebec episcopal chapter. He had long been dean of arts, a theoretical faculty that grouped the classical colleges, where he had nothing to do but enjoy the prestige of his post until the day came when an attempt was made to transform the arts faculty into an active body, as in the Anglo-Saxon world. He opposed all change. In order to get rid of him gracefully, his superiors promoted him to the deanship of the faculty of letters, where it was thought he would have no problems. One day, therefore, he was to be seen wandering along the Rue de l'Université, looking for his faculty. Meeting a social sciences professor (Jean-Charles Falardeau, as legend has it), he asked him in his broad Québécois, "Where's that faculty of letters? I've just been named dean, and I've been *sarching* and *sarching* and I can't find it!" He did find it in the end, alas, and there served as a vigorous brake to all change. When, during his reign, an effort was made to introduce folklore as a new academic subject, he declared during a board meeting—this, the successor to Camille Roy—"Oh yeah, folklore: it's just sheepshit!"

I presented myself at the canon's door full of enthusiasm. I should mention that he was also director of a residence for student abbés, and his office was there. Once inside, I thought I was in a general store at first, amid a clutter of paint cans, various boxes, and potato sacks. He proudly informed me that he had received everything needed to paint the bedrooms and had brought in his supply of potatoes for the winter.

"All my *pataques!* What do you think of that?" Not having foreseen the need to delve into this subject, I proceeded to discuss my own concerns and what I would be teaching in the faculty. "But *mon pov' monsieur,* what do I know about it, eh?" was his response. In any event, I had paid my official visit.

Monseigneur Parent soon told me what to do, when to do it, and how. He was a short dumpling of a man with the round white face of a choirboy, but he could freeze his interlocutor with a stony expression. I always felt like a college kid in his presence, as did many of my colleagues. It took me some years to learn to look beyond his shell. Once he travelled with me from Quebec to Montreal to hear my maiden speech before the Académie canadienne-française. He was a shy, very sensitive man with a good-natured side, and above all loved to laugh at tricks played on someone. He became a different person at such moments. I myself even dared, one April Fool's Day, to send my secretary (who was momentarily distracted) to ask him for the key to the old seminary sundial. He laughed all day! But alone with him I wouldn't have dared be so familiar.

Parent was an extraordinarily efficient man. Whether he occupied the post of secretary-general, vice-rector, or rector, according to the game of administrative musical chairs, he was always the key person with whom it was best to consult. Whatever his title, his actual job became the one most essential to the university. He knew about everything that was going on in the various faculties. I consulted him constantly in my capacity as secretary and then director of the institute, and also as secretary of the faculty of letters. I never had time to explain the object of my visit: he knew it already, and if I insisted on explaining the details, I felt I was boring him. He answered instantly, in an involuntarily curt tone, as though I'd asked him to get me a quart of milk. On each of my frequent visits I barely had time to go in and out. His very brief comments didn't call for any development of the conversation, and I felt like a fool. For a number of years I was responsible for the faculty calendar. As soon as the handbook was printed, I made an occasion (being very proud of my publishing experience) of giving him the first copy in person. Parent would open it at random. "*Tiens*, here's a typo you've missed," he would say. Or else he would happen at first glance upon a small change I'd made without consulting him. The summer courses that he had founded and kept going under difficult conditions had earned the university renown throughout the Americas.Under his long reign the university went from being a small business of the mind to a great industry.

It was thanks also to Parent's efficiency and undeniable authority that the new discipline of history was able to make a place for itself within Laval's faculty of letters and to develop rapidly thereafter. He overcame opposition, recruited the professorial staff, invited guest lecturers from Europe, and found the money for everything.

The titular director of Laval's newly formed Institut d'histoire et de géographie was Abbé Arthur Maheux, one of the most unconventional priests in the Quebec Seminary. He came from the Beauce region, as did his friend Parent, as well as Rector Vandry, Provost, the assistant archivist, Luc Lacourcière, chairman of the folklore program, and so many others. Beaucerons, as we call them, occupied every level of the hierarchy, and if you wanted to rise it was a good idea to come from the Beauce. Maheux was tall—or I should say long, *very* long—and used the longest cigarette holder the market had to offer, into which he would stick the longest cigarette available. As he never bothered to flick the ash off the end, there was always a curved tip of burnt tobacco constantly threatening the visage of whomever he was talking to. If you dodged at just the right moment you could avoid the shower of ash. His smoking apparatus may have been long, but his paragraphs were extremely short. When he had formulated a brief sentence, with subject, verb, and object, he had given his all and would start a new paragraph. His basic method of writing never changed, and his books consisted of rapid annotations, rather like spontaneous thoughts jotted down in haste or the cigarette ash that he let fall everywhere.

Unlike his rival, Lionel Groulx, Maheux had absolutely no use for eloquence. In his rare public lectures, he was content to hand out mimeographed sheets that he would comment on for the audience. Indeed, he was the first in French Canada, and perhaps in Canada as a whole, to transform a formal lecture into an analysis of texts. It was quite something to hear the rustle of foolscap sheets in the large amphitheatre, much like the flutter of wild geese on the Saint-Joachim flats. Still, it was an excellent way of talking about history.

Maheux often met with the Protestant historians of Toronto, something that was frowned on by many of the seminary priests and by Quebec society generally. To add to the juicy gossip, he boasted about his Toronto connections. On his prolonged visits to Ontario he would send back mimeographed pages of his personal diary to all and sundry. If he caught a cold, the whole of Quebec City knew how many handkerchiefs he'd used.

Abbé Maheux was an organizer. During the time of Camille Roy (whose protégé he was), he was asked to organize the secretary-general's office. Until then, everything had been administered literally from the bedrooms of those who occupied the various posts. If you wanted to see the rector, you went to his private room. Maheux acquired a large area of office space, bought a great deal of furniture, installed filing cabinets, scattered typewriters everywhere, and recruited personnel. The habitués of the old corner-grocery-store approach declared war on these delusions of grandeur. Once Roy was gone, Maheux was immediately eliminated. In the Quebec Seminary, where the priests formed a distinct community, closely-knit cliques and unrelenting hatreds arose. One could say of the inmates, as is said of monks and nuns who are constantly together, "They meet without knowing one another, live without loving one another, and die without being regretted." An abbé might go through life never speaking to his neighbour. When Abbé Maheux had to repair his fireplace, which shared a common chimney with his neighbour and colleague, he went to a third person to get arrangements started.

After his fall from power Maheux's superiors relegated him to the archives, hoping he would soon be forgotten. They didn't know Maheux! The seminary archives were perhaps the largest and oldest private archives in Canada and bore directly on the country's history. The seminary's own documents reflected its considerable role in the Church and, because of its Beaupré seigneurie, on the economy. In addition, the collection had somehow acquired the Contrecoeur papers recording the French occupation of the Ohio Valley, the papers of the American revolutionary Benedict Arnold, and papers relating to Chiniquy's long quarrels. In short, it was an inexhaustible mine of primary material for historians.

It happened that these archives had been banished to the basement of the building, and it was the rare visitor who gained access to them. Maheux decided that everyone should benefit from the archives. He hired personnel, undertook an initial sorting, organized a card catalogue, and had all these treasures moved to vast new quarters—just before the old basement suffered water damage after a fire. Maheux had a room set aside for researchers and organized staff to help them find what they were looking for right away—something no religious order in Canada had yet done. Finally, he began the publication of all documents, beginning with *Les Papiers Contrecoeur*. He well deserved to be named director of the new history and geography institute, even though he had no teaching duties.

The new history, or what was presented as "scientific history," began in French Canada in 1947. Before September 1947 this discipline didn't exist as a regular subject leading to a degree in our French-language universities. History studies ended with the baccalauréat, but before completing the philosophy year prior to university, the student had to write the exam described in an earlier chapter, which consisted of producing, from memory and without any documentation, the most stirring piece possible on the subject of Canada's history.

There had been talk for several years of finally making history a subject taught in French-Canadian universities. That it took so long is rather strange, seeing as how history had long been a tool of survival for French Canadians and a source of arguments to bolster the struggle for distinct recognition. There was very little organization in the history field. Apart from the *Bulletin de recherches*, which dealt with only minor details, the *Mémoires de la Société généalogique*, entirely devoted to the history of families or individuals, and *The Canadian Historical Review*, published only in English by the University of Toronto, there were no periodicals specializing in history. There were plenty of historical societies (sixteen in Quebec in 1943), some inactive, others moribund, and all limited to their immediate milieu, which was fairly restricted. They were kept going by people of good will, and in rare instances by intelligent, self-taught individuals. The French-language Quebec City historical society limped along, trying without much success to save the old quarter. Montreal's historical society made much of its past, which had been brilliant a half-century earlier, but its present was lacklustre. The Canadian Historical Association (known in French as *La Société historique du Canada*) was the work of English-speaking enthusiasts and mainly valuable for its annual congress. Few French-speaking Canadians took an interest in its various works.

This disorganized and improvised approach to history was rectified by Abbé Lionel Groulx. In December 1946, at a banquet given by the Saint-Jean-Baptiste Society, he announced the creation of a history institute of French America (l'Institut d'histoire de l'Amérique française), that is, "a team of historical researchers and writers who would focus on studying the French fact in North America." At the same time, he launched the *Revue d'histoire de l'Amérique française*, its letters patent dated April 10, 1947. The particular aim of this journal was "re-establish the true idea of history by making the rules and strict discipline" of the subject better known, and also by publishing reviews written by specialists, thus "raising, we believe, historical criticism among us and by the same token the level of historical works."

These two events heralded an immediate renaissance of history as a subject. But things didn't end there. Dissension arose over who had first thought of having a regular history program within the university curriculum. Was it Laval University in Quebec City or the University of Montreal? Who first wanted to train professional scientific history teachers? Groulx said his history project dated back thirty years. The Gentlemen of the Quebec Seminary (to use their ancient title) claimed that this project went back to Abbé Ferland in the first half of the nineteenth century, while the Quebec historical society spoke of its very long preoccupation with the subject. Abbé Maheux, Groulx's rival, claimed that the project had been simmering at Laval for many years. Everyone wanted the credit of having originated the program, thereby admitting that they had certainly taken their time about setting one up.

Be that as it may, in 1947 the University of Montreal established its history institute within the faculty of letters. According to its first chairman, Guy Frégault, this was "a group of *professors* for the *teaching* of universal history." Groulx's history institute of French America, by contrast, lay outside the university and aimed at convening *historians* who would *write* history. In that year of 1947, Laval University also inaugurated a history and geography institute within its faculty of letters. French Canada, from having no history institute at all before 1947, now suddenly had three!

The geographers were also going to experience an organized teaching program for the first time, but they didn't have to endure the burden of a subject considered as having a special mission. We historians wanted a truly *new* history. This meant history free of any nationalistic claims, because history is not a tool for lobbying (otherwise it would be distorted) but a reconstitution and analysis of the past. It is a history that is free from emotion and rhetoric, that will not ignore any field or aspect of human activity, and that at each stage supplies documentary evidence of what it states. Opposing us was *la belle histoire*, the only one then recognized in French Canada—edifying, revitalizing, exalting, and used basically to "form" the young. Another of our burdens was the mystical nature of Groulx's style, contrasting oddly with this respected historian's great willingness to be counted among the supporters of scientific history. We were also up against all those textbooks, from elementary school ("Cartier brought little Jesus to the savages") to the post-secondary level. Among these was Gérard Filteau's famous textbook of the 1930s, which only received the stamp of approval from Quebec's department of public instruction (of which the bishops were members) by mixing as much religion with history as possible.

It was the era (and not so long ago at that) when a high-ranking personage in Quebec stated, "To write the history of French Canada, one must first be French Canadian and second a practising Catholic," stipulations that eliminated a good many of the historical fraternity, including our friend W.J. Eccles of Toronto. The annual general meeting of the Société historique de Québec began with an obligatory high mass. The Société nationale Samuel de Champlain opened its sessions with a prayer to Champlain. Its founding president, Georges Boulanger, even had the following *ex voto* placed in *Le Devoir*: "Thanks to Samuel de Champlain. For favour obtained with promise to publish." Lucky geographers—they weren't condemned to practising a Catholic geography!

Because we wanted to make a more accurate assessment of well known historical personalities, Frégault, Eccles, and myself were accused of trying to topple hallowed figures such as Cartier, Champlain, Dollard, Frontenac, and Montcalm. Those who strolled irreverently through the halls of the great were called to order for crimes that, seen from today's standpoint, are nothing more than choirboy antics. In our day, the historian who considers these men from a critical perspective is performing an honourable function. Thirty years ago, he would have been putting a revolver to his head.

The fact was, we were surrounded by elders who watched carefully to see what we might be cooking up. When Frégault, for example, questioned certain of Frontenac's qualities and wished to show his faults, he was accused of being an iconoclast, of wanting to tear things down. Abbé Albert Tessier denounced me in the *Cahiers des Dix* if I showed Champlain being in the pay of the Protestant Pierre de Monts or when I spoke of his commercial ventures—the same Champlain who had been elevated to the status of missionary or (which was equally noble) the defender of a farming colony. In the abbé's view, I was deflating a figure of national glory whom "the old historians had taught us to love and venerate." He reproached me for saying Champlain wasn't an agricultural colonizer, a civilizing influence, or an evangelist. When I published my work on slavery, *L'esclavage au Canada français*, the reaction was the same: "He's still amusing himself by cheapening our history."

Respect was mandatory not only for great men of the past but for the "old historians." We were referred to the work of François-Xavier Garneau as to a bible. As late as 1935 you didn't speak of New France in classical colleges without citing Garneau. If it came from Garneau, it could only be the truth. This veneration resulted in a falsified edition of Garneau's work. Since his 1845 *Histoire du Canada* had become somewhat outdated in the light of more recent information, the author's grandson rewrote the work in 1913, adding and correcting, but at least being careful to put square brackets around material not written by his grandfather. But in 1944, what should appear but a new edition with these same additions and corrections, but without the square brackets to distinguish the original Garneau from the work of his revisors. I created a certain amount of scandal in the university by teaching that, although Garneau marked a decisive and admirable stage of our historical writing, he should be put aside as he was now only a historical monument.

I took the same approach to Thomas Chapais, another bible that was forced on us. I admired the man as a representative of a cultivated bourgeoisie. Around 1945, shortly before he died at the age of eighty-eight, I spent an afternoon with him discussing history in his library on the Rue du Parloir. All the same, I put aside a body of work that no longer suited our time. My preference with regard to Canadian writers tended more toward various historians of the late nineteenth and early twentieth centuries who had advanced historical methodology, but who had become objects of scorn for the historical establishment in Quebec. These included Narcisse-Eutrope Dionne, a meticulous, matter-of-fact writer, and Benjamin Sulte, who published not a *Histoire du Canada* but a *Histoire des Canadiens-français*. People derided Sulte, but he represents an important stage because his work marks the advent of ordinary people—*le petit peuple*—as a subject for historians, a sort of social history before its time.

Among our predecessors, we found highly cultivated men who had written the kind of works expected of them in their day, but we considered them too engaged in a religious and nationalist ideology, too inclined to show French-Canadian society as perfect and New France a Paradise Lost. However, they too were above reproach. When Frégault criticized an archivist-cum-historian with whom he had worked, the newspaper *L'Action* delivered this crushing salvo: "It's a dirty bird that fouls its own nest."

Some of these predecessors were still around and, like good fathers, took it upon themselves to set us on the right path. "Your teaching is too down-to-earth and your subjects lack exaltation," said one to me. "Read *Caesars of the Wilderness* [Grace Lee Nute, *circa* 1943], and you'll see how your courses will take on life by exploiting Radisson's great adventures!" I had no taste for history *à la* Buffalo Bill. Some would register surprise at my telling students to learn how the people lived under the French Régime, how they dressed, or what they ate, not seeing much connection between the mission of the French people in North America and what they had on their plates.

What young historians of today tend to forget is that we didn't live with impunity under the régime of a Church triumphant. An entire generation, Frégault and myself among others, had to reckon with the weight of a religious ideology that sometimes was applied openly, sometimes in a more subtle way. I remember one day receiving a message from the diocesan office while doing research in the archives of the Trois-Rivières Seminary, certain that I alone knew of my whereabouts. The message was from the bishop's palace: the bishop wanted to meet me in order to discuss history! I had no idea bishops were so keen on history. Nevertheless I accepted the invitation and listened politely (as I'd become used to doing at the university) while the bishop treated me to a long historical monologue that contained no hint of the Quiet Revolution.

Our elders considered us insolent for another reason. We refused to take them at their word and demanded proof of their statements in footnotes! Their answer was that our footnotes only cluttered the book and made it unreadable. Furthermore, footnotes added to printing costs! And where did we get the preposterous idea that a history book needed a bibliography "Why have a bibliography?" an abbé of established reputation asked me one day. "Those interested in the sources already know what I could list, and those who aren't will simply skip it; *ergo*—"

Our new approach was finally accepted in some circles. In 1953, Gérard Martin had this to say in a review of one of my books on the post-Conquest Military Régime: "[Trudel] never hesitates when confronted with the truth of a document, even if sentimental or nationalist tradition has to suffer. This takes nerve." Note well that even in 1953 the reviewer took the trouble to add, "This takes nerve." Today it's not in the least remarkable.

I began working with Lionel Groulx as soon as I returned from Harvard in 1947. Early in 1948 I became a member of the board of the Institut d'histoire de l'Amérique française. Although my personal collaboration was unhesitating, the same wasn't true of official relations between the Laval institute and those in Montreal. Laval's external relationships tended to favour English-speaking universities (with the exception of McGill, for reasons I've never understood). This was a long-standing tradition in Quebec City, strengthened by Monseigneur Roy and much more by Abbé Maheux. As a result, Laval professors cultivated a view of Canadian history that went beyond the traditional limits of French Canada.

Immediate and generous communication between the only French-language university history institutes in Canada would normally be a given. But for many years (I'd say for *centuries*) Montreal and Quebec had maintained a bitter rivalry. This dated from the early days of New France, and the enmity hardened with the contentious university question in the nineteenth century. Montreal wanted its own French-language university, but Quebec City vetoed it. All Montreal got was a branch operation with the humiliating title of "Laval University in Montreal," a state of affairs that lasted into the twentieth century! While attending a history banquet in Montreal, I was preparing to allude to this episode in our squabbles when an abbé advised me, with a highly confidential air, to leave the subject strictly alone. Even in 1950, the century-old wounds had not healed.

In those days French Canada listened to two unswerving opponents, Lionel Groulx and Arthur Maheux. Groulx looked his foes straight in the eye as he said, at a major public festival, "We are the generation of the living; you are the last generation of the dead"—a remark that chilled relations between the two camps and did little to promote co-operation. In 1943 Maheux had written a brochure directed at "the others" entitled *Pourquoi sommes nous divisés* (literally, "Why are we divided," although it appeared in English in 1944 as *Canadian Unity: What Keeps us Apart*?) In the same year Groulx replied on behalf of "the others" with *Pourquoi nous sommes divisés* (immediately translated as *Why We are Divided*). Like Voltaire in his dealings with God, these two clerics had a nodding acquaintance but didn't speak.

As I wasn't involved in the squabbles of preceding generations, I thought it idiotic to collaborate with Toronto and not with Montreal. Moreover, I admired Groulx and said so in a review of his *Histoire du Canada français* (1954), and when introducing him at a symposium. When he received the Léo Parizeau Medal I was asked to speak in his praise. I even wrote a similar speech (ghost-writer for once in my life) for Quebec education minister Paul Gérin-Lajoie. This being said, I didn't agree with Groulx's historical theses or his mantras. It was mainly his incantatory style that made his work age suddenly. He was a natural orator. Even in conversation, he seemed to think he was treading the boards. His voice would swell and he would stand as tall as his little body would allow, his breath sustained, the embodiment of Demosthenes. For me, however, history is not expressed by the urgency of words. It is calm, well thought out, nuanced, hesitant—the word seeking the truth, not untruth splitting the word.

Although not a partisan, I nevertheless admired Groulx. Here was a man who had devoted his life to history in the service of nationalism, yet at an age when others are retiring he accepted the fact that history had taken a scientific turn. He had set up two entities to foster a new history: the Institut d'histoire de l'Amérique française and the periodical (*Revue d'histoire de l'Amérique française*) that he wanted to be of the highest quality and independent of any ideology. If he had left us nothing else, we would have to say, "Bravo, Monsieur Groulx!" (but not too loudly).

I therefore became a member of the *Revue*'s editorial board, travelling from Quebec City for editorial meetings. They weren't frequent, and our power of decision counted for very little. Like the high-ranking ecclesiastics of his time (Groulx had become a canon, but Maheux had been promoted to *monseigneur*), he made up his mind before consulting others. He generously left us to decide the cases that he found genuinely perplexing.

Dating from my time as secretary of the Laval institute under Maheux, I had wanted to arrange a meeting between Groulx and my students. I expected it to take place at Laval. What could be more natural? However, the sages of Laval got into quite a stew about it, seeing such a meeting as a challenge to Maheux and all those Quebec Seminary abbés whom Groulx had relegated to "the last generation of the dead." I was given to understand that it would be preferable not to give the matter too high a profile. I should meet Groulx as though by accident, and above all I should not receive him on university premises. I therefore took Groulx and my students to the off-campus faculty club, and we spent a pleasant afternoon lurking in the underbrush.

I also needed to create a bridge between the Laval institute and the one headed by Frégault at the University of Montreal. Frégault, Brunet, and Séguin, men of about my own age, were the pillars of this institute.

Guy Frégault, like myself, had first been trained in letters and had dabbled in literary criticism while being a nationalist activist. He was a highly cultivated man with a methodical but subtle intellect, balanced judgment, and the courtesy of an aristocrat. He seemed cold because he was shy and reserved in his friendships. We quickly came to an understanding because I respect cultured people as well as liking calm discussion that takes account of nuances, and also because, as I myself love to laugh, I made this hypertense man roar with laughter. We talked much of history, not bouncing ideas off one another, but rather enjoying a joint exploration of the various possibilities of a question seen from the same side of the fence. And we talked just as much about literature and art. We visited each other's homes, and I was even a sponsor at his son's confirmation.

Frégault's career as a historian was brief. He left his university, dissatisfied with the treatment he'd received. The University of Montreal couldn't have cared less, displaying the same indifference as Laval later showed toward me. He took refuge at the University of Ottawa and was immediately retrieved by the Quebec government as deputy minister to organize its newly created ministry of culture. He devoted himself totally to his job and had a high conception of government service. People called him a veritable Colbert. Frégault wasn't cut out for the world of politicians, however, and cabinet shuffles brought him bitter disappointments. I was aware of this. When I was chairman of the history department at the University of Ottawa I tried two or three times to bring him back to teaching and research. He preferred to stay on, although he had been shunted aside and now occupied a tiny room in a wretched basement in Old Quebec. He died after long years of being away from history, as he himself recounted in his *Chronique des années perdues*.

Michel Brunet, Frégault's colleague at the University of Montreal history institute, was the exact opposite. A ready but not eloquent speaker, he was a thickset, stocky man with little culture who loftily condemned anyone who disagreed with him. "He hasn't understood a thing!" he would say. He seemed keen to impress people with trenchant and therefore excessive formulae, most often originating with Séguin. He was considered an excellent teacher, all the same, and I'm told his students were very fond of him. For the rest, when he wasn't talking about history, he proved to be a jovial companion.

Jovial, Maurice Séguin was not. He was excessively shy, especially when there were women around. He used to close his eyes when talking to us—perhaps the better to concentrate. Chatting wasn't his *forte*. He would reply with short, jerky sentences, tossed off as though his thoughts were elsewhere. All this may have been due to the pills he had to take for his health. Like his two colleagues, he had the reputation of being an excellent teacher. His courses and rare public lectures displayed a rigorous sense of logic. In fact his whole scheme of thought, constructed around a single event, the British Conquest of 1760, as the determining factor in French Canada's history, rested on the same rigorous logic. It was a tightly woven system, impregnable in its various parts. The basic premise was everything: either you accepted it or you didn't. Séguin wrote little, leaving it to his disciples (always a dangerous practice) to spread his ideas.

People used to say of the Montreal "school" that Séguin was the thinker, Frégault the writer, and Brunet the broadcaster. As with all formulae, this was overstating the case. Frégault didn't really concur with Séguin's system of thought. As an individualist, he wasn't about to be subjected to someone else's historical theory. He had written his masterworks before Séguin's system had been fully developed, and could stand on his own two feet. In contrast, it is difficult to imagine Brunet without the support of Séguin. Brunet used to say to me, jokingly, "Frégault took a long time to catch on." My private reaction was, "I can well see why."As a historian, Frégault didn't like categorical statements and narrow viewpoints. He took what he thought worthwhile from all sources. Frégault was on the same side as Séguin and Brunet, but not necessarily with them. This became very clear when he left Montreal. As for Brunet, the "broadcaster" of the system, he didn't always realize that he was repeating what had been suggested to him, and moreover he repeated it without the nuances of argument or the finely-woven logic of the original. If Brunet heard a conclusion, he trumpeted it abroad. The Montreal school was Séguin expounded by Brunet in a manner that must have made Frégault shiver.

Séguin had the great merit of making several generations of students rethink the British Conquest and take stock of its consequences for the future of French Canadians as a group. However, he is also responsible for the resulting fixation on the idea of the Conquest as a "catastrophe" that "decapitated the bourgeoisie," coupled with a failure to try to find other historical explanations.

Séguin's approach, which could be argued from a strongly logical standpoint, had the grave drawback of not being checked against the facts before being broadcast. At Laval our approach was, first let's look at an inventory of these forty millionaires that the Montreal institute claims to have found at the end of the French Régime. Let's see if they were really wealthy, and on what their wealth was based. A further question followed: was it the Conquest that destroyed our merchant bourgeoisie or simply the collapse of the fur trade at the end of the eighteenth century? Let's do some initial research, we said. To which Brunet responded, "The Quebec City people haven't understood a thing!"

We at Laval in turn criticized the Montreal school's approach for being exclusive rather than inclusive. Montreal was sure that it had the one and only key to French-Canadian history—the unique interpretation. How lucky they were to have found the answer so quickly! Brunet never missed a chance to add, with amicable mockery, "Trudel is trying to find himself." Along with many others, we couldn't help noticing the regrettable atmosphere of nationalism that surrounded the Montreal school's approach to history. What was the use, we felt, of having thrown overboard the erstwhile *belle histoire* only to replace it with a historical approach even more intensely ideological and politically contentious? We saw it as burdened by an absolutist perspective: the master had found the truth; he taught it, and the student had to repeat it or die unshriven. It seemed an unlikely method of developing a critical sense in future historians.

As director of the Laval institute, I did my best to maintain relations with Montreal. Frégault was invited to give a series of lectures at Laval, and Séguin also came to give a lecture, but throughout my professorial career I was never invited to teach at the University of Montreal or even sit on a thesis jury. They exported their gospel without admitting the existence of another Church in return.

Because the University of Montreal group was turned in upon itself, perpetually dwelling on the subject of the Conquest, it cut itself off for many years from current developments in historical writing, taking exception to anything that came from outside its ranks. The Montreal institute's situation didn't help, it must be admitted. It formed part of a faculty of letters run by professors of European origin. The historians were in a state of constant revolt against them. Were these relatively new Canadians less than tactful in their dealings with *pure-laine* French Canadians? In any case, it was really something to hear Brunet badmouthing what he called *les métèques*—the scornful equivalent of "dagoes."

Collaboration between Montreal and Quebec City historians generally took place on a one-to-one basis, facilitated by the neutral territory provided by Groulx's institute and his *Revue d'histoire de l'Amérique française*. This collaborative effort gained a certain amount of publicity through a common publication, *L'Histoire du Canada par les textes*. Its *raison d'être* was the fact that classical college students had no access to source texts illustrating various periods. We wanted to make these available. In 1952, following an initiative by Fides, which was interested in encouraging participation by the province's two French-language universities, Frégault, Brunet, and myself set to work. The project reproduced texts, preceded by a short introduction and a brief bibliography. Frégault, known as a specialist in the history of New France, was assigned the French Régime. As my own research was then focussed on the British Régime, I handled the period 1760-1854. Brunet, whose specialty was politics, covered the modern period. This was the first textbook of its kind in Canadian history studies. It sold successfully for many years and brought me the highest income of all the books I've been involved in, although it wasn't the one that gave me most pleasure to write. In terms of co-operation between the two institutes, an edition of texts with three contributors was feasible, but if we'd tried to produce a history textbook together the result would probably have been three different works.

So there we were with a Montreal school, and as a result people talked of a Quebec school. If this meant a system of thought, a historical *corpus*, a distinct field of enquiry propagated by a cohesive group of historians at Laval, no such school existed. However, if "school" meant a particular approach to history, a particular behaviour in relation to a document, and a systematically open-minded attitude to all research and interpretation, then I would say there was indeed a Quebec school.

Such a school, however, existed only in opposition to a Montreal school.

What we practised wasn't invented by us. We received it from the great schools outside Canada, and also from meeting the master historians who came each year to Laval as guest professors. Since I was the only one teaching Canadian history (at that time the major subject for a history degree) I was able to focus the course according to my own standards of historical science. This role was all the more important because our first generations of students would later, as professors and writers, need to maintain the orientation I'd given them, if indeed it was the right one. I didn't want to repeat errors practised elsewhere.

To begin with, I made sure students felt a sense of freedom vis-à-vis the professor. Was it my instinct, arising from how I'd always hated having a mind-set imposed upon me? Or did I lack confidence in my teaching? I was certain that I didn't have a monopoly on historical truth. I had studied enough historiography at Harvard to know what an illusion it is to imagine history as definitive and the historian as infallible. What can be more disastrous for the progress of history studies than this *magister dixit?* The study of history is a perpetual search, forever renewed with each generation. At the outset, therefore, I humbly admitted my fallibility. I had no respect for the student who followed the course without questioning what was taught.

Another concern followed from this. From one generation to another, the same line of thinking had been handed down as to the origin, role, and nature of the French-Canadian people. The French had come to evangelize, the English to trade. The mission of the French Canadians in North America was guided by providence and our historical figures had acquired angelic proportions. University students had to undergo a thorough mental house-cleaning to get rid of these entrenched attitudes. This amused the lay students, but it was less to the taste of clerics. I had in my course a zealous Jesuit who watched fiercely over the orthodoxy of my teaching. He often dozed off, since I gave my courses in the early afternoon, but if by chance I said the word "Jesuit," he awoke with a start, instinctively on his guard. I wanted my course to be an exercise in questioning accepted wisdom, in clearing the decks before beginning serious work and breaking free from naïve credulity. It was, if you prefer, a course in methodical skepticism (and the shortest route to finding myself out of a job).

I wanted to reach a point where I could practise the greatest possible objectivity, unbiased by previous attitudes toward people or facts, so that history would not be the first victim of the historian. To speak of objectivity around 1950, at a time when clerico-nationalist ideology was at its height, was to give the impression of condemning what had gone before and refusing to make history serve traditional claims in a society that clung to history as though it held the ultimate weapon for a people's salvation. In 1967 I wrote, on the subject of textbooks:

> [The] authors have been exposed only to an atmosphere of superheated provincial nationalism and have been inculcated with the conviction that history should serve what they call "la cause nationale" (the national cause), and so they have made their textbooks vehicles of a French and Catholic apologia. When we consider that today's French-speaking youth has received its historical education from these books, we can hardly wonder at the great vogue for the separatist movement among young people.
>
> [Marcel Trudel and Geneviève Jain, *Canadian History Textbooks: A Comparative Study* (1970), 131]

This certainly wasn't the only cause of separatism, but our schoolchildren, educated by these textbooks, were bound to become separatists. Their only training had been nationalistic; they didn't see what was happening elsewhere and learned nothing about the history of Ontario, the Canadian West, or the Maritimes. They only knew Quebec history really well, and what they remembered was a history of grievances, revenge, and survival. In my teaching and writing, I maintained that history should not be made to serve any combat.

For me, objectivity was based on understanding. Before adopting any attitude, people needed to understand the point of view and mentality of "the other," in our case the English-speaking society with which we began a joint venture in 1760. The education given in certain classical colleges (I speak of those with which I was familiar) didn't further such understanding, although it was and is an essential qualification for the historian who wants to make an accurate analysis of the past. What contribution, for example, did the newly-arrived English-speaking society of the eighteenth century make to our own society? Why did various groups in our society respond positively to this contribution? Were they betraying their own people in so doing? Why were some groups accused of betrayal? Why did others respond negatively? Were they right to do so?

The *bonne entente* movement was active when I was teaching. It had its ridiculous side, but in the teaching of history it was merely an attempt to understand in order to develop an objective approach. With this goal in mind, I agreed to study French-language textbooks for the Laurendeau-Dunton Commission on bilingualism and biculturalism so as to show where we differed and where we concurred in our views of Canada's history. With the same goal in mind, I added a course to the Laval institute's curriculum that was a great novelty: the history of Canada since 1867—a perfectly normal subject now, but unheard of until then in our French-language universities in Quebec, and in the classical colleges of my day and preceding generations. Our study of history ended with Confederation in 1867. Why? Was it lack of class time? Or because what followed wasn't our own history? No French-language historian in Canada had yet specialized in the modern period. While awaiting better sources, I had to rely on a legal historian. He could at least initiate students into the juridical aspects of modern Canada.

Since my aim was to enlarge our field of vision, I set in motion and for many years maintained a practical collaboration between the Laval institute and various historical bodies in English-speaking Canada. We needed to take every opportunity of making the history of New France and our French-Canadian society better known.

As the centennial celebration of Canada's Confederation drew near, the historians W.L. Morton and D.G. Creighton wanted to produce a series of specialized volumes covering the general history of Canada, entitled *Canadian Centenary Series*. It was to our institute that they came for French-Canadian participation. The project wasn't on as large a scale as we would have liked, due to lack of human resources, but at last we began really working with English-language historians.

Our participation increased with another wide-ranging project: the *Dictionary of Canadian Biography*, similar to publications in other countries. Historian George Brown of the University of Toronto had been given the task of creating a multi-volume work of great scholarly value containing biographies of those who had marked Canada's history from its origins up to the twentieth century. For so vast a project, an army of historians was needed from both the English and French communities. Brown, who didn't know Quebec well, seemed overwhelmed by the size of the undertaking when he came to see me in Quebec City. I was enthusiastic about the project, having always loved to create dictionaries. As an adjunct to the Toronto branch of the organization in Toronto, I established a committee in Quebec City to direct the entire French-language version.

As work progressed and successive volumes were undertaken, the Quebec team grew in importance and the Laval institute became a considerable centre of documentation, providing a very useful opening for many of our young historians. Above all, Laval became one of the two biographical poles in Canada—an advantage that could have belonged to the University of Montreal history institute if it hadn't consciously restricted its range, refusing all opportunities to work with the English-speaking world.

In the eyes of our nationalist colleagues at this period, working with English-speaking Canadians meant working *for* them and taking the *Canadian* (as against *Canadien*) side. However, we at Laval didn't become more federalist for doing so. I never allowed myself to use history to support the federal cause. To do so (or to use it to support Quebec nationalism) would mean failing to achieve my historical goal: knowledge free of all preconceived ideas, and uninfluenced by the need to serve any immediate cause. Politicians may pose as national guides, but the historian who chooses to play this role (whether in favour of Quebec or Canada) repudiates history, or is repudiated by it.

Because of this active collaboration, as much with Toronto as Montreal, and also because of the important subject that I taught, I appeared to be occupying centre stage. It therefore happened that I was presented as the founder and first director of the institute. I protest, although I don't insist too much. One should never aggressively refuse merits wrongly attributed, since they compensate for the wrongs unjustly laid at one's door. The real founder of the Laval institute, if it wasn't Monseigneur Parent, was Arthur Maheux. He was the first chairman of what was initially the Institut d'histoire et géographie. It was he who was the *de facto* organizer, and an excellent one at that. The ambiguity of my situation arose from the way in which the institute developed. I was the principal professor and a very active (if not agitated) secretary as Maheux's involvement lessened, and I ended by being promoted to the chairmanship in 1954. The secretary's position was filled by the equally active Louis-Edmond Hamelin, a geographer who had just graduated from the University of Grenoble. Geography soon found itself somewhat constrained within the institute's framework as well as being treated as a poor cousin. It was agreed that there should be two distinct bodies: a geography institute chaired by Hamelin and a history institute, of which I found myself the first director.

The history degree was based on the model used at the Sorbonne: three *certificats* in history and one in geography. This made good sense, since historians are not well trained unless they have studied geography—for what is history if not human geography? Well-known guest professors at Laval such as Raoul Blanchard and Pierre Deffontaines contributed as much to history as to geography. Deffontaines marvelled at the subjects for study that he discovered in this country. He never tired of saying to both historians and geographers, "But we must quickly study this or that," or "You haven't seen this? Come on, let's have some theses on the subject!" or "What? No one here has yet studied the problem of heating in winter? What are you waiting for?" In their first encounter with North America these Europeans showed us new fields for historical and geographical study.

The *certificat* of modern history, covering the period from the Renaissance to the French Revolution, was another basic requirement. How could we understand the French Régime in Canada, for example, if we didn't have a sound knowledge of events in France, the land of our origin, in England, and in Europe generally? We were able to take advantage of the presence of major French historians like André Latreille, Roland Mousnier, and Robert Mandrou. Others, less prestigious, used their spare time to produce works on the history of Canada. Alfred Rambaud wrote a thesis on Monseigneur de Saint-Vallier, which at long last provided a different view from the 1911 biography by our historian, Auguste-Honoré Gosselin. André Labarrère-Paulé, who became a deputy minister under Mitterand, left us a book on nineteenth-century lay educators, revealing to us that before Bishop Bourget's monopoly, our elementary schooling was in the hands of extremely well-organized teachers. These relationships with French university professors also gave us easy access to French universities. The students whom we sent abroad to prepare for post-secondary teaching were received in France with particular attention, and had privileged contact with the VIPs of the milieu that French students couldn't even dream about.

We had the added advantage of being in a position to consult various disciplines related to history—in the faculty of letters to begin with, where I was secretary for several years, which made liaison easier. I also took the initiative of creating a bridge between our institute and faculties such as social sciences and law, so that our students could visit them and their students come to us. With social sciences there was a meeting of minds, and interchange went well. (In the English-speaking world, history was in fact classed among the social sciences.) However, the law faculty, confined by its rigid structure, refused all reciprocity. The problem here was that all life under the French Régime and right up to our own day, from the cradle to the grave, was regulated by the Coutume de Paris, the basis of our Quebec Civil Code. How could we understand our ancestors' outlook without studying the laws that governed them, and how could we understand these laws without studying the outlook of the French Régime? Only two or three students from law visited the institute, but they merely audited the courses (among them was Clément Richard, future Quebec minister of cultural affairs).

All the same, I profited from my relations with the law faculty, thanks to Maître Marie-Louis Beaulieu, who was always available to explain some point in the Coutume de Paris. People in the bus going to the university must have wondered where on earth these odd people came from who discussed dowries, gifts *inter vivos*, exclusion from partition, and how fish in a pond are immovable but once out of the water become movable.

To provide students with an additional working tool, I tried to make the study of German obligatory, as in the science faculty. They already knew Latin (very useful, because many of our historical documents are in the language of the Church), but German is essential for the European historical writer or for reading much of our material relating to the American Revolution. It didn't become obligatory, but some students took courses, and I went with them. German is a marvellous tool, with its tightly-knit logic and Greek syntax.

Historians should extend their cultural field as much as possible. In his first course, André Latreille, our visiting French historian, took as his text a painting by Greuze to be analyzed like a written document. Everything is food for history, including works of literature and art, all necessary to one's understanding a period. In fact, sensitivity is among the primary requirements for being a historian. Without it, a historian is simply a manipulator of statistics and graphs. Alas, I have known a number who have remained closed to everything outside the well-fenced field of their specialty. One must be capable of expressing this sensitivity in writing, in a vivid, completely clear way. I repeatedly told my students, read, read—and not only history. Read Voltaire, Anatole France, or any writer who can inspire your pen.

Although I had a free hand in constructing the Canadian history program, I still had to have the necessary tools. We had the space, but no maps and no historical texts. First, I bought outline maps (then the last word in pedagogical methods) to hang on the wall. These were black canvas screens with the outline of a country already drawn on them. They could be written on with chalk. The suppliers had nothing available for Quebec, however, and I finally had a special set made. I also sent away for coloured wall maps of the United States published by Denoyer-Geppert. These were the best they had for my purpose, even though they dealt with American history. I prepared mock-ups and got Denoyer-Geppert to produce the equivalent for Canada.

If I wanted to explain Canada's development starting in the sixteenth century to my students, I needed a greater selection of contemporary maps. Nothing is more graphic than the experience of following the historical progress of the North American world on old maps. First come the Terra Nova—the New Lands—in the north, then, after a great gap, Florida. Later we see a shoreline joining the two. With Cartier, a river appears leading deep into the continent's interior. Then here are the Great Lakes and Hudson Bay from Champlain's time, and so it goes up to the nineteenth century. What a spectacle!

The Quebec Seminary happened to have many of these old maps in its archives and in enormous atlases. I did an inventory and reproduced the most useful. I drew others myself, especially those illustrating the seigneurial régime. This led in 1949 to the publication, in a rather awkward format, of my *Collection de cartes anciennes et modernes*, which, after various recastings became an *Atlas historique du Canada français*, and finally an *Atlas de la Nouvelle-France*. For the first time in French Canada, students and researchers could look at maps from various periods as well as maps of towns as they developed. I'm fairly pleased with my contribution in this field.

This preoccupation with cartography was already an indication of my concern, in teaching, for the real, the concrete, the down-to-earth. Neither in the classroom nor my books am I a man of the heights, the orator of great visions, the professor with dazzling hypotheses. I detest those who are gluttons for abstractions, who speak so as not to be understood and therefore pass for being profound. I analyze, I spread my wares on the counter. When I talked about the currency of the Old Régime, I brought samples of *écus* and *deniers*, and I even made copies of the "playing-card money" used as paper currency. I enjoy dismantling the mechanism of human activity, and I call a spade a spade. And I'm happy to note that today students of mine who are now historians and professors have the same concern for analyzing the data, whether it be a document or an artifact, and like to use the same concrete, simple language.

Throughout my career it has been this human activity, above all, that I have sought to bring to light. I taught a course on what was then called "institutions"—the boundaries of New France, its demographics, the defence of the territory, the seigneurial régime or the way in which land was held, economic life, the justice system, material comfort, intellectual life, and religion—in short, setting the scene before encountering the people who lived in it. In 1968, after twenty years of teaching, I turned this course into a textbook, *Initiation à la Nouvelle-France*, published in English the same year as *Introduction to New France*.

The analysis of texts was a European method that I had used when preparing for my *licence ès lettres*. It was also on the institute curriculum. In order to train my students in critiquing works, I would use material dealing with subjects that in my day and for the previous century had bolstered myths. Questioning such myths inevitably caused a scandal. Take the matter of Dollard des Ormeaux, considered the saviour of Montreal from the predatory Iroquois. How did this myth, the most sacrosanct in our history, arise? And how did it develop into a legend of epic proportions over the course of the nineteenth century, reaching a high point in 1918, when it invaded our classical colleges. After that, May 24 became an obligatory annual festival with speeches and bands playing. It is fairly significant that this myth was the creation of four successive priests: Vachon de Belmont, Étienne Faillon, Jean-Baptiste Ferland, and Lionel Groulx. Each tried to outdo the other in writing the most pages on the Battle of the Long-Sault, inserting the greatest number of religious elements, or drawing the most ennobling lessons from the story. Vachon de Belmont was outdone by Faillon, Faillon by Ferland, and Ferland (outdistanced by far) by Groulx. Lay historians had less to say on the matter and were the first to attack the myth. Attacked by *les Anglais*—imagine! That was enough to make the myth as solid as Gibraltar among French Canadians. Then came the agreeably shocking business, around 1940, when one of our own dared to treat Dollard as a "joyous brigand"! With my students, the debate was carried on in an atmosphere worthy of history. The first priority was gather the documents in the case, make a critical analysis, and evaluate the reliability of witnesses. These exercises resulted later on in one of my former students writing an excellent article on Dollard in the *Dictionary of Canadian Biography*.

We went through the same process with the myth of Madeleine de Verchères. This myth wasn't the work of churchmen. There was already a plethora of religious heroines for one thing, and it would have been difficult to make a saintly woman of Madeleine de Verchères. Various people persisted, without the slightest misgivings, in promoting a version of events given by the fifty-four-year-old Madeleine forty years after the incidents in question, at a time when all awkward witnesses had died. This later version, packed with all sorts of unlikely details, was retold in France by a professional writer. Still, it was a fine story, far more apt to excite cries of admiration than the very brief and simple version Madeleine had given at the age of twenty-one, only a few years after the events, when all the witnesses were still alive.

Another subject that I used for documentary analysis was "the Jumonville affair," a historical conundrum into which Canon Georges Robitaille had waded with fiercely partisan emotion in order to prove that George Washington, a Freemason, was a murderer. We also looked into the deportation of the Acadians. Here we were indeed walking on eggshells! I wanted to approach the question from a wider perspective by studying the phenomenon of deporting groups of people under France's Old Régime. In a public lecture I sketched the outline of the project initiated by Louis XIV and Governor Frontenac in 1689 to deport the Dutch population of New York "together or separately" and disperse its members in other colonies to make room for a French colony. The parallel between 1689 and the Acadian exodus of 1755 became evident. I was accused of trying to justify the tragedy of Grand-Pré. "Now he wants to deport the Acadians a second time!" critics exclaimed. Not being a candidate for suicide, I dropped the matter.

I also had to set up a course in methodology. Students coming from the classical colleges knew how to prepare a dissertation and compose an essay under three headings in the traditional French way, but they hadn't yet done any research. They had never before gathered information from documentation, transcribed it into a card file, and expressed the results of this research. Drawing on my experience in writing a thesis and preparing books for publication, I enthusiastically undertook an introductory course in research: how to reproduce or summarize an archival document, how to compile notes, and how to move from the card file to writing up the subject. All students were free to use any other method that suited them. I also taught them how to polish a manuscript, correct proofs, and even (why not?) details about book distribution. If my students were to be professors one day, I also saw in them future writers, since I felt that reconstituting a slice of the past could only lead to publication of some kind.

With this in mind, I encouraged my students to publish as soon as possible and made an effort to find publishing venues whenever they produced some interesting research, such as an essay on the building of the first road between Quebec and Montreal. In it was an account of the rebuilding of a bridge from the French colonial period (a significant discovery, in my view). The essay was published without a word changed in Groulx's *Revue d'histoire de l'Amérique française.* Another student prepared a critical inventory of royal notaries that was published serially in the same journal. Yet another wrote a paper on the sacrament of confession. To facilitate this policy of publication, I founded the *Cahiers de l'Institut d'histoire*, a series that is still going and includes some twenty works.

Critics often reproached me for publishing papers by students who were relativity inexperienced, accusing me of not being sufficiently demanding. My aim was to give students the taste for publishing, certain that once they'd done it there'd be no stopping them. Out of twenty full-time students between 1947 and 1957, half have published books. All of them began by getting articles into print. Did they become authors because they took my courses? Or did the initial nudge come from somewhere else? For students who published nothing, my course was still useful. In taking up a book, they knew what it represented in sustained effort, and what problems needed to be solved, from the initial archival research until the final book was off the press.

I began my career as a teacher of Canadian history with very meagre classes. The institute's opening in September 1947 had been a mad rush, with no time to advertise its existence. A lone full-time student presented himself. This was Claude Galarneau, *primogenitus* of the institute. Abbé Maheux had dug up a few people to audit courses, all of them with names ending in the sound *ô*—Arteau, Boissonnault, Boiteau, Noreau, Provost. The most original of these was Georges Boiteau, who had Amerindian ancestry and had already published two books of poems in the style of Alfred Desrochers. He earned pocket money by hunting fur-bearing animals. Occasionally he would be absent from class in winter. He was checking his traps and would dress the skins himself before taking them to the Hudson's Bay Company post. He would return to class, his pockets well-lined. As a history professor I couldn't say just anything about the fur trade to this particular student—nor about fire-water. In my second year at the institute, three full-time students registered. The next year there were eight. The institute was launched.

Most of those going in for the newly-established profession of historian in French Canada were lay people. Occasionally a brother or a secular priest, or a Jesuit appeared. The first nun to register as a student was a cloistered Ursuline. Because of her restricted status, her superiors had imposed conditions. She had to make the journey between the convent and the institute (five minutes' walk at most) in a taxi, accompanied by another nun (it was unthinkable for cloistered nuns to walk around the centre of town). The taxi dropped them at the institute door and picked them up at the same spot, much to the amazement of passing lay students. The chaperoning nun sat at a desk a little apart from the rest and spent her time saying her rosary. The following year, the student nun managed to have a lay female student as her companion. This new chaperone would fetch her from the convent, take her to class, and see her home again—in a taxi as before. The other students used to tease the Ursuline, especially after she said to them one day, "When I came back to the convent last week, one of our mothers said to me, '*Ma mère*, you smell of man.'" The good sister no doubt meant, "You smell of tobacco," but our students' interpretation was less innocent. A few years later I met the same nun, all alone this time, and in a bus. I made it clear how surprised I was to see her wandering around Quebec City in complete freedom. The Quiet Revolution had begun.

The Ursuline was soon succeeded at the institute by another nun, a non-cloistered one and therefore at home in the twentieth century. However, since she came from one of those small convents with no intellectual tradition that were just beginning the race for university degrees, she found herself in a completely strange world in my course. To help discussion, I gave my courses around a big table. The fashion for seminars had just begun. The sister installed herself at the table, but sat right beside the professor, either to show her greater interest or because she considered it a place of honour and her due. She sat very straight, her hands folded, in the pose of the perfect listener. The class progressed, the students wrote, interrupted the professor, and made comments to each other, but the nun kept her contemplative posture. At the end, a little out of patience, I stopped. "But Sister, aren't you taking any notes?" I asked. She replied in the most deferential voice, "Can one take notes while you are speaking?"

It was through these nuns that I saw how the Holy Spirit operates during oral exams. They took care to inform me that, on the very morning of the exam, all the sisters had been asked to pray for the success of one of their number. I felt my back to the wall, as though threatened by the convent firing squad. At least once I was privileged to witness the transmission of grace. On that day several nuns were to be interrogated one after the other, but in private. As soon as one nun came out of the room, she handed something to the next, who held it tightly in her fist throughout the oral exam.

Intrigued by these goings on, I asked the last nun rather gruffly, "Sister, would you kindly tell me what you're passing to one another? I'm concerned about this little game."

"Oh sir, you mustn't see anything wrong in it. It's just a relic of our venerable founding mother!"

Heaven was still arrayed against me.

It must be admitted that the candidates in these early years were very much in need of heaven's assistance, since marks were handed out with the faculty's traditional parsimony. For his first paper, an excellent student like Galarneau received four out of twenty. Abbé Provost, the Quebec Seminary's assistant archivist, had to be satisfied with a meagre one out of twenty. I was applying the system that I myself had been subjected to eight years earlier. In this respect, the Quiet Revolution hadn't yet begun.

8

Delight and Disillusion

I TAUGHT, BUT I ALSO WROTE. It is impossible, however, to prepare university courses and write history without doing research, and this was no easy matter in those days. Salaries were meagre around 1950 (I earned about $3000 a year), and there was no paid time off every seven years for what would eventually be called a *sabbatique*, after the sabbatical already enjoyed by English-speaking academics. Nevertheless, grants for short periods were beginning to flow as we waited for the Golden Age of the Canada Council for the Arts.

Researching documents required great patience. Public archives in Quebec City or Ottawa kept office hours, and if you happened to be in Ottawa (then the most boring city imaginable), you had further arduous research trying to discover how to kill time from five in the evening until nine in the morning. At least the public archives had a welcoming staff. Such was not the case in archives that were private, or considered as such.

I think I must have been one of the first lay people to want to dig into the archives of the Archdiocese of Quebec and of religious communities and presbyteries. Marius Barbeau and Gérard Morisset had gone before me, but they were civil servants who could go almost anywhere without difficulty. Becoming a mobile historian had its perils.

Need I remind those of my generation how difficult it was to gain access to documents of the Catholic Church? Difficult, primarily, because the archdiocesan archivist seemed to be carrying on a fulltime ministry elsewhere, and you had to wait a long time for an appointment. Difficult also because *garder les archives* was the archivist's job, and guard them he did, like the angel with the fiery sword. You were obliged to explain your research plan at length, prove the information existed nowhere else, and state clearly that the subject hadn't been dealt with already. (One day a worthy abbé answered me with the comment, "No, this subject has been covered by Monseigneur Gosselin, and there's no need to go into it again.") Finally, you had to reassure the archivist that Church history would benefit from your research. Only then would he bring you documents—*bring*, but not necessarily *hand over*. Seated on the other side of the table, he would read an initial document to himself, then tell you, "No, this letter won't be of any use to you." He would read another. "Yes, this might help you." He would carry off at least half of the documents and historical truth had to be satisfied with what remained. And yet we were frequently told that "Pope Leo XIII wasn't afraid of the truth; he opened the Church's archives." But that was in Rome, not Quebec City.

Gathering source material from nuns in those early days proved equally stressful. The good sisters weren't yet accustomed to opening their archives and they seemed to think we were poking around for their little secrets. In those far-off times I didn't have permission to enter the Ursuline cloister, but instead had to remain in the parlour, in front of the grillwork (even though I had an Ursuline nun as a student and my two daughters were being educated there). Mother Barnard, an old nun (a vaguely archival personage and the niece of the old historian Thomas Chapais) was sent to deal with me. As a kind of preamble, she felt obliged to recount the history of her religious community through the grillwork, from the soup in which Mother Marguerite de l'Incarnation found the old shoes of the *sauvagesses* to Montcalm's skull. As my research focused on the period of the Military Régime, we finally got around to 1760, but only by making a detour to visit Thomas Chapais, treating me on the way to the genealogy of the Chapais and Barnard families. At last, her store of knowledge exhausted, the good nun went off to fetch the documents. She was a long time finding them.

The said documents were handed to me through the *tour*, a small cylindrical, revolving cupboard set in the wall, which made it possible to avoid all direct contact. Because those great convents were always bathed in a mysterious half-light, I installed myself at a little table near the window. One day, perhaps because I had made something of a reputation for myself, Mother Barnard refused to let me handle the documents. At the time I was researching seventeenth-century scholarships. She would only agree to show me the old notebook through the grillwork. I squinted through first one square opening, then another, trying to decipher the tiny, antique writing. Moving my eye like this, I finally managed to complete the lines. Years later, the Ursulines had their own professional archivist and a huge, well-lit reading room with numerous documents on a large table. I was even served *sucre à la crême,* a treat that I imagine heralded the advent of the Quiet Revolution.

Consulting material at Quebec City's Hôtel-Dieu convent was an equally formidable task in the early days of the new history. The archivist wasn't always available, and the corner where you worked was very small. The nun did her best to help us, however, and I remember that one day, when she heard me coughing, she brought me a marvellous little syrup. Later on, like the Ursulines and the Quebec Seminary, the Hôtel-Dieu set aside a fine study room with a permanent staff. Today's researchers are indeed coddled

My most trying research projects involved rural presbyteries. I did two rounds of the old parishes of the French Régime—some fifty of them. The first round was to research the accounts of the parish council for 1760; the second was to make a list of slaves recorded in the registers of civil status. If I'd been looking into the tithe registers I would have understood the curés' hesitation. Since the tithe belonged to the curé, the registers involved their personal property. The parish council accounts that I was researching on my first trip were in the domain of public administration. I was armed with a letter from the rector of Laval and an introduction from the province's attorney-general—in other words the minister of justice—who was in charge of public archives. As I had kept my childhood image of the traditional country curé, kindly, devoted, studious, and always ready to receive callers, I felt I could present myself at any hour and be cordially welcomed—all the more so for being a university professor and an established writer—for I thought myself famous after publishing three books.

Having no car and relying on bus and train, I started with my own region of Trois-Rivières, feeling I was one of its eminent natives. I presented myself at the Batiscan presbytery, but the curé politely refused me all access to the archives on the pretext that he was alone and had no time to keep an eye on me. This was a bad beginning for my journey. I hurried back to Trois-Rivières and my uncle, the vicar-general of the diocese. He encouraged me to return to Batiscan. This time the curé made me very welcome in the huge parish attic. I was left completely alone in the presbytery, and once my work was done there wasn't a soul to thank. I wasn't even sure whether or not I should lock the door behind me.

When I reached Verchères and knocked on the presbytery door, I met with the kind of welcome given an Iroquois of 1692.

"What do you want?" asked the curé through the screen door before I could say a word. He didn't invite me in. I reeled off my name and my letters of recommendation, explaining that I was a historian and wanted to consult the parish council accounts for 1760.

"Go away!" he cried in his rich country accent. "I'm accountable to nobody!" And so saying, he left me on the doorstep.

There must be a vicar around somewhere, I thought. I'll knock on another door, the vicar will answer, and I'll explain what I want.

As I stood there, the curé suddenly loomed up again. "Go away!" he cried once more, and locked the door.

I called on the bishop for help, and he suggested I go back to Verchères to consult the parish council accounts. However I couldn't in all conscience run to the bishop each time someone shut a presbytery door in my face.

In Grondines, where I arrived by bus, hungry and thirsty, the curé had just sat down to table. He was furious at being interrupted. "I have to eat," he said. "You can wait if you like." I waited in the front hall while the aroma of hot soup and a roast wafted through the presbytery like a blessing. Only once, in Ancienne-Lorette, did the curé show an interest in history. He had just come in from fishing, and invited me to dinner. The trout, done to a turn, consoled me for many miseries.

In the end I succeeded in consulting the necessary documents, proof of which is the fact that I did indeed write a chapter on the financial state of parish councils in 1760. But what a lot of palaver and bowing and scraping had to be gone through each time! Usually the curé's answer was clear and made it difficult to insist further. "No, monsieur, we don't have that," he would say. The trick was to get into the office. I would praise the presbytery, commenting on the venerable age of the parish and the reputed wealth of its archives. Finally the curé would admit that, "Yes, we have quite a lot," and show me the cupboard in which they were kept. I would marvel at the sight of this edifice, particularly if I found out that he'd built it himself, and he would proudly open it. Continuing my praise, I would run my eye over the contents, looking for old books bound with yellowed parchment. Without seeming to contradict the curé, I would say, "Look, up there on the right—you've got some things that seem quite old to me." The astonished curé would get the book down and open it reverently, for it was an account book dating from the French Régime! At almost every presbytery I had to conduct a similarly lengthy siege, progressing to the storage cupboard where, despite, the curé's denials, we would discover the old notebook I was looking for. It being summertime, I would say to myself as I entered a parish, "Oh, if only the curé is on holiday!" I knew that curés asked "a child of the parish"—that is, a member of a religious order—to substitute for them in their absence. I would watch from afar, hoping to see a Franciscan cowl on the porch or the white habit of a Dominican. If I did, what a feast it was! Together we would give ourselves up to the delight of inspecting the archives.

As I hadn't drawn up a long-term agenda for my historical writing, I had to go over the same ground some years later, this time to check the number of Amerindian or black slaves whose existence might be revealed in records of baptism, marriage, or burial. The subject of my research was a strike against me, as it was then considered unseemly to dredge up this page of eighteenth-century history. A further strike against me was my recently-published book, *Chiniquy*, frowned on by the clergy. In the circumstances, I simply announced, "I'm looking for Amerindians." Even then, one curé, indignant at my suggestion of racial intermingling, replied "Monsieur, there are no savages *icitte* [here]!" In some places my name rang a bell and I was immediately upbraided with, "So you're the one who wrote *Chiniquy*!"

This tour of old parishes revealed to me an unsuspected world of sepulchral presbyteries that smelled of death, intellectually barren, redolent of the boredom of solitude and of curés who, with rare exceptions, were horrified at the thought of having to get out of their rocking chairs and had no idea what was in the precious archives in their custody. As I left I would wonder what on earth they did in their long winter months. The thought came unbidden that this was what I would have become, had I persisted in the choice I made in 1938. These two rounds of presbyteries, in 1950 and 1956, made me question my relationship with the Church. I was still a member, but my conviction was waning. Despite all this, however, I was still trying to see the Church as useful and sincere. Looking back now, I view this time as a decisive stage leading to my final withdrawal in 1963.

My first research trip outside Canada was to the United States. This was mainly a pleasure trip. My object was not to find documents but landscapes. Part of my teaching dealt with North American colonial history, and I owed it to myself to become familiar with the actual setting. I had already encountered New England during my two years at Harvard, but I hadn't visited the other early colonies. Funded by a grant, I undertook a historian's tour, visiting the Hudson Valley, old New York, the old section of Philadelphia, and Washington with its imposing monuments and public buildings (especially the Library of Congress), the Potomac River, and George Washington's home at Mount Vernon. Promising myself to venture further toward Virginia and Louisiana at a later date, I returned by way of the Allegheny Mountains and along the Monongahela River (the celebrated "Malengueulée" of the French) that flows into the Ohio or Belle-Rivière where the French built Fort Duquesne, now Pittsburgh. My aim on this return journey was to comprehend how the barrier of the Alleghenies could have kept the English from pushing westward, thereby allowing the French from the St. Lawrence Valley to make themselves at home as far south as the Gulf of Mexico. From Fort Duquesne, I came back by Fort Niagara, a marvellous eighteenth-century fortress, some thirty kilometres from the falls, that absolutely shouldn't be missed. I wound up my trip south of Lake Ontario, traversing ancient Iroquoia, the land of the narrow little Finger Lakes. This historical and geographical ramble was to add depth to my teaching.

At last, in 1957, I made the voyage to France planned for 1939 (but which the war prevented), then for 1947, again put off because of the sudden creation of the Laval history institute. Travel stories are no longer of much interest. Today the astonishing thing is not to travel, but to stay home. There are almost no adventures worth recounting nowadays, apart from tales of lost luggage destined for the Caribbean that ends up in Vancouver. The return of the traveller is a very ordinary event. When I went to the Sahara and wanted to describe it to my teenage children, they looked at me in amazement. These children of the television age seemed to be saying, "Good lord, you'd think he'd never seen anything!"

What took me to France in 1957 wasn't research exactly. In my view, this first visit was to be something like my ramble through the old American colonies—a voyage of observation, the better to understand the background of our past. The Institut scientifique franco-canadien had chosen me to give a series of lectures at the Sorbonne and in other universities over a period of two months, all expenses paid. As a favour I asked to be given as much free time as possible to allow me to really see France. My hosts graciously agreed, and my program was reduced to the minimum: three lectures at the Sorbonne, two at the Institut catholique de Paris, and one each in Poitiers and Lyons. Marvellous! I would have a month to roam around Paris and another to wander through provincial France.

I took off from Dorval on January 30. The night flight lasted ten hours, at the end of which a gap in the clouds revealed the Seine winding through the countryside—my first glimpse of France! My lodging was on the quais across from the Louvre, and my first days were a series of delirious promenades from one end of Paris to the other. To see! See! Guide in hand, I walked all over Paris, entering doorways, sauntering, trying to capture everything at once out of so many centuries of history. I climbed Notre Dame's bell towers to examine the gargoyles and walked for hours in the Père Lachaise cemetery, greeting the illustrious dead who had charmed my teenage years: Colette, Alfred de Musset, the Comtesse de Noailles, Maréchal Ney, La Fontaine, Sarah Bernhardt, Balzac. At last I was within arm's length of Balzac! I hurried to the Picpus cemetery to pay tribute to La Fayette. After that I visited everything: the Louvre, of course; the Musée de l'Homme (and the skull of Descartes); Les Invalides (with the tombs of Turenne, Napoleon, and Foch); the Pantheon and its crypts with the bodies of Voltaire, Hugo, and Zola; the Church of Saint-Étienne-du-Mont where Pascal and Racine lay; the Basilica of Saint-Étienne, the fortress of Vincennes with its famous keep; and Versailles!

At the Sorbonne, where I was introduced by the historian Roland Mousnier, I dealt with three subjects: the seigneurial régime in Canada, slavery in the St. Lawrence region, and the formation and development of the French-Canadian population. In the audience was Judith Jasmin, Canada's pioneer woman political and foreign correspondent in the forties and fifties. At the Institut catholique I met the dean, A. Dain, the celebrated Greek scholar. His office was sadly shabby, as the Institut was only funded by the French clergy at the time. Its professors were heroic compared to our prosperous bourgeois university teachers. There were several French-Canadian abbés at the institute. They had to do their *licence* there, as our bishops didn't allow student priests to register at the Sorbonne.

Finally I set out on my tour of France. In the Perche region, where Canadians were always welcomed with great ceremony, a week of special events beginning with a high mass and a procession outside the church had initially been planned for me. I persuaded my hosts to reduce the program to three days. I was treated like an ambassador. From morning to evening I was followed around by a cortège of mayors. I was transported from one place to another, taken to lunch at one home, to dinner at another. I was led with great pomp to the home of the *sous-préfet* and installed in a bedroom where Napoleon, so I was told, had slept. No one, alas, will ever say that I too slept in the same room.

Each visit was the occasion for a *vin d'honneur*, with flag-draped walls and speeches to which I had to reply, making use of all the tricks of rhetoric at my disposal. At Montligeon, where I was to give a lecture, the entire basilica was illuminated for me alone. The banquet presided over by the deputy prefect lasted for hours, complete with *trou normand* (a glass of Calvados drunk between courses), speeches, and the hunting horns of Reno giving a concert beneath the banquet hall windows. The next day we visited schools (with speeches of welcome and replies), a number of farms, and the forest of Reno where oaks were cultivated. A luncheon followed at a mayor's home, then dinner at the home of the prefect. All this was merely a preamble to the lecture that I was to give on the crossing of the Atlantic in the eighteenth century. The visits continued next day—twelfth-century Romanesque churches, a public washhouse, the tomb of Sully, and the tiny hamlet of Parfondeval, from where my ancestor Jean Trudel left for Canada around 1650. When I boarded the train for Rennes, I wanted to see nothing more, no Romanesque churches, nothing and nobody. I locked myself in my hotel room for a long rest.

Once I'd recovered from this whirlwind tour, I felt the journey to Perche had been a marvellous experience. I had sensed the presence of the seventeenth century in that small province, the home of so many colonists who had come to New France from its earliest days and who had left so many descendants in Canada. The emigrant Jean Trudel was the sole ancestor of some fifty thousand Trudels now spread over the whole of North America. I found in Perche the same family names we have at home, the same faces, the same timbre in their voices, the same long *a* (the Perche notary said to me, "C'est *pâ* beau"). The old men I met were exact replicas of old men I'd seen in the Lower St. Lawrence.

I can't forget another delightful encounter with the past. This was at La Rochelle, the starting point for the yearly voyage of the king's ship with its emigrants, basic provisions for the colony, and the year's mail. A letter that missed the boat had to wait until the following year. Seated on a bench in the old port, I spent an afternoon summoning up those ships with their great sails. I was to witness the real thing in 1984 in the old port of Saint-Malo, where, beneath the light of a full moon, I saw and heard the sails of these olden-day ships snapping in the wind. Life sometimes holds unique experiences.

A second stay in France, this time for a whole year (1959-1960), enabled me to gain a deeper knowledge of the country. I went there to do research on the Hundred Associates, also making time for short trips to the various regions of France as well as the traditional journey to Italy. This time my family came with me.

In Paris I encountered problems with schooling. My two daughters, Jeanne and Madeleine, were in the letters course and adapted quickly, getting top marks even in French, just as they had at the Ursuline convent in Quebec City. Nonetheless, their English teacher, a London man, couldn't get over the fact that these Canadian girls were so weak in English. However my daughters did have the advantage of having travelled. It was well known, at least in those days, that the French didn't like to leave home. When I say "leave home," I'm referring not only to their country, but their neighbourhood. One day Madeleine was coming back from the lycée with a Parisian friend. She led the friend toward the Seine as they chatted. Suddenly they found themselves facing Notre Dame Cathedral. The friend gave a cry of surprise. "So *that's* Notre Dame!" Truth is often stranger than fiction. When I told my Parisian neighbours about my visits to the Eiffel Tower, the interior of the Arc de Triomphe, or to various museums, they almost always commented, "Oh, one of these Sundays we really must head that way!" My son Marc, who was twelve, immediately fell afoul of the French education system. He had to wear the well-known blue smock, a hangover from the nineteenth century, and from the very first day he was taken to task by the lady in charge of first-year letters. It was because of his handwriting. In France, all students are taught to write in the same way. Faced with Marc's individual but perfectly legible style, she reacted publicly with the typical cry of a Frenchwoman, "But you write like a little pig!" Marc was determined not to set foot in that school again. He was old enough to begin what we in Canada call the *cours classique*. Since the first year in France was very different from our *éléments latins* year, I decided simply to coach him myself in preparation for the Jesuit College in Quebec City. Marc profited from an initiation into general culture through a program of visits to the great museums, including, of course, the Louvre. When he arrived at the Jesuit College, he would have actually seen the beautiful things that other students would only know from their textbooks.

As a professional researcher, I, like so many others, was subjected to the occult system prevailing in French archives. At the Bibliothèque nationale, as at the Archives in the Rue des Francs-Bourgeois, a draconian discipline reigned. Beneath the eye of a supervisor perched on a high platform against a side wall of the great reading room, we waited for the documents requested. They were always long in coming and dispensed in niggardly portions. We had the right to three volumes of papers per day. It didn't matter how crowded or empty the room was, and it made no difference whether or not you got through your material quickly. I was working on an inventory of documents that would be useful for studying the period of the Hundred Associates. Often I would finish looking at my three volumes in an hour. In vain did I negotiate with the supervisor. He wouldn't budge. At ten in the morning my day was finished unless I hurried to another archive where I would have to register anew and wait again, always for the same limited number of volumes. Even then I'd be finished in an hour or two. I wondered how on earth they managed, those French historians who produced fat tomes based on historical documents! I later learned that those with fatter purses provided themselves with *nègres*—in other words, research assistants—to do this tedious chore.

And the lighting! Whether the day was cloudy or not (and in Paris the clouds are always very low in winter), the lights in the reading room came on at precisely four o'clock. One day, almost unable to see, I complained to the supervisor. After a long confabulation (it became known that this Canadian had been accorded the honour of a visit with *monsieur le conservateur*), consent was given to turn on one light, but only the one right above my head. My table was bathed in light amid the outer darkness, and my neighbours found themselves in even deeper shadow than before. There was much muttering. "*Ah non!* What's this?" The next day I kept my complaints to myself, realizing that in France any exception to the rule causes social upheaval.

When it came to lighting, the French were used to a régime of austerity. They used all sorts of devices for saving electricity—for example, the *minuterie* installed on the staircases of large buildings. Before walking up, you pressed a switch. The lights came on, but watch it! If you lingered to say hello here or there, the lights would go out, and you had no choice but to feel your way back down to the switch and start again. Did you need to go to the cellar? You opened the heavy door, and the cellar was lit. You closed it, and the lights went out—something I didn't know. On my first visit to the cellar I thought that someone had forgotten to switch off the lights. After I came up, I wanted to check that everything was turned off. I opened the door to find the lights still on and no switch in sight, so I thought it my duty to alert the concierge. I took him to the cellar: he saw that everything was normal and told me off.

"Why are you bothering me for nothing, monsieur? Look: you open the door, the lights come on; you close it, the lights go out." He walked off grumbling, "Where does that guy come from?"

And the sacred lunchtime! From noon to two o'clock, France is at table. You think it a good idea to save your errands for lunchtime? Everything's closed and all economic activity is at a standstill. If you insist on being served by a shopkeeper who is already on his doorstep, you will hear, "What's this? I'm not allowed to take time for lunch now?" Two hours for lunch! I understand why the French find it funny that we North Americans set aside a bare fifteen minutes for lunch.

I discovered the hedonistic appeal that sitting down to a meal had for the French. To eat at noon and in the evening seemed to me the two high points of a Frenchman's day. This is why Molière makes people laugh so much when he has the Miser say, "One must eat to live, not live to eat," and why the complaint, "You know, we were hungry during the war," is so pathetic. As the statistics of 1960 made clear, a Frenchman eats three times as much as a Canadian, and I tried to calculate at what moment a Frenchman stopped being hungry.

The French simply couldn't understand why Canadians, reputedly hardened by severe winters, could be cold in France. You had to describe our overheated houses, our public buildings, and churches that were as com-fortable in winter as in summer. At home the Frenchman covered himself with thick pullovers (referred to as *les pulls*) and woollen socks (for both men and women). There was no need for heating. When the sun appeared, he opened the windows wide (no matter that it was January or February), and rubbed his hands with relish. "How fine it is today! Very fine!"

I had made provision for the cold, bringing a supply of woollen blankets. I thought I had been farsighted in renting an expensive apartment "with central heating." I was sadly disappointed. In this apartment, which consisted of a living room, a dining room, two bedrooms, a kitchenette, and a tiny bathroom, the only "central heating" was a kind of ball, about as big as a grapefruit, from which issued a little gas flame. This was in the living room in front of a false fireplace. On winter evenings we used to gather around this ball as though it were a campfire. As I had much writing to do, I installed myself at the dining room table, far from the "central heating" but well wrapped up in a woollen blanket, the hand that pushed the pen being the only thing to emerge. As for taking a bath in an unheated bathroom, it became an act of heroism on each occasion. The average Frenchman had a simpler solution. In winter he didn't take a bath, and the bathtub served as a catchall.

During these ten months in France, I read voraciously to broaden my general culture, particularly in anthropology and archeology. This changed the history of Canada for me. What a wealth of books there was to read about Cro-Magnon man or the contemporaries of the artists of the Lascaux caves, that marvel which I visited shortly before it was closed to the public for good.

In the fourteenth arrondissement where we lived there was a neighbourhood library—and what a library! It easily surpassed Laval's library in history, literature, and other fields. However, I first had to convince the administration that I was a worthy borrower. I presented myself, explaining that I was a visiting foreigner, and asked to borrow books. I was dealing with a lady. Frenchwomen are very pleasant, you know, but put them in authority behind a wicket and they become hard as nails and crushingly caustic. Despite all the forms I had filled out at the Préfecture de Police, her brusque comment was, "But monsieur, did no one tell you? You must show me the receipt for last year's rent!"

"But madame, I wasn't here last year. I've just arrived from Canada."

"It that my fault, monsieur? I need the receipt. Next! *Au suivant de ces messieurs!*" she said to the waiting line. I insisted, the waiting *messieurs* joined in the discussion, and everyone debated my case. The lady then conceded: "*Eh bien!* I could make do with a letter of introduction. Yes, that's it. Bring me a letter signed by a local resident."

This sounded easy enough, but I didn't know anyone as yet. Then I had a stroke of genius: my concierge! I had him sign a paper and hurried back to the library, feeling triumphant. Ah, liberty, equality, fraternity, if you could have heard the laughter from behind the wicket!

"Can you imagine! Just look at what he's brought me, this gentleman from Canada: a letter from a concierge! Do you realize—a concierge!"

This time I'd had my fill (I lose my temper once a year, but then I really lose it) and finished up by threatening the lady in question to take the matter up with my embassy. That was the magic word. Much as these feminine functionaries take a mightier-than-thou attitude when they are in charge, they are equally shrinking when it comes to avoiding trouble with their superiors. "Listen, monsieur, there must be some misunderstanding. You know, I have to apply the rules; it's idiotic, but that's the way it is. All right, I'll try to arrange things for you. The head librarian will surely understand."

And what wonderful books I was able to carry home every week after that!

We always have a particular image of France because of the fine phrases that the French have spread world-wide until they've become clichés. The French Revolution apparently overthrew the Old Régime with it absolutism, its minutely graded social hierarchy, its excessive privileges, and the positions that could be bought. Free, equal, and fraternal: this is how I imagined the French. I was in for repeated shocks. The French government seized books and suspended opposition newspapers with the greatest ease in the world. All television was state-run, controlled by the party in power. Tobacco was also a government monopoly: no one could buy it except through the state. If you became a notary, you couldn't practice unless—as under the Old Régime—you bought the *greffe* from a notary who had decided to retire. This republic was a hotbed of monarchists and would-be monarchs! The covers of best-selling magazines constantly ran photographs of kings, queens, and princesses. De Gaulle, elected by universal suffrage, had more power than Louis XIV. When he appeared on television, the streets emptied and everyone went home in order not to miss a word of his speech. What need had such a man of a crown?

As the product of North America's level social horizon, I discovered the chasm that separates masters and servants in France, the latter usually being treated with the greatest disdain. I saw absolute social cleavages between, for example, professional men and labourers that made it impossible for people of different classes to have a serious love relationship, let alone marry. One day Professor Mousnier walked over to meet me near the Seine. He stopped to say a word of encouragement to a sweeper, but he was so ostentatious and paternalistic in the way he tapped the man on the shoulder that I felt extremely uncomfortable. And then there is the absolutism of parental authority among the bourgeoisie. Whether of minor or major age, the fate of the child depends on what its father and mother decide. An example was a young university student leaving for a position at Laval University. His parents, who were also university professors, made him marry the young lady whom they had chosen—a marriage that satisfied all the *convenances*, it is true, but need I add that in Quebec City we soon realized the couple's incompatibility? Another surprise for me was the fact that if you reach a certain level in the French public hierarchy, you keep your title. Even when you no longer occupy the post, you are still addressed as "monsieur le président," "monsieur le ministre," or "monsieur le conseiller." And what privileges come with such posts—apartments, cars, and chauffeurs, to name a few.

I was at least pleased to see that university professors—unlike their Canadian counterparts—occupied a position of respect in the social hierarchy, greater than even a member of parliament, for example. No one bothered about whether he had a doctorate or not, as people do in North America, where being called "Doctor so-and-so" is quite a status symbol. It was enough to know that someone was a university professor for people to bow and say "monsieur le professeur" with every sentence. As I was not even forty at the time, I felt a little awkward about this.

In December 1959 I had the advantage of seeing Algeria in its last days of colonialism, as the final crisis began. The University of Algiers was celebrating its fiftieth anniversary. I was in Paris, and Laval chose me to represent it. My first surprise was that Algeria, which the French claimed was an integral part of their territory, had an Algerian franc that wasn't acceptable currency in France. The second surprise for a relatively uninformed Canadian was to find that all the policing was done by soldiers toting submachine guns. The white city of Algiers existed in a state of occupation by the French army. There were soldiers everywhere, on every street corner and at the doors of public buildings and shops. Only after being searched could you enter. I say "you," but there was a clear distinction: the French were given a merely symbolic frisk, whereas Algerians were subjected to a fairly rough search, often accompanied by kicks. This shocked me, but I was forgetting that for the French soldier, Algerians had become the enemy. Once inside a cinema or a lecture hall, you had to stay in your seat until the very end, a regulation that discouraged terrorists from entering just long enough to leave a bomb. The casbah was charming as long as you ended your promenade the minute you lost sight of the soldiers on duty. An "accident" could so easily happen at the entrance to some courtyard. There were grand receptions in palaces, but, protruding from the ceiling-high wall hangings, we could see the boots of the soldiers who were trying to protect us as unobtrusively as possible. Necessary precautions. The very morning of the opening celebrations, as the long ceremonial parade neared the university, a bomb hidden under some flowers killed some of the students who were waiting for us. Luckily I was near the end of the cortège. Danger lurked everywhere, although this didn't stop me from accepting a student's invitation to visit a Roman archeological dig at Tipasa in the countryside some distance from Algiers. As with those who are unthinking, nothing happened to us, but a few hours after our return a van on the same road was blown up by a mine.

I was ill-prepared to judge the Algerian problem. What I saw mainly was the dramatic predicament of the French settlers for whom Algeria had become their homeland. Even though it was only a hundred years since their forebears had arrived, France had become a foreign country in their eyes, despite the fact that Algeria was a French *département*. I talked to these French Algerians as a Canadian who saw a historical parallel in the present context. Only a century after settling in the St. Lawrence Valley, my ancestors feared being forced to return to France. They, too, regarded it as a foreign land. Meanwhile the Acadians of Canada's east coast suffered the hardships of being sent back to the Poitou region and Belle-Isle-en-Mer. In 1959 French Algerians were not yet being forced to choose between a suitcase and the grave, but things were beginning to heat up and they would soon have to sever their almost century-old roots to return to mainland France, where they would live as exiles. In the dazzling white of Algiers we were still somehow in a European city. The crowning aspect of our trip was the Sahara. In the oases of Ouargla and Gardaïa we were at last in an alien land. Oases, those masterpieces of civilization, are the thousand-year-old cultivation and development of a single waterhole on three levels. Vegetables are grown on the ground, fruit trees above them, and above these again, protecting the whole area from the burning heat, rise the date palms. We stopped to visit the Mzabites, a strict Muslim sect. The women could not show even the slightest part of their faces. They wore long white veils covering their bodies from head to toe and moved around like statues wrapped up for some mysterious expedition, phantoms shrouded in silence. And then there was the desert—dunes as far as the eye could see, shifting with the wind like snowdrifts in Canada, blocking a road at midday that was clear in the morning. And the eternally blue sky that holds a man motionless in the infinite vastness, a feeling I also discovered in the solitude of the Yukon. It's impossible to escape the fascination of desert places, whether they be of sand or lichen.

My study year ended and it was time to go back to Quebec City, the classroom, and the daily toil of research and writing.

Of my own free will (and, I admit, ambition), I had accepted administrative duties outside the history institute. Through the summer courses in thesis preparation that I gave, my role in the faculty of letters had expanded considerably. In 1952 I became faculty secretary, a very important function because of the traditional absenteeism of the dean. This was usually some high-ranking person from the Quebec Seminary who had neither the time or inclination to visit the faculty kitchen, so to speak. If the secretary had the slightest wish to increase his sphere of responsibility, he could become an almost independent CEO. The dean got the prestige, but the secretary held the reins of power. I took office right after Félix-Antoine Savard had been made dean of the faculty of letters. He was not from the Quebec Seminary, but rather a mere abbé with no academic degree beyond his baccalauréat. Against him was the fact that he had not come up through the university ranks to the deanship; in other words, he wasn't "from the shop." Savard was the author of major literary works such as *Menaud, maître draveur* and *L'Abatis*. He had first been invited to give several lectures, then hired as a lecturer, although he was no more ready to be a teacher than an administrator. His courses on Claudel are still renowned for his constant digressions on "the good peasants of Quebec," on their speech "which came from the Renaissance," on the greatness of "the tiller of the soil," and on "this great and noble land that we must take over for ourselves." He used to turn toward the window and speak of the green of the trees, the birds' song, and then cry out abruptly, his voice suddenly very loud, "How beautiful it is, don't you think, my children!" He never had time to get very far into Claudel.

In his native Charlevoix region, he played at being a Francis Jammes or Frédéric Mistral. He even adopted their costume, an unexpected sight in Canada, consisting of an extremely wide-brimmed straw hat, worn with a shepherd's cloak and long crook. He was an artist with considerable talent in drawing. His signature alone was a work of art. He was a jeweller of words, turning them this way and that, making them sparkle, often revealing treasures of invention, but his thought had no power or depth. In this respect his published *Journal* is a wasteland. Like all artists, he was alarmingly susceptible. The slightest scratch became a wound that never healed, and the guilty party an object of bitter and unremitting resentment. He dripped paternalism from every pore, adopting a tone of an "understanding papa," bending toward his interlocutor, a comprehending hand resting on the latter's shoulder in a perfect expression of the curé-cum-*paterfamilias* who sees himself as God's intermediary.

Then came the day when the faculty freed itself of Canon Laliberté (who blocked all change) by promoting him to the honourary post of vice-rector. Abbé Savard obtained the deanship through the influence of his close friends, Monseigneur Alphonse-Marie Parent and Luc Lacourcière, with whom he formed a triumvirate. In moving from the uncouth Laliberté to an accomplished man of letters like Savard, the faculty had a distinguished dean in the tradition of Camille Roy. However, Savard had no experience of university administration to prepare him for the deanship. He easily became lost in the mechanics of the system, a circumstance that suited me as faculty secretary. In any case, he only came to Quebec City occasionally, spending a day or two there, mainly taken up with the Société de colonisation, which he had already served by directing groups of settlers to the Abitibi region. Between two errands in town, he would find time to see me. I dragged out of him the decisions needed for the academic side or to make it easier for me to exercise power. This I managed to do by making the question under discussion as complicated as I could, wearing him down so that he finally replied, "Fine, fine! Work something out. I leave it to you, my dear man."

In these circumstances, to be faculty secretary meant being the boss, and this I was between 1952 and 1957, while also running the history institute. I had wide-ranging powers, only limited by rare board meetings—the dates and frequency of these being set by myself. Like all bosses, I made my quota of blunders and occasionally sacrificed the principles of democracy. Basically, I focused on improving the academic program, recruiting specialists, tactfully moving on two or three incompetent members of staff, insisting on professors doing their work punctually and efficiently, and developing a series of public lectures called "Faculty Wednesdays," in which professors took turns talking about a subject in their special field.

As the faculty of letters was getting too big for its locale, I took advantage of the offices vacated by the Faculty of Medicine. This time, however, since my colleagues were busy elsewhere (or so they said), I had to take care of moving the furniture myself. Picture it: the boss, historian, doctor of letters, etc., heads for the Quebec Seminary stables and returns leading a horse and cart, then carries armloads of stuff to the cart, climbs up the Rue de l'Université, and unloads everything into the elevator. Finally, completing the rent-a-cart service, he leads the horse back to the stables. The academic profession requires knowledge of all kinds: if you want to lead men, you must also know how to lead a horse by its bridle.

I flatter myself that I was attentive to students' needs. Throughout my career I have given students priority, making sure they weren't bullied and that their claims were listened to. As the proceeds from the Faculty Wednesdays went into a small slush fund, I often dipped into it to help a student who hadn't enough money to eat. The little fund dropped, rose, and dropped again, but I was accountable to no one but myself.

This was the era of a sudden surge in the student population. Among them was one Gilles Vigneault, a poet living on next to nothing and reverberating with freedom. He came to ask me for a letter of reference for a teaching post in mathematics at the technical college. Can you imagine Vigneault explaining the principles of arithmetic? He had his letter, but I made the following remark which, ever since, has covered me with shame and would indeed embarrass any wise advisor: "Monsieur Vigneault," said I, "you are not cut out to be a teacher. You have no voice."

As a historian, I couldn't limit myself continually to the internal activities of the Faculty; I had to join various associations connected with my discipline. I owed it to myself to take part in the activities of the Canadian Historical Association, for example. It was in 1947 that I talked about history in public for the first time. My subject was international thinking about historical writing, and the ideas concerning history put forward from 1922 to 1947. I was given an hour to speak at the annual meeting. I prepared for months, rehearsing, exercising my jaws, wanting to conquer this audience of scholars from every part of Canada—including those who had dealt me hard blows concerning my thesis on the influence of Voltaire. Alas! The historian who preceded me on the podium spoke well over his allotted time, leaving me a scant ten minutes before lunch, which the audience was looking forward to far more than my speech. I gave an overview, but hummed and hawed in doing so, stammering as I tried to say everything in ten minutes. My first extramural appearance was a catastrophe.

I continued to work with English-speaking scholars. It was considered a sin in some quarters, but it was my way of claiming the share that French-speaking society should have in this field. One day I agreed to review a book for the *Canadian Historical Review*. I sent my article in French, and it came back to me translated into English. I protested, wanting my article to appear in French. I was told that the review didn't belong to the Canadian Historical Association (which had a bilingual policy) but to the University of Toronto. I persisted, refusing to accept this explanation, and withdrew my manuscript. Technically, I was wrong, but I was determined to be published in French. Later, the *Canadian Historical Review* agreed to publish French papers.

It was in this same stubborn spirit that I agreed to take part in a venture launched by the University of Toronto. The aim was to create a multi-volume biographical dictionary. From the outset, the *Dictionary of Canadian Biography* was seen as a strictly bilingual work. But having our articles translated into English and proofreading the French versions of English articles was nothing compared to working out the actual content. Who would we include, and how would we make sure there was a fair division between English and French subjects? How long should each article be in relation to the importance of the subject? Who would we get to write the articles? How would we gather documentation and make sure it was the best? We in Quebec were well-placed to deal with these questions. The first volume would cover the history of Canada from the earliest days to 1700, and this was familiar terrain for us. Over the years I had prepared a bibliographical card index of considerable size, and I placed it at the disposal of the team. We hired full-time researchers and prepared a list of people who could be called upon to help. It was actually the first time that a list of historians in Quebec had been drawn up according to their particular fields of interest. This collaboration wasn't always easy, given the language difficulties and differences in outlook. We weren't in the habit of working as a team with English-speaking colleagues and we didn't have the same approach. Take editing, for example. On the English side, an article paid for by the publisher belongs to the publisher, who can change it at will. In French-Canadian society, we feel that the author remains the absolute owner of his or her text, and that the publisher who pays for it can't change anything. For us, it was a revolution—allowing our work to be corrected by a third party before it was printed! In other respects, it wasn't easy to agree on articles that would be published in two languages. One day I received an English text from Toronto, to be translated into French as a common introduction to the work of the two teams. When the translation was done, I found the introduction confused and disordered, and my French brain felt very uncomfortable with this English concoction. I therefore changed the order of the paragraphs, bringing some nearer to the opening, placing others further back, and changing the style of various sentences: in a word, producing the same dish with another recipe. I showed it to the people in Toronto, and everyone was delighted. The spirit of Descartes had prevailed.

In 1961, I made my contribution to a campaign against separatism. In the course of a public lecture I demonstrated that separatism was a solution of denial that amounted to making Canada a kind of medieval Italy. Because various African nations were gaining independence, the scandalized cry had gone up in Quebec that "The blacks are independent and we aren't!" But

Canada was already a small minority within the mass of English-speaking North Americans; to break it up would be suicidal. I didn't want a Berlin wall around Quebec, the territory to which the separatists wanted to restrict French Canada. The separatist option was even becoming an electoral issue. "That's a good thing," I added. "It will be the downfall of separatism." The subsequent referendum confirmed this hypothesis. However, once separatism became a political issue I stayed away from the debate out of professional concern as a historian. It was from this moment on that I was considered a federalist. In the eyes of some, if you weren't a separatist, you must be a federalist. Following my "Berlin Wall" lecture, I received several anonymous letters accusing me of selling out.

Along with other colleagues, I joined the campaign to save the old quarter of Quebec City, especially in 1951-52, when there was question of disfiguring the historic quarter with a tall concrete box added to the Hôtel-Dieu, and of tearing down a crumbling old wall in this neighbourhood, the sort of thing that gives the old cities of Europe their distinctive atmosphere. I persuaded Canon Groulx to join with us in saving a heritage that we considered of national value (today it is officially recognized as having world value). We didn't win, and today the square tower still rises above the cityscape.

I wanted a law to protect historic buildings. My friend Gérard Morisset talked more of educating the public. In vain I said to him, "Old Quebec may be gone by the time you've finished their education!" Premier Duplessis had been against us on the Hôtel-Dieu matter and he opposed all legislation, being—in the legal tradition—a great respecter of private property. To touch or presume to want to touch private property was a crime in his eyes. Moreover the residents of Old Quebec were no help. It was a disastrous time. We watched the old city collapsing wall by wall, stone by stone. The old Cadet house was demolished in full view of everyone, with all the necessary blessings. If the demolition permit was slow to come, the dirty work was done secretly. There was an old house from the French Régime on the Rue Couillard, very well preserved on the outside, a charming house with the outer wall bulging onto on the street. The demolition crew quietly began work on the inside. When we realized what was happening it was too late. The historic house was in ruins, and a "fine new house" soon took its place.

The Côte Sainte-Famille was paved with the cobblestones needed in olden days for horse-drawn traffic. With the advent of the automobile, cobbles no longer had any practical value, and so they were taken up to be replaced with asphalt along the whole street. It was modern and clean, but the city lost another element of its authentic old look. Lately, with the realization of how foolish this had been, the asphalt was dug up and the old cobblestones put back. Idiocy is an expensive luxury!

We had to wage a major battle to save the Saint-Pierre Church on the Île d'Orléans. This is a marvellous little church dating from 1717, all of it well preserved. The curé, having found lots of money in the coffers of the parish council, convinced himself that the church was too small for midnight mass on Christmas and New Year's Eve and decided to build an addition. An architect said that it could be done without changing the overall look of the building. We were able to prove to Archbishop Roy that, on the basis of statistics, the curé had room for all his parishioners, and that in any case the butchery in store shouldn't be tolerated. The opposition carried the day, and the old church wasn't touched. However, the curé built himself a modern church facing the historic one, thus changing the traditional landscape. The new church is still there, but its parishioners are fast fading. The old church, now a museum, is perhaps visited by more of the faithful.

Colbert wrote to Frontenac, "Let each one speak for himself, and let no one speak for all." We were familiar with this régime at Laval. There was indeed an official ruling: the annual salary began at $2000 and rose by $200 each year to a ceiling of $3000. How were we to know if this pay scale was respected? Was your salary insufficient to pay the mortgage instalments on your new house? Was there a new mouth to feed (it was the time of large families—the song of the cradle).The thing to do was to go and see Monseigneur Parent, tell him your needs, and you would emerge from his office with an increase in salary, unbenownst to your colleagues.

I was one of seven or eight professors who, in the early 1950s, got together in an attempt to put an end to this paternalistic, every-man-for-himself system. Guy Frégault, then a young historian at the Université de Montréal headed up a similar movement. We in Quebec City wanted to found not a union (who would have dared do such a thing in those days?) but simply a harmless association of professors. First we had to visit Rector Vandry and ask his permission. We feared the worst. To prevent things from getting nasty, we were wise enough to ask Professor De Koninck to join our delegation. He was an internationally known Thomist, an advisor to the cardinal, and a close friend of Monseigneur Parent. We arrived at the rector's office. As he was not yet there, his secretary asked us to be seated. At last the door opened. Through it appeared a tray of *sucre à la crème* followed by the arm of the rector, famous in Quebec City for his love of rich food. For a moment I thought we were about to have a party. But no, the tray passed right in front of us, at eye-level, followed by the rector, and disappeared into the next room. When Monseigneur Vandry came out again, his tastebuds blissful, the conversation at once became very pleasant and the gentlemen of the university left as happy as urchins who have obtained the permission they sought. Please don't scold us, you union leaders of today—Laberge, Chartrand, and Larose! Think of the risk we thought we were taking.

The association took shape, regular meetings were held, and the authorities received our demands. The first procedure to be established—something completely new at Laval—was to have the professors' monthly dues collected by the university. We had an official existence, which counted for much. After this, the association worked toward getting health and life insurance on good terms, although it would be a long time before the adoption of a strict salary scale, uniform course loads, and rules about time off. We had made a very small start.

In 1964 the professors wanted to create a larger association that included teachers in Quebec French-language universities. A special committee of five was struck. François-Albert Angers was the chair, and I was asked to write a discussion paper on the concept of a university teacher for a subsequent meeting. The result of these cogitations was simple—I got my definition adopted as follows: "The university teacher is both a researcher and a teacher: a researcher because he must advance knowledge in a particular discipline, a teacher because he must communicate the results of his research." I had initially suggested, "is primarily a researcher and then a teacher," but this hierarchy seemed too revolutionary. From all this came lengthy memoranda and many discussions in committee. After my departure for Ottawa, however, I lost sight of its workings.

The Académie canadienne-française, founded in 1944 by a group of Montrealers, was then considered an exclusively Montreal-based institution. Because of the attitudes of some of its members, it had earned an undeserved reputation for narrow-minded nationalism. There were those who suggested that it was trying to rival the Royal Society of Canada, even though you could be a member of both organizations at the same time. In order to extend the Académie's membership to Quebec City, I submitted my candidacy for the twenty-second seat (out of twenty-four), for which no occupant had yet been named. I was inducted in 1951. There being no predecessor, I was spared the traditional eulogy for "the dear departed." In my maiden speech, to which I was driven with Félix-Antoine Savard and Monseigneur Parent, I spoke on French-Canadian civilization (these being the days before talk of "Quebec civilization"). The Académie wanted to be the Canadian equivalent of the Académie française—a most noble dream. It remained a provincial academy, however, like its counterpart with the comical name of "Académie bérrichonne," to which all members of the Académie canadienne-française automatically belonged *ex officio*. There were dreams of producing a dictionary, but the Académie published only linguistic newsletters. These were very well done. Victor Barbeau carried the entire load of this project, from editing to stuffing envelopes and mailing. However they disappeared when Quebec's cultural affairs ministry began publishing newsletters of a similar nature. The Académie had its *Cahiers*, which grouped members' articles on a given subject. These have appeared on average every two years—a respectable rate of publication for an author. The sixteenth *Cahier* came at the time of writing these memoirs.

Founded and at first chaired by Victor Barbeau, the Académie had another chair from 1947 to 1953, Philippe Panneton, who wrote using the *nom de plume* of Ringuet. He organized meetings during which we discussed French words. He left to become a career ambassador, and Barbeau resumed the chair, replacing the lexicographical sessions with a monthly dinner instead of regular meetings. It's always pleasant to meet colleagues around a well-laden table. This is where you get to know them best, and I spent some pleasant moments in the company of Jean-Louis Gagnon and Paul Toupin. The intellectual menu offered by the chair was always the same, however: when would we get funding from the ministry of cultural affairs, where would we house our library, and when should we publish another *Cahier*?

Panneton (whom I used to tease about his brother, the canon and former vicar of the little village of my youth) was what we call *bon prince*—easy-going, discriminating, and always affable. Barbeau was the complete opposite. He directed the Académie, cane in hand, as absolute master (it was his creation), with a ringing voice, speaking in austere, grammatically impeccable sentences (imagine Barbeau making a mistake in syntax!). He treated anyone younger than himself as a lesser being. Whenever we spoke, we sensed the dictation teacher watching us, lips pursed. Can you see yourself, an academician, committing a stylistic error in Barbeau's presence? Once seated at table, we discussed business. No more chatting and joking. Barbeau tolerated no opposition. He would cut discussion short because he knew he was right. If you insisted out of bravado, the final cut of the cleaver would descend from the head of the table: "Trudel, shut up!"

Our treasurer, Robert Rumilly, felt his honour or competence had been put into question concerning his report (quite what the problem was, I'm not sure). But God in heaven, what a sudden uproar! Rumilly drew himself up, ready to defend his reputation in a grandiloquent tirade. Then Barbeau drew himself up in turn, riposting with great blows of academic verbiage, after which, each having exhausted his lexicon and absorbed the shock, they resumed battle stations. Our confrère Roger Brian, who had not graced the meetings for ages and was not to reappear, calmed the emotional storm by invoking longstanding friendships and the noble virtues of working together. Rumilly stood up again, and in a classic sentence declared there had been a misunderstanding and he was ready to withdraw his immoderate words. Barbeau rose grandly from his chair to speak of dignity and greatness of soul. Then, as though French Canada were only waiting for the curtain to fall, the two men, convinced that they were posing for posterity, shook hands. And so we returned to the evening's agenda.

With Barbeau's retirement, the Académie experienced a few dull years. Members didn't turn out for meetings—maybe three or four would show up. Sometimes I would travel from Ottawa to Montreal for nothing, as there weren't enough members to form a quorum. The *Cahiers* no longer came out regularly. In any case, there were too many elderly members, and there wasn't much to attract younger candidates. But under the leadership of Jean-Guy Pilon, a dynamic intellectual, the Académie revived. The first task was to bring in younger members. I was among the few intrepid academicians who proposed that members should liberate their seats at sixty-five (which was also my age) by becoming honourary members. Suddenly thirteen members were obliged to retire. There was some gnashing of teeth, but the motion passed. Younger candidates presented themselves, and their reception (as they weren't obliged to make speeches praising their predecessors) became a feast for the mind. The *Cahiers* began appearing again, the Académie acted as an intermediary for distributing major prizes, meetings were well attended, and the prestige of old was restored.

My participation in the Conseil des arts du Québec of the 1960s was an enriching experience. Here I met men and women from every cultural milieu and became familiar with all the issues concerning intellectual and artistic activity in the province. When setting up the council alongside the cultural affairs ministry, Georges Lapalme, the minister, told us, "It's up to you to define your role," by which he meant that we should determine the nature and sphere of the arts council in relation to the ministry. Under the guidance of the first chair, Jean-Charles Falardeau, this is what we did, and this was the cause of all our tribulations.

The new minister was also busy defining his own role and organizing the ministry. It happened that his role and organization were established parallel to those of the arts council. Guy Frégault, the deputy minister, was not one to tolerate this kind of competition, on top of which there was a relative lack of communication between Frégault and our chairman.

The first cultural affairs ministers (Lapalme, followed by Pierre Laporte) were very comfortable with the situation, and during their time in office the arts council was able to act as a counsellor in matters of culture and art. Then came Jean-Noël Tremblay, who wanted to crush both his deputy minister and the arts council. At this juncture I became chairman of the council and had to call on the minister in my official capacity. This former colleague from Laval, where we had enjoyed each other's company so much, now saw me as merely the chairman of an organization he detested. He treated me with enormous condescension—for example, offering me a cigarette which he then lit for me, obliging me to bow very low before him. The council's funds were cut, our secretary, Léon-Z. Patenaude, found himself with nothing, we no longer had the money to hold our meetings, and vacancies weren't filled. The Quebec arts council quietly faded from public life. Since it was created by an act, it still exists in law, and twenty years later I wonder whether I'm still chairman.

I made an effort to be useful to the historian's profession by sitting for several years on the Federal Commission for Historic Sites and Monuments. I have no great merit in this respect, because the commission had at its disposal a team of highly competent researchers who supplied us with all the material needed. We, the pundits, were content to suggest to the government solutions that had already been found. However, the commission gave me a great deal in the way of magnificent journeys, royally paid for. I stayed in fine hotels and ate well in Newfoundland (especially in beautiful Plaisance Bay where I reconnected with French history), in the Maritimes (above all in Louisbourg, where we had to oversee the historical reconstruction), in Fort Garry in

Manitoba, in Vancouver, and on the Klondike River in the Yukon where we had to give an opinion on the restoration of Dawson City. These long trips enabled me to spend time with historians from all parts of Canada, among them Donald Creighton. I never heard a word of French from his lips and I couldn't understand his spoken English because of his particular way of pronouncing words, so my relations with the celebrated Toronto professor were limited to the ritual "Good morning."

I embarked on an adventure completely outside the university milieu when I joined the Mouvement laïque de langue française. It was to change the course of my career.

This organization, known by its acronym, MLF, was shaking up Montreal society with its demands. They were audacious, considering the period. The MLF wanted obligatory civil marriage, non-denominational schools, hospitals and orphanages run and staffed by laypeople instead of members of religious orders—in other words, the entire laicization of society. Montreal was a cosmopolitan city that felt the urgent need for social change and offered a fertile field for MLF activity. Quebec City, by contrast, lived under the watchful eyes of the archdiocese, Laval, and the newspaper *L'Action*. It considered itself safe from the threat of such social upheaval, and with respect to criminal activity cited the words of an Upper Town judge: "Quebec must not become a second Montreal."

One evening in 1963, a meeting was convened by Robert Cliche in the home of a friend of the MLF, with a number of university teachers from all faculties, including mine. We talked about the demands for laicization and of founding a branch of the MLF in Quebec City the next day. Hearing the way some of my colleagues castigated clerical power, I said to myself, "Tomorrow, we'll see some action in public; the MLF workers will be out in strength!" The next day we met in a large hall in the Chateau Frontenac. But where were yesterday's enthusiasts, the virulent critics of the clergy? Only about a dozen were left. When it came time for elections, someone, to my great surprise, proposed Trudel for chairman, and the rest supported the motion. Without reflecting or weighing the consequences, with neither heroism nor bravado, I accepted. Journalists crowded around me, radio stations asked for interviews, and everyone was agitated. "The MLF has come to Quebec City and a Laval professor is heading it!"

Immediately I realized what consternation we had just created. I tried to calm public opinion: "No, you won't have to get married again before the mayor, we are asking for civil marriage for those who would be accommodated by it; no, we don't want to hound nuns and brothers from the schools, we only want an education system that is more in tune with our pluralistic society. No, we don't want . . ."—and so it went for days. In this Quebec milieu, I wanted to fight for the right of the non-Catholic or non-believing minority to marry without adopting the subterfuge of conversion, to go to a school where religious difference was respected, and to stay in a hospital without being peremptorily summoned to say the rosary by the loudspeaker.

We issued mitigating statements, tried to avoid a head-on confrontation with a society emotionally attuned to the idea of the Church triumphant, and organized public debates where we featured men of recognized prudence and integrity—but in vain. For my part I relied on the philosopher De Koninck, whom I consulted regularly. He encouraged me in my theories and supplied supporting arguments. It was all to no purpose: the public could only see the face of the Beast of the Apocalypse.

Denunciations came from various sides. A woman friend went to the archdiocese to tell them what a sad case I was. A Jesuit friend (ah, my dear friends!) with whom I had spent many, many hours chatting in my home, climbed into the pulpit of my parish church and, in my presence, denounced the MLF. I was still going to Sunday mass as a social obligation. I left the church, and at the same time I left the Church.

The height of opposition came during a debate we'd organized at Beauport, presided over by a church dignitary, the former dean of the theology faculty and an open-minded man. Everything proceeded at first in a sympathetic atmosphere, but then a young abbé stood up and stated that, during a journey between Ottawa and Quebec City, some well-informed person had assured him that the MLF was financed by the Freemasons. Here was newsworthy material indeed, and it was all that the city's newspaper, *Le Soleil,* cared to note in its edition of March 11, 1963, under the fascinating header "MLF started by Masonic lodges." After this solemn preamble came the proof of the pudding: "It seems the abbé has in hand all the evidence to back up his statement. Moreover, he is president of the Eastern Townships Archaeological Society." There was clearly no point demanding photocopies of cheques sent by the Freemasons. The harm was done. Parents telephoned the rector of Laval to say they wouldn't send their teenagers to an institution where professors were Freemasons. By a curious turn of fate, this same young abbé who crusaded against anything not on the extreme right ended by renouncing his sacred calling and taking a wife.

The MLF campaign coincided with the publication of my book, *L'esclavage au Canada français*, about which I was still giving interviews for the radio and newspapers. I talked of bishops and priests who had owned slaves. Even if I made it clear that, in a society where slavery was the custom, the clergy had only owned 1.6 percent of the slaves, what was remembered (and what was considered newsworthy) was my basic statement about slave-owning ecclesiastics. Others, without bothering to read the book, thought it dealt with the enslaving of Quebecers by the powers of the Church under the Duplessis government. Frequent reference was made to the fact that it was I who'd revived the story of Chiniquy, the apostate priest.

Every so often I had to meet the university rector. Each time, he appeared friendly and admiring of my historical work. At no time did he speak to me of the MLF. I felt justified in concluding that, at the university, liberty was at last triumphing or that at least my actions hadn't upset anyone. One day, however, an abbé who was not a close acquaintance came to my office. He closed the door firmly and confided to me that the university authorities were extremely disturbed and that I should not have. . . His voice dropped. I assumed he'd been entrusted with the task of approaching me. Also, I had become aware that my private life was the object of some scrutiny—it might always be useful. Today's readers will say that all this happened at the beginning of the sixties, in the middle of the Quiet Revolution. But who will tell me at what moment this revolution began?

I was still director of the history institute. Someone remembered that I'd held this post for quite some time—as though I weren't contributing to the progress of the institute and establishing its reputation throughout Canada, especially by means of the French side of the Dictionary of Canadian Biography, a project beyond my already heavy workload. The years were counted up. "*Tiens!* He's been there for nine years." A rule was found stating that a director could not exceed nine years in office. The dean of letters, a layman who came to the deanship by the back door but who was known for his obedience to the powers of the Church, announced to me that, "unfortunately," my mandate couldn't be extended. "It's really too bad, *mon cher collègue*," said he. There was indeed another director who had held his post for a good fifteen years, but this was a man beyond reproach, and no one remembered to count the years in his case. I knew perfectly well why my own years in office had been counted, and I didn't press the point. I had witnessed the far more dramatic ordeal undergone by Father Georges-Henri Lévesque in similar circumstances. Mine was a very minor affair by comparison. I lost no time leaving the post vacant for someone else.

I remained president of the Quebec City branch of the MLF. From then on I was passed over for university promotion, and salary increases were meagre or less than those of various colleagues who knew how to respect the established order of things. Those who had any reason to resent me (and such reasons are not lacking with regard to anyone who has chaired a body for years) quietly created a vacuum around me. Some of my friends became aloof in their manner, as the hour was approaching when they would have to show which side they were on. I felt myself becoming a visiting professor.

Gradually I came to a decision that would have been unthinkable five years earlier, so completely had I identified with Laval. I resolved to go elsewhere and begin something new. The news spread quickly. Offers came from various universities, even from British Columbia. I hesitated between the University of Ottawa and Carleton University in the same city. Carleton offered me the directorship of the Institute of Canadian Studies. I would be the first French-Canadian to occupy the post. The University of Ottawa offered me the chance to revive the history department that Guy Frégault had briefly chaired before becoming Quebec's deputy minister of cultural affairs. I visited both institutions.

At the University of Ottawa the Oblates still wore cassocks, as at Laval. The corridors were dark, and there was a boarding school odour everywhere. I was received in a large, bare room by the dean of arts, Father Lavigne, who wore a grimy cassock. He was seated behind a desk laden with piles of student assignments and scattered with large tobacco pipes. The dean introduced me to the acting director whom I would replace. He too was dirty and his expression not one to reflect the presence of a lively mind. I replied that I would come back another time.

Carleton was a marvel for me. I found myself in a young institution. One felt its dynamism and above all the good organization, the cleanliness. At Laval the rector wore the red sash and spoke in a paternalistic tone, his voice pastoral and his gestures ecclesiastic. At Carleton I had before me a businessman-president who didn't bother with platitudes, who talked to me in a relaxed manner, one leg thrown over the arm of his chair. I discovered a new world and opted for Carleton. It will be a challenge to teach in English, I said to myself. I want to face this challenge for at least a year and try to make the history of New France popular among English-speaking people. Later we'll see.

My choosing Carleton created almost as great a commotion in Quebec City as the arrival of the MLF. Already, for many, the French Canada that covered a good half of English-speaking Canada no longer existed: there was only Quebec on one side and *les Anglais* on the other. By teaching the history of New France to the latter, I was depriving Quebecers. Again I received at least one anonymous letter calling me a *vendu*.

I handed in my resignation to Laval. No one made any attempt to keep me on staff. Only my friend and colleague, Louis-Edmond Hamelin, director of the Centre for Northern Studies, offered me a post as a researcher, similar to one occupied at the time by Jacques Rousseau. However, I would have been in the same physical surroundings and atmosphere as before. The rector and the dean of the faculty replied to my letter of resignation with brief notes of acceptance. Between the lines of official regret I could hear the sighs of relief. The university would regain its purity, the city of Quebec would no longer have its lay movement, and the Quiet Revolution would not happen.

Haste was made to find my replacement. My post was immediately offered to Frégault. He told me that, knowing the circumstances surrounding my departure, he refused out of friendship to take my place. Laval reportedly even approached W.J. Eccles, the University of Toronto historian—the scholar whom I had described as "the most French of English-Canadian historians" and with whom I was on the best of terms. He too refused out of friendship.

Laval had a Parthian shot in store. In the course of my career I had developed a bibliographical file of about seventeen thousand items for my personal research. It took a second to find just about any study or document published here on the history of French Canada. I had made a copy for use by my students in the institute's research room. When my departure was announced, someone placed the cabinet containing all this under lock and key, and no one seemed to have any idea of its whereabouts. Even the dean, it appeared, didn't know where this large piece of furniture had gone. It was claimed that what I had done as a professor, with the help of a secretary, belonged to the university. I sent formal notice summoning the university to either return this copy of my personal work or buy it from me at a suitable price. The university opted for the second solution and thus ended an affair of the most doubtful taste.

In changing universities, I had wanted to make a new beginning. Little did I know how very new this beginning would be. In September 1965 I suffered the worst accident that can befall a university teacher: the loss of all my papers and books by fire.

I had already heard about an English-speaking professor who had lost everything during a move. The truck had gone missing. What amazed me when I heard this was that the truck had never been found. I didn't give much thought to the professor. In my case, the huge trailer-truck on which I had loaded everything wasn't lost; it caught fire on the way to Ottawa. One of its many tires burst and rubbed against the others for some time. The rubber caught fire and the whole truck burned, far from any habitation.

In it was everything I had gathered in the way of personal papers since childhood (and I'm a collector): my correspondence (I answer every letter and keep a copy of the reply), my public lectures (I always write out the text), the courses prepared over eighteen years of teaching, and all the documentation for forthcoming books. There was enough material to prepare a general study of the Military Régime (1759-1764). During a year spent in France, I had amassed a trunkful of material covering the period of the Hundred Associates (1627-1663). Lastly, I had a thousand-page manuscript all ready to submit for printing. This was the *Dictionnaire des esclaves au Canada français et de leur propriétaires.*

For years I had preached to my students about the need to keep a copy of their theses in a safe place outside the home. One never knew what might happen. In the stress of packing (and what beautiful packages I had made!) I forgot this golden rule. I put the five copies of my dictionary listing the slaves of French Canada and their owners into the truck.

Apart from these papers, there was my specialized library on the history of New France collected with so much effort over twenty years. I was proud of some of the collections or single volumes in this library, such as an edition of Garneau's 1845 history of Canada, autographed by the painter Théophile Hamel. And how much more? It's impossible to remember in detail what one has accumulated during an entire career. For all this—books, course notes, manuscripts, and personal souvenirs, I had an insurance policy. In vain did I point out the precious value of everything. I was reimbursed by weight. This weighs so much, and you'll get so much per kilogram!

When the telephone rang in Ottawa bringing the news, I was doing my morning exercises. I had the choice of throwing myself out the window (but I was living on the fifth floor) or continuing as though nothing had happened.

I took the easiest solution and finished my exercises, ate my breakfast, and sat down at my desk to continue working on a chapter of my *Histoire de la Nouvelle-France*. The fire . . . the terrible fire? Oh yes, it all came back to me. I tried to push the thought away. "All right, that's the way it is," I said to myself, "but yesterday is yesterday and I have my program for today and tomorrow."

It is commonplace to say that misfortunes never come singly. There was one final disaster. I had kept in my care, to look over when I had a moment, a file of teaching materials for Carleton. It was all I had left of eighteen years of courses and research. Becoming wise after the fact, I gave it to the university to be photocopied. It got lost in the administrative shuffle and I had to begin my courses by improvising. At the end of a week, the dean of arts having personally became involved in hunting down this file, office by office, shelf by shelf, the lost file was found.

I cannot forget all those colleagues who, on hearing about the fire, sent me a kind word, knowing what those tons of paper were worth—André Vachon, Pierre Savard, Maurice Lebel, Jean-Jacques Lefebvre, Gustave Lanctot, Jacques Rousseau, Victor Barbeau, and David Dunton. The historian Gustave Lanctot, whom I had so often attacked, sent a very sympathetic message written by his wife, as he had become blind. Jacques Rousseau sent a long letter saying, "Over the years you have accumulated a fund of documentation that is not to be found in cardboard boxes, but in yourself!" And he added, "You'll have to delve more deeply into yourself rather than into a painstakingly amassed collection of documentation, but you'll be able to develop ideas that you've allowed to hover in your mind until now without ever setting them down on paper. If you so desire, this misfortune may be the stimulus for your best works." Rousseau reminded me of his own experience. "Rejected in my own country and living in a kind of exile in a foreign land," he wrote, he found himself cut off from his research material. But he added, "I discovered that I could see the problem from a higher perspective; I no longer felt myself a prisoner of my old notes," and "in this way I experienced the most fruitful period of my career." In short, he was saying that I had undergone a major cleanout that would do me good, since I would be forced to start afresh. I later understood that he was right. We end up being the slaves of what we have gathered for years. The mass of documentation imposes its historical method and we get caught up in it. I began my research anew in a different spirit, concentrating on bringing myself up to date on historical writing and focusing more on social history. Perhaps I'm wrong, but it seems to me that my work after 1965 is of better quality.

Certain not very productive colleagues who felt embarrassed by my energetic career were, I was told, glad about this accident. At last Trudel has got his comeuppance! Some students, it seems, even thought the fire was the result of a plot. If nothing else, their overactive imaginations proved their loyalty.

People from various places helped me reconstitute my library on New France. Someone sent me an old book, another gave me a tip about a bookseller specializing in Canadiana. In the name of the ministry of cultural affairs, Guy Frégault acquired various government historical publications for me and lent me a number of precious books from his own library for an indefinite time. A special grant from the Canada Council for the Arts enabled me to buy many volumes as well as microfilmed copies of all the notarial registers prior to 1663.

As my shelves gradually filled, I felt a growing enthusiasm for continuing my work.

Marcel Trudel at Louisbourg, as advisor to the team overseeing historical reconstruction of the fort in Nova Scotia.

9

The Ottawa Sequel

I ARRIVED IN OTTAWA feeling like Sinbad after he'd shed the old man from his back. The fire had freed me from thirty years' professional baggage. At the age of forty-eight I was beginning anew with a wonderful enthusiasm, in an atmosphere of freedom such as I had never known. Here in Ottawa I no longer felt the *diktat* of religious authority hovering over me; no corridor stretched out before me through which I must pass, whether I wished to or not. At no moment would I be confronted by the gossip-mongers and tittle-tattle of the Cap-aux-Diamants. I was reminded of the historian Benjamin Sulte, who had to leave his hometown of Trois-Rivières to find liberty and freedom of speech in Ottawa.

More than this, I felt surrounded by a sense of warm sympathy. The ordeal I had just undergone, the fact that I had been much talked about, my promotion to the chairmanship of the Conseil des arts du Québec (can you imagine the head of the Quebec arts council in Ottawa?), and a major prize that Quebec had just awarded me—all these circumstances gave me prestige and helped me become part of my new surroundings more quickly.

In Ottawa I followed a second career lasting seventeen years, uniquely devoted to the history of New France. It was here that I really earned the nickname "Mr. New France," jokingly given me by my friend Robert Lahaise. This second career equalled in length my professional life in Quebec but was more abundant in terms of published books, public lectures, and various other initiatives.

Canada's capital has changed enormously since my arrival in 1965. In those days you reached it by a dreadful road, narrow and crowded. With its 300,000 inhabitants Ottawa seemed like a small provincial town, and not much bigger than most. It was a city of little, single-family dwellings spread over a large area. Once out of the city centre you entered the most drab suburbia. The architecture was dreary and there were few European restaurants or French cinemas. On Sundays the city was as dead as a doornail because of its idiotic by-laws. Hull, its neighbour across the Ottawa River, was still a miserable working-class city of antiquated houses of no historic or architectural interest—a big, dismal village. A depressing metal bridge linked or separated these two worlds, depending on your point of view.

Twenty years have seen remarkable improvements. Hull received a modern facelift after the church, city hall, and law courts burned down. The policy of bilingualism resulted in civil servants working on both sides of the river and new office buildings being constructed to accommodate them. European cuisine made its appearance at the same time as French cinema. Magnificent edifices arose, particularly the National Library and the Public Archives. Some streets were set aside for pedestrian traffic, and outdoor cafés sprang up. Ottawa became famous for its tulips, and a new superhighway linked it to Montreal. The capital has become a city that is pleasant to live in. Alphonse Allais used to talk of creating cities in the countryside. In the Ottawa-Hull-Aylmer-Gatineau area, this has been achieved: a tree-shaded urban grouping beside the water, five minutes from a national park that runs for kilometres.

In this city of provincial manners I initially found two distinct societies living side by side, one English-speaking, the other French-speaking. I was reminded of Lord Durham's comment of 1839: "I expected to find a contest between a government and a people; I found two nations warring within the bosom of a single state"—but with this difference, that in Ottawa it wasn't two warring nations that I found, but two ethnic groups eyeing each other warily. The French were the first to arrive in what was originally a lumberjack town, and they were still encamped in the section where they had first settled, known as Lowertown. It was a neighbourhood of pitiful little houses and no greenery. In Sandy Hill there was a small section of better-off homes where the French-Canadian middle class lived. The English-speaking citizens, powerful in business and the civil service, occupied the better neighbourhoods, not only in the Glebe with its Rideau Canal and lagoons, but farther out in the greener area between the Ottawa River, the canal, and the Rideau River. Each of these two societies had its own institutions and never mixed with the other. Two solitudes indeed!

Obviously, each group had its university, but the French-Canadian institution resembled an English-speaking university in many ways. The former classical college of Bytown (this being Ottawa's original name), run by Oblates, was organized on bilingual lines so as to serve English-speaking Catholics. (At the time, Catholics couldn't send their children to Protestant or non-confessional schools.) The University of Ottawa was obliged to introduce academic subjects such as Common Law that could only be taught in English. Moreover, as physicians were trained for service in an English-speaking province, medical courses were given in English, as were many others. Some departments were more English than French. In this Ontario environment, degrees were given in the Anglo-American style: B.A., B.A. Honours, M.A., and so on. At graduation ceremonies every sentence, long or short, was imme-diately repeated in English. The result was a bewildering spectacle, sometimes rather childish in its concern for bilingualism to the last drop.

In 1965, the university was still pervaded by an atmosphere of old-style Catholicism. The Oblates, who were present at every level—it was, after all, their university—wore cassocks with the distinctive crucifix stuck through the belt like a sword. You would see flotillas of nuns in voluminous habits, complete with wimple and veil, and note the amazing designation of the three washrooms: *Gentlemen*, *Ladies*, and *Nuns*. Lacking any government subsidies, the University of Ottawa had kept its old classical college atmosphere, including the quadrangle in front of the main building—although it wasn't the magnificent green space of today. The first time I saw it, on a gloomy autumn day, I felt myself once more in the inner courtyards of my former boarding schools.

English-speaking society had its own university, Carleton. A cluster of well-spaced modern buildings had been built on the outskirts of Ottawa, between the Rideau River and Dow's Lake. Everything needed for daily life was there, and as the buildings were connected by underground passages, a student could enter the university in September and not stick his or her nose outside until the following summer. The University of Ottawa was old-hat, and Carleton was in equal measure the epitome of all that was ultramodern, dynamic, overflowing with the spirit of youth (as much in its architecture as in its teaching staff), and free from the constraining traditions that weighed on the old institutions. Carleton University proclaimed the success of English-speaking society.

Although not officially bilingual, French had its place at Carleton. Its president spoke excellent French, and it had a French department staffed by professors whose mother-tongue was French—not always the case in some institutions. In teaching history, I was surprised to meet a high proportion of English-speaking students who spoke impeccable French, learned in Toronto, of all places. I was supposed to teach in English, but it happened that students would ask me to give this or that course in French. Was it to get a rest from my English? I don't think so. Among my students was a Franco-Ontarian who, like all French-speaking Ontarians, was a victim of Rule 17 that forced him to have English-language schooling and learn French at home. Occasionally he would say something in French. I felt distinctly uncomfortable each time. The thought had already occurred to me that, outside Quebec, good French would survive mainly thanks to the English-speaking élite, and here was yet further proof.

I noticed something else. One day I said to my students, "You English people," only to evoke the protest, "We're not English, we're Canadian." One of them reminded me that among English-speaking Canadians there are those whose forebears came from England, but others are descended from Irish, Scottish, German, and many other backgrounds. It was a mistake to confuse "English" with "English-speaking."

The existence of two universities in a city that was hours away from the large population centres seemed absurd to me. Equally absurd was their indifference toward each other. Was someone already trying to encourage collaboration, I wondered? I hoped so, and in any case ventured to get something going between the two history departments. As professors and students from the University of Ottawa came to consult me, and as I wanted to establish links between the two institutions, I arranged various occasions for getting together. When I invited guest lecturers from France, such as Robert Mandrou, to Carleton I would make sure the neighbouring history department profited from the visit.

These relationships gradually brought me closer to the University of Ottawa. As it turned out, the first French-Canadian chairman of the Institute of Canadian Studies was to remain in office for only a year. Somewhat unexpectedly, great changes were taking place at the University of Ottawa. The wave of laicization had reached the Oblates. They put aside their cassocks, a move that already changed the landscape considerably. It was no longer necessary to belong to a religious order in order to get promotion, and the Ontario government was going to provide the necessary funding to help modernize the university. Moreover, a new dean was appointed to the faculty of arts—an important change from my point of view, since the history department was part of this faculty. Instead of a dean who worked in a messy office and wore a grubby cassock, here was a university graduate from London, a modern man of business, Father Joseph-Marie Quirion.

The headquarters of this cultivated CEO were transformed into a properly organized office, with carefully chosen curtains and carpet. Instead of a mess of papers on his desk, a single file concerning the matter to be discussed lay on one side. This was the dean who, in 1966, invited me to revive the history department, giving me *carte blanche*.

The history department didn't have its own locale. At that time it shared quarters as best it could with other parts of the faculty, and hadn't even its own secretarial staff. Professors didn't have individual offices (one shared an office with a professor from another discipline who kept her baby with her), nor were there special classrooms or a designated room for daily meetings. In fact, the history department didn't exist from the physical standpoint. I had the university turn over two neighbouring houses where I would have the space needed to set up secretarial services with the necessary personnel, give every professor a private office, and provide common rooms, including one for professors' meetings. As with the history institute at Laval, I went on a buying spree: wall maps for courses, tables, chairs, filing cabinets, the works. At last the department was properly equipped. True, the two houses were somewhat old-fashioned. The halls were narrow and we had more bathtubs than we needed, but the necessary space was there, plus a small Romeo-and-Juliet balcony, as charming as could be.

Even more urgent was the need to put together a strong team of professors. More by accident than design, there were teachers on staff who didn't really fill the requirements for history. On my list I found the name of Séraphin Marion, for example, a man I respected highly for his work in literary history, but who had ventured into the realm of Canadian history where, with the zeal of a Joan of Arc, he was busy attacking *les Anglais*. We especially needed to strengthen the French-speaking team. Since the history department had to cater to students in both languages, two groups of professors had been formed. For various reasons, the French-speaking group had cause to feel neglected. I therefore turned to my former Laval students, and the recruitment ritual became very easy. A telephone call to the dean of arts, and I had the green light. I offered tempting salaries, and in a matter of minutes I had a new recruit. Soon I was surrounded in the French section by former students who had gone through the traditional French system, talented people who were beginning to make their mark in history with their publications.

In order to give a French framework to the teaching, I wanted to establish the types of degrees given in France or Quebec (*licence ès lettres, diplôme d'études supérieures, doctorat ès lettres*) alongside the Anglo-American system. This initiative fell flat. There was no place for such things in the Ontario system. In fact, even in Quebec where the Parent Commission's education reform was in progress, the trend was toward the Anglo-American system. I therefore had to adjust to a situation that was well ensconced in Ottawa.

Another of my initiatives also came to naught. On staff were several specialists in the period of New France or the Old Régime. As we were at last in the era when the Public Archives of Canada was launching a huge program to microfilm documents of the seventeenth and eighteenth centuries in France, we were going to have a rich source of documentation in Ottawa. I dreamed of setting up a research centre in the history of New France. It would have made Ottawa the hub of this discipline in Canada. But my colleagues weren't as keen, and I had to drop the project.

I had greater success with other new ventures. At Laval I had launched the *Cahiers de l'Institut d'histoire,* and by the time I left Quebec some fifteen issues had appeared. In Ottawa, I founded the *Cahiers d'histoire* in 1967. At the same time, the rector of St. Paul University in Ottawa asked me to found a centre for research in religious history, supported by a library with enormous resources. The centre had its first meeting on April 6, 1967. In December of the same year, it held a joint session in Toronto with the American Catholic History Association. A program of public lectures was started, and a first volume of religious history appeared under the auspices of the centre. The enterprise was off to a good start, and I subsequently handed on the flame, concerned about spreading myself too thin.

Another new endeavour of greater scope was the founding of the journal *Histoire sociale—Social History*. In 1967, after becoming a professor at the University of Ottawa, I invited colleagues to my home from both Ottawa and Carleton. These were academics who were interested in social history, and I proposed that we set up a periodical specializing in this subject. It could be the joint effort of both institutions, and we would try to get all Canadian universities involved, as I'd been able to do for the *Dictionary of Canadian Biography*. With Dean Quirion's support, I managed to get the two universities to contribute a set amount of money each year. The University of Ottawa also undertook to defray the costs of printing and distribution, and the Canada Council for the Arts promised grants. The first number appeared in April 1968. I assumed the editorship for the first three years in tandem with my Carleton colleague, Stan Mealing. At the time of writing, this journal has thirty-three volumes to its credit, each over two hundred pages.

Histoire sociale—Social History, a bilingual review appearing twice yearly, was the only journal of its kind in Canada because of its exclusive interest in social history. With contributors from Newfoundland to British Columbia, its range was transcontinental. There were even articles by American and European scholars. Thanks to this journal, Ottawa became the centre for social history and the University of Ottawa moved to the forefront of intellectual life. True, one may wonder at the present juncture whether the review will survive, but it has lasted twenty years, not a negligible record, after all.

In the history department, along with my colleague Micheline D'Allaire (who to this day has remained my best friend), I set myself to develop the kind of atmosphere that would enable teams in our two languages to work congenially together, after years of existing far apart from each other. For a while a little magazine circulated in the department that, unbeknownst to me, was called *Trudelia*. It contained funny and serious offerings from professors and appeared for over a year, a lifespan not much shorter than that of many historical journals. At the appropriate times of year we met for more social gatherings. Instead of everyone standing around the whole evening, glass in hand, as is the custom in English-speaking circles, there would be singing, dancing, games, and skits. Among other events, we organized a mock investiture to celebrate the recent doctorate awarded our colleague Marcel Hamelin. It featured a Molièresque ceremony, complete with the *dignus, dignus est intrare* and the conferring of doctoral paraphernalia. There was the blessing of new wine made by a Slav colleague. As high priest, I invoked the spirits in a long incantation: the spirit of wine, the spirit of method, the spirit of parochialism, the spirit of the occasion, l'Esprit des Lois, Pierre-Esprit Radisson, the spirit that is willing when the flesh is weak—in other words a protracted litany, including everything that contained the word *vin*: *ravin*, *chauvin*, Boivin, Calvin, and the inevitable *Amène . . . à boire.* The wine wasn't necessarily the better for all this, but the other departments envied us our historians' *soirées*.

For a time we had a "Fine Tastebuds Club." Each member took turns preparing a gastronomic repast, a prerequisite to the solemn reception of the apron, soup ladle, and title of *chevalier*. Although master of ceremonies, I still had to prepare my own gourmet meal. The description of each dish on a most erudite menu was more appetizing than the actual food, but the members, being very polite, emitted oohs and ahs with each mouthful that I took to indicate sincere approval.

It was, alas, the Last Supper, for my time as chairman of the history department covered a brief two years. I had been asked to reorganize and rebuild an effective teaching staff in both languages and bring it up to at least the level of history departments in other universities. I considered my mission accomplished, and in any case I was under pressure from my works-in-progress (this was the period in which I was working on reconstituting the St. Lawrence cadastral survey of 1663). Moreover, I was becoming ever less enamoured of administration with its growing number of committee meetings—a system not at all to my taste. I left the post to Marcel Hamelin, one of my former students, and returned to the ranks where I could work at my ease.

The loss I had sustained in 1965 obliged me to reconstruct my teaching program. I had already published several books and had others in preparation. However, except as a novice teacher, I had never wanted to give students material that I felt was too specialized and too limited in scope. What they needed were more general courses. When I arrived in Ottawa, I once again set about explaining the institutions of New France. Then, as this material came out in a book (*Initiation à la Nouvelle-France)*, I adopted a new formula that for about ten years worked very well for me—always supposing that it did the same for my students.

From seventeenth-century archives I extracted documents depicting all the acts connected with life in New France, from the cradle to the grave. These covered the way in which the population was established (immigrants' contracts of engagement, registers of civil status, censuses, marriage contracts); the formation of social groups such as the nobility (letters patent of nobility); business activities (farm leases, the purchase of slaves); the activities of "the little people" (apprenticeship, contracts for clearing land); transmission of property (the concession and sale of land, gifts *inter vivos*, wills, inventory after death, partition of succession); seigneurial activities (the concession of land given in fief, rendering fealty and homage, admission and enumeration); and religious activities. Every student got a photocopy of the original documents to help them learn to decipher old handwriting. These pre-1663 texts were mostly notarial acts inscribed by those old notaries who, like Audouart, are the despair of scholars. Students had to learn to read the document, study its structure, and then exploit the content, in other words to wring from it everything that could help us learn about the life and outlook of people in New France. They were looking directly at history as it was lived, working with original source material instead of listening to theoretical considerations, however scholarly. Seated in the classroom, they got the feel of being historians.

I also had to do some teaching outside my own university. The University of Toronto invited me to conduct a seminar, and I visited Louisbourg in Nova Scotia, where restorations of the fort were in progress, to explain various points of history to the research team. I was even asked to talk about New France in Italy—in Genoa in the north and Messina in the south. But never once was I invited as a visiting professor to the nearby University of Montreal or to Laval, my former university. I should say, however, that Laval made a generous gesture by awarding me an honourary doctorate. Much had changed in twenty years, and I was given this signal honour during a public gathering.

My extramural teaching took an unexpected turn. On the initiative of Micheline D'Allaire, a professor of well-established reputation, the *Club des voyages historiques* was born. The students wanted to see Old Quebec and all those spots so reminiscent of the history we were telling them about. The first trip was to Quebec City, where I acted as guide from one end of Cap-aux-Diamants to the other. This initial attempt was a success. We organized another, this time going as far as Tadoussac, and later made short outings to the Papineau manor-house in Montebello, to Montreal, and to the Richelieu River.

There was even a three-day midwinter visit to Sainte-Marie-Among-the-Hurons in Midland, Ontario, to see buildings reconstructed in the seventeenth-century manner, where we would live like the olden-day French. We left with some forty students for three days of history experienced under historic conditions. You can imagine the spectacle at night: professors and students mixed, lying on the floor, their feet against the fireplace, heads covered with tuques (for between the door and the sill there was a good inch allowing the cold to pass through), each taking a watch for replenishing the fire. Almost everyone became a cook.

After this expedition to Huronia, the group took the opportunity of visiting not only Niagara Falls, but what, alas, very few Canadian tourists go to see. I'm speaking of the old French fort, some thirty kilometres beyond the American border. Here, at the end of Lake Ontario, is a fort from the French Régime that the Americans have kept just as it was: with picket barricade, parade ground, and buildings, including the central pavilion where the garrison was lodged. It's a magnificent architectural document that allows viewers to relive the military circumstances of this period, deep in what was then the wilderness.

The club was to go much further afield. In 1977 a trip to France was organized, Micheline having found the necessary funding. There we were, with some forty students, launched on the great adventure. I acted as guide for this tour, since I had gone over it several times. It included Paris, Chartres, the Perche region, Brittany, La Rochelle, Provence, and the Côte d'Azur, returning through the Auvergne and the Loire country. On our last evening in Paris we had a splendid dinner in a Montmartre restaurant to use up any leftover funds. The next morning, the day we were to leave for Canada, a catastrophe befell us. A general strike kept us in Paris for another twenty-four hours, with no reservations and not much money. We had to rely on what the French call System D (for *débrouiller*) and cope as best we could.

The next year we organized another major trip, this time to the West and the Yukon, also familiar territory since I had already travelled there. This time we wanted to make it a combination trip and course, with an exam at the end that would count in the regular curriculum. Some colleagues, bound by the constraints of formal classes, put a number of obstacles in the way of this project, and life became a bit complicated as a result. Finally, the faculty gave its *nihil obstat* and we were on board our plane for Calgary, where the train would take us over the Rockies to Vancouver. From Seattle, we flew to Juneau. A cruise boat took us to Skagway where the "little train" carried us upward in a series of long loops as far as Whitehorse. Finally, we took a plane to Dawson City and the Klondike River where we panned the gravel and gathered gold-dust. On each day of this marvellous trip I gave a class on the history of the West. It was a serious class, but the classroom was more or less potluck: dance hall, church, hotel room (the thirty students squeezed in, sitting on the beds or the floor, or standing, facing a professor whose lectern was the television set). Sometimes the classroom was the great outdoors, as with the class I gave at Banff, overlooking the Rockies gleaming in the sun. On the last evening, despite our Paris experience, we held another feast to empty the cashbox, and the next day the gods visited upon us a further punishment. By mistake, we had been sold return tickets, not from Dawson City in the Yukon, but from Fort Dawson in Alberta! The difference in distance and cost was enormous, and we had only a few hours to find the money and reservations for thirty people.

Since Micheline occasionally gave a course on the Caribbean islands, where I had a holiday house and a brother-in-law who ran a hotel, the idea quite naturally came up of organizing a trip to Martinique combined with a course. It took place in 1979. The hotel was in a rural setting on the south shore of the large Fort-de-France Bay, beside one of the finest beaches on the island. The Hotel Calalou à l'Âne was the site of a peripatetic university for three weeks. Classes were held each day beneath a canopy of palms and mango trees. From Calalou, our group of thirty would board a bus for a guided tour or a reception by various planters. On the eve of the exam, the boys and girls in their bathing suits stretched out on the sand to go over their notes. The next day they visited me one by one on the bluff (or *morne* as they say in Martinique). This time they wore clothes more compatible with academic dignity, and gave an account of their study-visit.

It was the club's last major trip. After each journey Micheline and I would return exhausted and pretty well burnt out. Living with students twenty-four hours a day for three weeks was a very tiring experience. Day and night we bore the weight of their problems: women students who kept the others from sleeping because their room had become a hairdressing salon; one who had a heart attack; another who wanted to kill herself because she was too old for the good-looking twenty-year-old male students; a young man who had run through his travel money too quickly; another who had been left behind, despite our care in keeping count of our people at each stop; a young woman who couldn't find her plane ticket. We also had to check continually that we were duly expected at the next stage and that there was enough accommodation for everybody, or even (as happened to us in the depths of the countryside), find a tow truck for the bus, which had backed into a ditch.

Apart from these considerations, I wanted to have time for my own trips. Each year I used to go to my house in Martinique—that Département d'Outre-Mer where one lives on French territory. It was the Côte d'Azur without the noise and crowds of the summer months.

Until then I had visited France several times and even lived there. I had travelled the length of Italy, from Venice to Sicily, but even though I was nearing sixty I had never seen Greece—the Greece of the books that had fascinated me as a teenager and made me dream of a career as a Hellenist.

I left for Greece in 1975, sure that I would not discover the land of my classics. I knew very well that modern Greece had been profoundly marked by the former Turkish occupation. It happened that Greece and Turkey were now at war, and this would prevent us from visiting Turkey's western coast, an area covered with Greek monuments. At least the great landscapes of Greece were unchanged. I saw the sky, the mountains, the olive groves, and the islands much as Plato, Sophocles, and Thucydides saw them. There, too, was the Peleponesian countryside and that sea on which I sailed one day at dusk, bound for the islands of Myconos and Delos, white rocks on blue waters. I saw Poseidon's temple at the tip of Cape Sounion, looking as though it had been built in the sky. These are scenes that we only delight in fully the first time, because then we approach them with the freshness of discovery, a unique moment in which we are inhabited by the gods. Later we remember, conjuring up images more beautiful than the real thing, like photographs poetically retouched. The finest part of a trip is that moment when, once more seated in our own little corner, we ruminate inwardly on the beautiful things that have moved us.

Since my last major trips, after France, Italy, Greece, the Sahara, and the fantastic Machu Pichu high in the Peruvian mountains, my great landscapes are now those of the Charlevoix region. From my house built high in these mountains that roll down to the sea, above ever-changing waters, I can follow a horizon that reaches to the Alleghenies, a panorama sixty kilometres wide, running from Les Éboulements as far as Rivière-du-Loup. I live there with my ducks, the white water lilies on the pond, the American goldfinches, the cedar waxwings, partridge, hares, and even the brown bear that watches us go by more often than we can glimpse him in the underbrush. In the spring, flying north after stopping at Cap Tourmente, the great geese form their trailing *V* in the sky, honking as they go. In autumn they fly back south, and I prepare for winter.

I looked forward with great impatience to my sixty-fifth birthday and to finding, at long last, total freedom in what I wanted to do. In the long run you tire of teaching the same subject, giving the same courses, hearing the same silly things in oral exams, and directing theses when there are so many things you want to write yourself. When you see so little progress from one generation of students to another, you look forward to the moment when you can let all the strings drop. It's true that my two hours of teaching per week (for the university granted me an ideal timetable) left me a fair amount of leisure. My career at the University of Ottawa had been very full, or one might say very agitated, depending how you look at it. Despite what it cost me in time lost for research, I had given a great many public lectures, each requiring nearly a month's work, even if they seemed like nothing more than facile popularization. In these seventeen years of my Ottawa sequel, I had produced some fifteen books, seven alone on the period of the Hundred Associates.

Retirement came in 1982. Free at last! I was a free man forever! But there was work to be done all the same. I thought I was finishing things, but I have the impression I was just beginning.

At home in Lucerne, Québec, 1977.
Photo by Roger Monahan

10

A Sympathetic Self-evaluation

According to the current criteria for recruitment, a historian who wishes to occupy a university chair must have a doctorate in history as well as an established reputation in a particular field. In 1947 I fulfilled none of these criteria.

A *licence ès lettres* followed by a *doctorat ès lettres* were my academic credentials. I had moved from the study of Greek to comparative literature and had published a novel. At the invitation of Laval University, I had shed my literary feathers and, without a history degree, had become a historian specializing in the history of Canada. Up to this point my career had proceeded by a series of unexpected leaps. There would be further such leaps in my career as a professional academic. I explored the British Régime, then the Military Régime, before at last finding my niche: the beginnings of New France. My friend Michel Brunet was right when he said, teasingly, "Trudel is trying to find himself." And Frégault was equally right when, in a 1947 review of my novel, he spoke of Trudel "whose progress is difficult to foresee." My colleagues in Montreal didn't waste much time trying to find themselves. At the first attempt, Maurice Séguin and Michel Brunet had pinpointed their quarry: *la Conquête*—the British Conquest of New France—as an explanation for the entire subsequent history of French Canada. Guy Frégault chose New France as his specialty, and although he took some time to find a focus for his scholarship, he soon joined Séguin and Brunet in highlighting the phenomenon of the Conquest. My background in literature (like Frégault's) surfaced in my first two publications, *L'Influence de Voltaire au Canada* and my novel *Vézine*. The former was not a masterwork. The style may seem pleasant (I had just spent four years reading Voltaire), and the book has plenty of energy, with a plot somewhat like a play. It was a best-seller for its day, although that isn't necessarily a guarantee of quality. Reviews were highly critical, coming mainly from Ottawa. Admirers of Garneau, and especially of Gustave Lanctot, were indignant at seeing their great men treated as Voltairians and accused of having plagiarized large chunks of that philosopher's work. The literary page of *Le Droit* was full of this contentious subject one day. I responded in the same aggressive tone, which didn't much help the search for truth.

Actually, this book was only a schoolboy's work, done with the meagre means at hand. In the years between 1941 and 1945 we were in the midst of the war, and intellectual contact with Europe was cut off. There was no question of having a critical edition of Voltaire sent from France, and the edition available at Laval was very out of date. I had no access to Voltaire studies published in Europe, and in Canada we had almost nothing on the notion of comparative literature. I therefore took the works of French-Canadian literature from 1764 to 1900, and compared them with the works of Voltaire.

This was easy work as far as the eighteenth century in Canada was concerned, but less so for the nineteenth, when people could express Voltaire's ideas without having actually known or read him. As a result my book was weakest in dealing with the years 1830 to 1900. My thesis director was reluctant to restrain his young student's enthusiasm, and I may have discovered more Voltairianism than really existed. Ideally, the parameters of the work should have been defined at the outset, and the basic terms—Voltairianism, anti-clericalism, and left-wing clericalism—should have been clearly understood. However, in our universities we hadn't yet developed this approach.

What strikes today's critic is more the spirit in which this thesis was written, reflecting an outlook that may surprise anyone unfamiliar with the social climate of French Canada in the 1940s. Here was a Quebec City student in his twenties who wanted to prove that our literature, remembered only for its devout pages, was the offspring of Voltaire. Here also was a young professor teaching in a college run by priests in Rigaud, who spent his leisure time reading and writing about Voltaire. The thesis was to be submitted to a fiercely Catholic institution with a papal charter. Of the two thesis directors, one was a Quebec Seminary abbé and teacher who would dictate part of my conclusion. The examining jury consisted of five professors, all practising Catholics, and my thesis would only receive the crowning title of "doctoral" after publication. The candidate had no choice but to submit to the demands of the system.

I had to show my pastors and masters that I had emerged unscathed from my reading of the forbidden author. The resulting religious overtones date this pre-Quiet Revolution thesis. Today critics are still judging my *Influence de Voltaire* as if it had been written in the post-1965 intellectual climate by a historian with several books to his credit, using the comparative literary method developed after its publication. I admit my guilt, but the guilt of the critics is no less then mine.

I profited from my time at Harvard to rework the entire thesis in depth, since the first edition had quickly sold out, but other work forced me to put the new manuscript aside and it disappeared completely in the fire of 1965. I don't intend to rewrite this thesis. There has been too much progress in literary history, too many specialists have focused in recent years on phenomena that I only touched on, and I now have other interests. If a new edition were to be published, it would have to be a faithful reproduction of the 1945 work presented as an example of what a young student could produce at that time, under the conditions and pressure of the prevailing mentality.

It was also at Harvard in my leisure moments that I put the final touches to *Vézine,* a novel begun in Rigaud. It didn't arouse the critical storm that greeted my book on Voltaire, but reviewers found much to complain about, all the same. Some saw it as a novel of the land, which had been fashionable before the Second World War but had fallen out of favour immediately afterward. *Vézine* is not such a novel; in fact there is no mention of farm life. It is a novel about village life against a logging background, a novel about the closed environment from which my hero escapes each morning and to which he returns each night. Balzac's influence is evident. The structure of the novel, the use of portraiture and description, the dialogues—all are reminiscent of Balzac, an author for whom I had a great fondness. I dreamed of being the Balzac of Canada.

I admit the weakness for which critics have reproached me: that this book seems to be made up of set pieces sprinkled with brilliant digressions in which I manipulated words at my pleasure. This description of an ear is the best example:

> Like a flower pinned in the hair, the ear is an ornament. It truly is a flower. The auricle turns in a delicate helix, the translucent shell takes on a deep rosy hue in the sunlight, the tragus curves like a petal, and this stemless bloom ends in a pendant, the lip of a brilliant wild

orchid. A flower open to the invisible pollen of music and words. A flower that, through its sound-bearing rhizome, brings to one's very soul light articulate!

I made great use of the device of the final word, a method I had taught my pupils in Rigaud, and of choosing the precise word, as did the Young Naturalists and Brother Marie-Victorin, the great Canadian botanist. My goal was to do in prose what Hérédia or Léo-Paul Morin had done in poetry.

In a word, as Jean-Charles Bonenfant noted, *Vézine* resembled a "series of well-developed *tableaux* by an author adept at writing prose." Guy Frégault, at that time literary critic for *L'Action nationale*, placed *Vézine* higher than Germaine Guèvremont's *Survenant* but criticized it for phonetically transcribing the dialogue. To sum up, he judged the novel "too fine for what is ugly, and too ugly for what is fine"—an opinion that showed Frégault and myself as equally precious when it came to style.

The novel was written while I was doing research on Canada and reflects a concern with history. My idea was to make it a documentary about an era, like a chapter of history, having kept a notebook in which I recorded, much as a historian makes file cards, what would be useful in portraying a certain social milieu. I had examined the old post office, the old general store with its jumble of goods, and the old grocery store before they all disappeared. I had scrupulously reconstituted the traditional speech read to parents on their silver wedding anniversary, the daily life of the Saint-Dominique orphanage, and the Ursuline parlour. I had consulted catalogues for early twentieth-century fashion so that I could describe exactly what women wore. In other words, I had followed the classic method of the historian.

This was to be my method throughout all my works once my career had begun. After writing a thesis in literature and a novel, I embarked on history the way people take up a religious vocation, with a total devotion to the most rigorous method. This is evident in my first genuinely historical work, *Louis XVI, le Congrès américain et le Canada, 1774-1789*.

Frégault was making New France his subject and his colleagues in Montreal were focusing on the question of the British Conquest. For my career in Quebec City, I chose to devote myself to studying the British Régime, a subject that had been studied by Thomas Chapais, but only from the political standpoint. Little was known about the society of the time—its structures, outlook, and commercial activity.

As Laval had sent me to Harvard, I began by studying the problem posed by Canada at the time of the American Revolution, in terms of relations between the United States, Britain, and France. What would become of Canada after the War of Independence? The Americans wanted to make it a fourteenth state. This would rid them of the threat of a British presence to the north and remove an obstacle to their expansion. France didn't want to take Canada back and perhaps be drawn into conflict with the former British colonies. The French preferred Canada to remain a British possession and a continued threat to the Americans, who would then be forced to maintain their alliance with France. All of these stratagems were of course played out in the greatest secrecy, but in the end everyone knew what the others wanted. To foil any unfavourable schemes, France alternately made French-Canadians believe it wanted to bring them under the French crown again, or that it wanted to help the Americans conquer Canada, with La Fayette leading the Congressional troops.

I wasn't the first to describe this diplomatic game, as I carefully reminded readers in my foreword. I simply wanted to reopen the question and try to probe deeper than my predecessors.

Above all, in this 1949 publication my aim was to make a resounding impression by practising what we called "scientific history" as against "eloquent" or "nostalgic" history, in a word, the old *belle histoire*. My foreword impressed Frégault, who understood its objectives. I wrote:

> My aim has been to apply scholarly methods to this study, although in some circles history is still considered a work of art, much as a play during which you would be shocked to see backstage paraphernalia and what was going on the wings. It's an odd thing for a historian to have to excuse himself for including footnotes and a bibliography. History in French Canada has always found a comfortable home in the rhetoric courses of our colleges and has looked down on the historian-cum-researcher whose aim is to be scientific. The former approach relies on fine phrases, the latter on sources, and it is this second option that, in the last analysis, will be more certain to reveal historical truth.

In 1949 such a statement amounted to a manifesto for the "new history," a declaration of war on the history that had gone before. Listing one's sources and works consulted was considered pretentious at the time, as though saying,

"See what a lot of things I know!" Putting footnotes on a page was tantamount to insisting that historians always back up their statements with proof—in other words, a refusal to take their word for it. "Gentlemen, your credentials!" Many of our elders felt this way, and many a cold shoulder resulted. They came round in the end, however. We were taking a step forward. The *Revue d'histoire de l'Amérique française* did a great deal toward generalizing the use of this method according to the precise rules that I taught at Laval (order in the bibliography, the reference system, and the use of abbreviations and initials). I like to think that I helped establish this method in Groulx's *Revue*. Today, even an amateur's first reaction, when looking at a work of this sort, is to check for a bibliography and footnotes. This isn't necessarily proof of quality, but the reader wants to feel secure. He seeks knowledge, not fine discourse.

In 1949, therefore, I appeared in print with a twenty-eight-page bibliography and copious footnotes that seemed designed to send the reader straight to sleep. The excessive zeal of the neophyte was evident in this presentation, as also in the meticulous dissection of international politics vis-à-vis Canada. For the 1976 edition I therefore got rid of everything that didn't deal directly with the subject at hand. The bibliography was reduced by half, and the voluminous footnotes drastically curtailed. The 1949 foreword, a declaration of war on fine rhetoric, was no longer useful, and I replaced it with a more usual presentation of the current state of historical writing. Let's hope that our fortunate present-day historians remember that we had to break down barriers to give them the greater freedom they now enjoy.

In 1952, immediately after this book appeared, I had a chance to work on another aspect of the British Régime. Fides invited me to contribute to *l'Histoire du Canada par les textes*. As I have said, Frégault, a recognized specialist in the French Régime, took care of the first part, covering the beginnings to 1759. I prepared the period 1760-1855, while Brunet dealt with the years 1855 to 1939. The idea was to publish the most significant texts, preceded by a brief introduction. It was designed as a textbook and therefore to be as simple and as brief as possible. However each author, through his choice of texts and the short commentaries that prefaced them, showed where his ideas and interests lay, although with the appearance of perfect objectivity. My part clearly had a very different approach from those of my two colleagues.

My interest in another field of history was already apparent. The questions I raised about the British Régime relative to French-Canadian society were based in large part on what had happened during the Military Régime in the years 1759-1764. To understand how the century-long British Régime got under way, you first needed to observe the Military Régime closely. The importance of this transition period had barely been recognized by our historians. I wanted to be the specialist of the Military rather than the British Régime.

This period would be more correctly described as a provisional government, since it was only in place until the treaty deciding Canada's fate was concluded. The expression "Military Régime" evokes a harsh rule that did not happen. In fact the French Régime continued, but since the country was entirely under the authority of military personnel and the militia (even in the area of justice), the term "Military Régime" is justified.

The question was, how to approach it? The occupying military government had strictly applied the traditional division of New France into three governmental districts (Quebec, Trois-Rivières, and Montreal) to the point of making them three autonomous regions. To get my hand in, I preferred to begin with the smallest, that is, with Trois-Rivières. This preliminary study became a book in 1952, *Le Régime militaire dans le gouvernement des Trois-Rivières, 1760-1764*, after which I felt experienced enough to attempt an overall study of the régime. New difficulties arose at this point. The scope of the subject was immense, and there was a wealth of documentation despite the short time span. I decided to study one aspect at a time and see how things went. I chose the Church, but this one aspect continually expanded as I advanced. In the end I had a two volume work, *L'Église canadienne sous le Régime militaire, 1759-1764.*

If a new edition of my work were to appear, these three volumes (long since out of print) would be the ones that I would retouch least—except, of course, if I got hold of new documents such as Jesuit or Recollet papers (both rare for this period), or correspondence by ordinary people. At present we have a great many documents relating to the Quebec Seminary, and this makes the study lopsided. The historian can't do anything about it, however, because this kind of a study depends entirely on the available archival documentation.

For the time being there would be little to change as far as information goes. The same is true for the tone of the work. I'm convinced that I achieved as objective, cool-headed, and detached an approach as is possible for a historian. The critics grasped this aspect of my work, and indeed they had begun to accept the fact that history, even if the subject is the Church, can be written according to strictly scientific principles.

Not everyone appreciated the neutral approach to history, as shown by the liberties taken with a preface that I wrote at this time. I had been asked to write it for the *Généalogie de la famille Trudel (Trudelle) en Amérique* prepared by Paul-Eugéne Trudel, a Franciscan. I therefore wrote a solemn text without any patriotic tirade, rather technical in fact. Imagine my surprise when the book appeared in 1955 to find that someone had inserted preachifying passages such as: "Our Canadian genealogists' only ambition is to seek out the noble virtues of our ancestors . . . who transformed a corner of the Canadian wilderness into a Christian land. What a moral comfort this is amid life's struggles. . . . These poor colonists . . .bore us, named us, and gave us treasures of moral worth." There were other interpolations in the same style that the author or editor had the temerity to insert under my name. This kind of editorial tampering clearly proves that people still felt the need for more heated rhetoric, rather than the historian's detached tone.

As a diversion from my work on the Military Régime, I took time out to write *Chiniquy,* published in 1955. Chiniquy had been a legendary figure for me since childhood. My parents spoke of him with religious terror, imputing to him the blackest deeds. Some old folk claimed in good faith (such are not always the most credible witnesses) that after Chiniquy's apostasy they had seen him jokingly blessing the bread in the baker's van as it went by. I encountered the pastor again when researching Voltaire's influence on French-Canadian literature, and I still sensed his presence in the Lower St. Lawrence region where my first wife lived.

When I read Chiniquy's books and polemical newspaper articles of the second half of the nineteenth century, I was staggered by the evidence of this man's extraordinary activity. Not only had he aroused the crowds of Lower Canada with his temperance campaigns as only great orators can, but after his apostasy he preached with increased energy against the Church of Rome in Canada, the United States, and as far away as Australia. Wherever he went, he caused riots. His writing reached an international readership, something no French-Canadian author had yet been able to do.

Among his other works were two massive autobiographies, published in both French and English, *Fifty Years in the Church of Rome*, followed by *Forty Years in the Church of Christ.* In the first work he wanted to prove that he had been a Protestant reader of the Bible from childhood in the rural world of Lower Canada and that, throughout his career as a Catholic, he had seen nothing but hypocrisy and scandal. In the second work he told the story of his campaigns as a Protestant convert as well as his persecution by Catholics. Posing as a martyr, he even brought in Christ, who appeared to him in person to ask him to leave the Roman Catholic Church. It was a rather blatant artifice, but Chiniquy had much to be forgiven by his new religious partners. Just before his "conversion" to the Protestant faith he had fiercely defended the papacy alongside Bishop Bourget of Montreal and fought the French-speaking Protestants of that city tooth and nail.

This man's astonishing life story had not yet been told as a biography. I therefore decided to devote a book to him. The clergy was more than reluctant to have the public reminded of Chiniquy. I would be telling the story of a famous preacher, showered with honours by bishops, who renounced his priestly vocation, married, and violently denounced his former Church. In 1955, when the Catholic clergy was in the midst of its triumphalist period, at a time when the *sacerdos in aeternum* was forever being extolled, French-Canadian society was unprepared for these historical flashbacks. In this unchanging social environment, the tragedy of Jean-Charles Harvey as told in *Les demi-civilisés*, a novel that was after all innocuous, was a recent event. In the atmosphere of the time, neither society nor its religious leaders could accept a book that wasn't a refutation of Chiniquy. As a result I was once more beset by the perils of my years of studying Voltaire.

It wasn't easy to gain access to documentation, although there was abundant material in the Quebec Seminary and archdiocesan archives. I often had to resort to some ruse or other, pretending to be interested only in Chiniquy's temperance campaign or in his great adversary, Vicar-general Mailloux. I also had to rein myself in when writing the book, not going too deeply into the causes of Chiniquy's apostasy and above all not insisting on the poor training of nineteenth-century priests as an explanation for his straying from the fold.

In addition to all this, I had to submit to religious censorship. When I had written on Voltaire's influence, I knew that one of the Quebec Seminary abbés was going through my paper with a fine tooth comb and that a jury of five Laval professors awaited me once the thesis was done. This time there was also surveillance. When a priest or other religious figure wrote on a religious subject, he had to submit his work to the censorship of his bishop (see the words *Nihil obstat* and *Imprimatur* in the front of such books). I was a layman and therefore exempt from episcopal scrutiny in principle. Nevertheless, as a university professor and author of several works including two on the Catholic Church in French Canada, I was informed by a member of the hierarchy that it would be to my advantage ("entirely of your own free will, of course," said this person condescendingly) to submit my work to the bishop's censorship. I was dependent on a salary and the good will of an authority that wasn't bound by any union. I therefore presented my manuscript, "entirely of my own free will," to a designated censor and obtained a passing grade.

Even this episcopal stamp of approval didn't necessarily earn me the clergy's blessing. I wanted to dedicate the book to my brother on the silver anniversary of his ordination, but I was told by indirect means that it would be in bad taste. When doing the rounds of presbyteries to consult archives after *Chiniquy* appeared, the priests were noticeably resentful toward me for having published it. And yet I hadn't treated the former temperance preacher with kid gloves. His deliberate fabrications were so glaring that a serious historian had no choice but to denounce them.

As a result the book was in a kind of limbo. Some critics reproached me for having said too much against Chiniquy, of letting myself be carried away by my concern for setting the record straight. Others accused me of not having said enough in favour of the Church or criticized me simply for disinterring the subject. Was it an anticlerical work? Was it a clerical or even "ultramontane" book (as recently described by a colleague whose capital virtue is not objectivity)? One doesn't judge a work written in 1955 by a 1985 yardstick.

A *Chiniquy* written in an atmosphere of academic freedom after the Quiet Revolution would have been different. Thirty years ago, we had to be content with simply setting forth the facts, and even so we had to sugar the pill. A biography of Chiniquy written today would be far greater in scope. There would be less attempt to share out the blame and more emphasis on trying to uncover the why and how. It would take into account the nineteenth-century mentality of aggressive Catholicism, inexorably opposed to the slightest deviation and expressed in the most violent rhetoric. It ought to describe the Church's massive recruitment of candidates for the priesthood, aimed at establishing its social prestige. The shoddy training of recruits and the superficial theology of the period deserve mention. The author would focus on gaining a better understanding of what was going on in Chiniquy's mind when he decided, after various much-publicized incidents, to jump ship from the Church of Rome to "the Church of Christ." Finally, a new biography would give more weight than I did to Chiniquy's very active Protestant career that lasted nearly forty years, and would make greater use of Presbyterian archives. I'm hoping to begin work on this book soon in collaboration with a Toronto historian.[1]

While researching the early days of New France, I also found time, as though wandering down an intriguing byway, to write a book on slavery in French Canada. Published in 1960, it wasn't as questionable a project as my *Chiniquy*, but it shocked readers almost as much. I demonstrated that eighteenth-century French Canada had not escaped the international use of slaves, despite the fact that there was no necessity for it from the economic standpoint.

From around 1700 to the British Conquest, we had slaves. A clause in the 1760 treaty guaranteed our ownership of them, and after the Conquest we owned more than the British in the colony. The first difference about this slavery was that it involved far more Amerindians than Black Africans, and these Amerindians belonged almost exclusively to French Canadians. The second difference was that, since slavery was an accepted social phenomenon, I found records of slaves owned by men of the Church—very few, it's true, only 1.6 percent. However, the clergy and right-wing individuals generally were lying in wait for me, and this piece of information gave them their chance. For them, Voltaire, Chiniquy, and slavery were all part of a programmed effort to sling mud at both the Church and our *belle histoire*. And yet my study on slavery was written in all impartiality. I accused no one; I didn't even condemn slavery, an indifference for which some were quick to censure me.

The harshest blows came not from critics, however. I had prepared a thousand-page biographical dictionary of the slaves and their owners. The five typed fair copies were all destroyed in the fire of 1965. When I retired in 1982, I began my research anew and began rewriting the dictionary, this time listing over four thousand slaves. The manuscript is now with a publisher, and I hope it will at last appear in print.[2]

Apart from my *Histoire de l'esclavage* and *Chiniquy*, both written as a diversion from my regular work, I had now published three books on the Military Régime, but they merely scratched the surface. I was preparing a general study of the régime and had gathered almost all my documentation. However I realized that for an in-depth study of this period, which was merely the continuation of the French Régime, I needed a comprehensive understanding of the problems of New France. My knowledge was relatively sparse in this respect. I immediately decided to give myself a refresher course in the French Régime, and with my painstaking mentality that meant beginning at the beginning, which is to say 1524.

There are periods in one's life where time really doesn't seem to press and we think ourselves eternal. At forty I took it upon myself to delve into the entire history of New France, from 1524 to 1760, period by period, year by year, in all its aspects. After this, I said to myself, I'll be able to speak with authority about the Military Régime, the concluding chapter of New France.

I therefore began. Thirty years later, I haven't yet reached the period 1663-1675. There's a century left to study, and I'm seventy years old!

I haven't lingered on the way, however. The first volume of this *Histoire de la Nouvelle-France* appeared in 1963 (*Les vaines tentatives, 1524-1663*), followed by *Le comptoir, 1604-1627* in 1966, and the two sections of the third volume, *La seigneurie des Cent-Associés, 1627-1663,* in 1979 and 1983.

Les vaines tentatives dealt with the sixteenth century and was the weakest of the series because it contributed the least amount of new material to the subject. Nevertheless it had the merit of integrating the New France of Brazil, and later of Florida, into our own history in a logical and natural way. It lacked originality because of the documentation available. Nothing new about Cartier has been discovered for at least fifty years (something that was fully acknowledged at the 1984 Rennes colloquium), so that writing on the sixteenth century of New France can seem to be something of an exercise in face-lifting.

It gave me greater pleasure to write the second volume, *Le comptoir, 1604-1627.* At first glance this period appears completely unexciting. The men of action were few. During these years Europeans were methodically seeking ways of going deeper into the North American continent, and this was when the culture shock of the encounter between Amerindians and French was most decisive. Documentation remains meagre in this area. How can we really understand a period in which Champlain was in fact the only and constant witness?

I then came to the period of the Hundred Associates, when a permanent European population settled in New France. Many of this period's characteristics would define the entire French Régime.

My approach was no more hurried than usual. Because of the period's supreme importance I felt the need to carry out unprecedented preliminary studies. *La population du Canada en 1663* (1973) was an attempt to reconstitute, person by person, the population of the St. Lawrence Valley on the basis of all available documents—a census of 1663 carried out by a man of 1973! *Le terrier du Saint-Laurent en 1663*, which also appeared in 1973, listed and described all the land conceded *en fief* or *en roture* from the Gaspé region to Montreal, illustrated with numerous maps and diagrams that I had drawn myself. *Les débuts du régime seigneurial au Canada* (1974) took as a starting date 1627, not 1663 as R.C. Harris had just done, demonstrated how the Hundred Associates laid the foundation of a system and launched a procedure that would remain in force for over two centuries. Then, in order to see how a society developed in a circumscribed environment, I wrote *Montréal: la formation d'une société, 1642-1663* (1976). Finally, as I needed to know who the individuals who had come to form the first French settlement were, I made an inventory, year by year, with biographical notes. There was a delay in publishing this, but it finally appeared in bookshops in 1983 as *Catalogue des immigrants, 1632-1662*. In the meantime I'd had to write an overview of the colony entitled *The Beginnings of New France* for a Toronto-based series.

These studies are not entirely satisfactory from my point of view, although, as in the case of my books on the Military Régime, I undertook exhaustive research and maintained the strictest objectivity. *Le terrier du Saint-Laurent* is an original work that has served scholars in all sorts of ways and should continue to do so for a number of years to come. Unfortunately errors will creep in. For example, I reversed the order of some of the seigneurial concessions on the Côte de Beaupré, and, because of insufficient information, my cadastral survey of Cap-de-la-Madeleine leaves something to be desired. I missed some people in the 1663 inventory and, from time to time, I've had to correct or complete my *Catalogue des immigrants*. This is the fate of all authors: the moment you open the book fresh from the printer, out pops a mistake. I'm especially unhappy with my *Beginnings of New France*. The Toronto publisher wanted a resumé of the years 1524-1663. When the contract was signed, the 1524-1627 part was already done and I merely had to condense it. However I had not yet covered the period 1627-1663 in depth, but as the publisher was in a hurry, I was forced to write it before finishing my research. As a result, in this volume I simply repeated what others had already said concerning the Hundred Associates.

However this may be, after all these preparatory studies I was in a position to attempt an exhaustive study of the years 1627-1663, published under the title, *La seigneurie des Cents-Associés*, the third instalment of my *Histoire de la*

Nouvelle-France. It consisted of two fairly thick volumes, one giving the chronology of events, the other intended as a social study.

My pleasure in reconstituting this thirty-year slice of history was diminished by insufficient documentation for some areas that prevented me from exploring all avenues. There are depressing gaps in the archives. The minutes of the Hundred Associates' deliberations, their account books, their correspondence—everything has disappeared, perhaps in the pillage by the Communards of 1871. Also missing are the letters of the governor, Huault de Montmagny, a man who apparently played a very active role for twelve years. Gone, too, are the papers and minutes of the first Quebec Council, as are many items from the original archives of the religious communities. The embarkation lists for French ports cannot be found. Yet despite all these missing elements, I believe I made the best possible use of what has survived, especially the notarial records. My successors may have the opportunity to add to this documentation. Better trained than I was, they will no doubt find new insights into this period. This is how the study of history advances.

Since I'm handing out compliments to myself without a great deal of modesty (one is best served by oneself), I have no hesitation in mentioning two works that are still useful. The first is my *Initiation à la Nouvelle-France*, published in 1968, which appeared in English as *Introduction to New France.* The opening segment is an overview of New France's history from what is perhaps a traditional perspective. The second part, however, is the fruit of some twenty years' research and teaching. It has the merit of describing the institutions—that is, the social mechanics of New France in its various sectors. Today's students are having more and more trouble understanding the vocabulary of the seigneurial régime, whether it be the justice system, marriage contracts, currency, weights and measures, what is meant by *la fabrique* (the parish council), the tithe, the *cure fixe*, a seminary, a Recollet, *une professe de choeur*, and so on. My *Initiation* is the textbook for those who truly want to explore life in New France, but like all textbooks, it will soon be out of date.

I am no less proud (I'm still in my crowing mode) of the second historical tool, the *Atlas de la Nouvelle-France.* After two or three editions of a *Collection des cartes* assembled for teaching and research purposes, I finally produced a bilingual atlas designed for easy consultation. It contains the basic cartographic material for New France: maps of the colony from the first explorations up to the military campaigns surrounding the British Conquest, regional maps from different periods, and maps of cities as they grew. Considering the lengthy preparation of this *Atlas*, the courses on sixteenth-century cartography that I gave for years, and all the maps I drew for my *Terrier du Saint-Laurent*, I sometimes wonder if I might have done better as a cartographer than as a historian.

Where did I find the time to write these works—some thirty of them—while carrying a considerable teaching load as well as handling the administrative duties that fell to my lot for a number of years? The production of works for publication demanded constant application, as nothing was left to chance. From a very young age I had learned to exercise rigorous self-discipline. I was a fulltime boarder from the age of eight and remained so for thirteen years. I had to learn to live on my own. There were elementary and secondary school teachers who gave me an appetite for study, and perhaps, in my long solitude, this was my one salvation.

Of necessity, or as a result of my upbringing, I always set myself difficult goals. From my first days in classical college I developed the habit of taking on additional studies just for pleasure—more Latin and Greek works, writing a verse tragedy, or compiling dictionaries. Because I had a very precise timetable, I managed to complete my various projects. No long-term undertaking could intimidate me (then or now), since from the outset I counted on it taking a certain number of months, of hours per week, and of minutes per day. In this way, working outside my regular schedule, I was able to create file cards on each of New France's inhabitants prior to 1663, listing all their legal acts as registered in the archives and every single land concession received. All of this went into two books, the *Catalogue des immigrants* and the *Terrier du Saint-Laurent*, without unduly affecting my regular work timetable.

This discipline has remained with me throughout my career. As with some of the great toilers, I got into the habit of setting aside the whole morning for this supplementary work. Except for Saturday mornings during one period, I never gave morning courses. As director, I could arrange my own timetable and I therefore scheduled my courses for two o'clock (I ended up being called "the two o'clock man"). This left me several hours in a row for supplementary projects during the morning, the best time of day. For a few years I even forbade morning courses at Laval's history institute, naively supposing that my students and colleagues kept the same working hours as myself. If I had an administrative task to perform (which was the case for nineteen out of the thirty-five years of my career), no supposedly urgent problem could make me budge from my work table.

At nine o'clock each morning (a late hour, as I am lazy in spite of everything) I sat down at my work table and didn't rise until the stroke of noon. As I explained to my students in my introductory course on research, when you sit down to your desk regularly at a given time, inspiration greets you on a daily basis. On the stroke of nine the god of creation (this *deus ecce deus,* as the poets say) is there each morning, all one's life. Even on New Year's Day, after the family ritual, I would go upstairs to my library with the most delightful feeling that I was beginning the new year, pen in hand.

Each day I wrote my five pages. Félix-Antoine Savard was greatly shocked when I told him, rather out of bravado, that any writer worth the name should write five pages a day. I knew very well that he aimed at only one page—but what a page! The artist in him was quite taken aback. What I didn't say was that I reworked those five pages extensively. All the books I have produced have been entirely rewritten three and sometimes four times. I like monumental tasks, but I also like to do them with care.

As the physical man must also be kept in shape, I resumed the habit early in my university career of doing morning exercises, something I picked up at the Franciscan college. How long have I faithfully done this half hour of exercises? Thirty-five years? Forty? When anything prevents me doing them I'm unhappy for the rest of the day. What wonderful sessions I've had on the bridge of the *Homeric* as the sun rose over the Atlantic! In a Paris villa, set in its own garden, I used to open the french doors giving onto the tops of chestnut trees and begin my day with this elixir of youth. Soon people who shared the villa were saying, "These Canadians are great athletes!" (a charitable generalization). In my introductory course on research I used to start with practical advice. University students were surprised at being taught to do a long session of exercises every morning.

Learning to relax is also important. Before the last and most difficult year of my *license ès lettres* I closed my books for four months—four months that I spent in the outdoors. The subsequent academic year was a success. During the most harried period of my career I set aside a month of *farniente* each summer. I would take my family camping in the Lac Saint-Jean region, on Lake Huron, in the Gaspé (I could draw you a map of the camping sites of eastern Canada!). For a month I left civilization behind: I didn't open a book or even a newspaper.

Physical workouts should be complemented by intellectual gymnastics.

For many years I would make myself study German for fifteen minutes after breakfast. During those years, always looking for a good mental exercise, I moved on to Russian. Now there's a difficult language! Each morning before sitting down at my desk I study Russian. When I feel this exercise is becoming too easy and doesn't require any painful effort, I'll move on to Arabic or perhaps Chinese.

[1] Published as *Chiniquy. Prêtre catholique, ministre presbytérien* (2001). JB

[2] Published as *Au Canada français. Dictionnaire des esclaves et de leurs propriétaires* (1990). JB

11

How Well Do Books Pay?

My thirty or so books have brought me endless joys of the mind. One writes mainly for the pleasure of the thing. If there are other consolations, so much the better.

For one also writes for fame. But what does it mean for a writer to be famous? If he doesn't appear on television frequently, he remains a name without a face. People meet him but don't know who he is. He walks along the street, unknown among the common herd. Sometimes readers are so taken by a book that they completely forget the man they are reading.

You write a number of books that get talked about. Do you think yourself famous? Do you believe people know who you are? It happens that your face resembles someone else's. "Bonjour, Monsieur Saulnier," I heard a passerby call one day. He took me for Lucien Saulnier, a Montreal city administrator. If he could at least have taken me for Mayor Drapeau! At a Paris cocktail party someone headed for me smiling broadly. "Ah! Monsieur Hertel, how are you?" I was François Hertel, and duly flattered, but I would have preferred to be recognized for my own face.

A more surprising metamorphosis occurred in 1960. I was to give a talk in a salon of Canada House in Paris. Apart from compatriots like Félix Leclerc and Michèle Rossignol, I had an audience of French guests. After fifteen years as a university professor and some ten books, I looked on the occasion as the crowning moment of my career. But after the ritual laudatory introduction of this "distinguished lecturer," the master of ceremonies announced, "And now I give you the great historian, Michel Brunet." Work hard to make a name for yourself and see where you get!

While people may easily put someone else's name to your face, you at least believe your works are your own. Don't be so sure. Recently the Institut québécois de recherche sur la culture (Quebec Institute for Research on Culture) published an exhaustive catalogue of works that appeared prior to 1960. My six books are there, but four of them are listed under another person's name. I should be grateful to be with two! It just goes to show the need for publishing in quantity if you want to survive: some get lost, but there's always something left.

You think you're front and centre and that all the world follows your every move? Count yourself lucky if people don't think you're already six feet under. Last winter I planned to attend the launch of a book with which I'd been closely involved. The invitation didn't arrive. "It must be an oversight," I said to myself. It was not. One of the organizers had heard I was dead and had crossed my name off the list. A stroke of the pen, and you're gone. Around the same time an Ottawa lady, alerted by someone newly arrived from Acadia, the French-speaking area of the Maritimes, telephoned the house. I answered the phone, and she gave a joyful shriek. "Oh, I'm so glad to hear your voice. Someone told me you'd died. How glad my children will be!"

All this time I hadn't known I was dead! But when you're dead, do you know it? I was writing my memoirs without realizing they were *Mémoires d'outre tombe.* After phoning two or three people to make sure I was alive, there was nothing for it but to get back to work. My inquiry completed (but not that of the coroner), I realized that once again, after a twenty-five year interval, I had been confused with the historian Michel Brunet. Oh yes, try to make a name for yourself!

Compensations come that make the author think his reputation is growing or his efforts are at least recognized. Among these compensations was the festschrift, *Mélanges d'histoire du Canada français offerts au professeur Marcel Trudel*, an honour accorded a professor at the end of his career in the form of a book of essays by colleagues and former students. Pierre Savard, a former student, had taken charge of the project. The book, with a map of New France on the cover, contained articles by eighteen university professors, eight of whom were my former students and now recognized historians. I was pleased to find among the contributors the name of geographer Pierre Deffontaines, whose visits to Quebec City were always a stimulus to research, along with geographer Louis-Edmond Hamelin, with whom I worked for so long at Laval, and the historian Serge Gagnon, who was soon to dedicate to me *Quebec and its Historians: 1840 to 1920*, the English edition of this book on Canadian historical writing.

Another compensation was short lived. I had long been an admirer of the Royal Society of Canada. Founded at the end of the nineteenth century, the French section had always brought together people whom French Canada considered to be great thinkers. For half a century it had published its *Mémoires*—heavy tomes that each year brought us various studies, many of great literary or scientific value. During the second half of the twentieth century, however, the society had sunk considerably from its former grandeur, only publishing new members' maiden speeches. It retained a certain prestige even so, because of its distinguished membership. Like many others (for many were chosen) I was admitted in 1967. Five years later I was expelled.

I had done nothing subversive or dishonourable. On the contrary, my expulsion was the result of my lofty conception of the society. For me, the Royal Society was an honourary body, selecting from the ordinary run of people those considered worthy of distinction. There could be no question of entering, cheque in hand, as one enters a sports club. This is why I was taken aback when asked for an annual payment of seventy-five dollars. I was being charged for being honoured in this society? There must be some mistake! In the Académie canadienne-française, the Order of Canada, or the Ordre national du Québec you don't pay a cent! I said no. The society sent me statements annually for five years. It threatened to throw me out. I wrote a memo stating my case, but in vain. In 1972 the president wrote me a long letter explaining that, when all was said and done (but he expressed it in more embarrassed terms), either I paid or I could no longer write the letters M.S.R.C. after my name. The postman always rings twice, it seems. This president was the same university professor who, as dean of the faculty of letters at Laval in 1965, played a role in my departure. I ignored the summons, which didn't deserve a reply, and dropped the precious initials. One does not buy honours nor rent them by the year.

The compensations, promotions to honourary societies, medals and monetary prizes aren't necessarily a guarantee of quality. Those who receive none may consider them rather empty formalities or be reminded of certain year-end ceremonies of their time in classical college. Nevertheless such compensations are always an essential stimulant for those who receive them. Stage actors receive applause and in this way know just how much they interest or charm their audiences. This is considered normal. We writers, however, don't hear our public's reactions. It is rare for us to glimpse one of our books in a reader's hands. Even more rare is something that happened to me while walking in the grounds of the Benedictine abbey of Saint-Benoît-du-Lac. Through the refectory windows came a voice reading *recto tomo*. As I walked toward it, the sentences became clearer. The subject was Jacques Cartier, and I recognized the text immediately. Someone was reading aloud from my *Vaines tentatives*! I did indeed have my public, one that listened to what I had to say; I was making an impression on it, I really existed! Hearing my work read aloud in the refectory of a religious community was for me the sweetest recompense. Such things bring self-forgiveness for the austerity of the writer's life and lessen the constant fear that research is futile.

When these compensations are accompanied by a cheque (particularly a cheque of five figures, such as the Molson Prize awarded by the Canada Council for the Arts), they make up for all the accumulated expense of gathering documentation, writing a manuscript, and getting it to the public. Usually this is the only material benefit you get from a book. The fact that there are financial consolations is all to the good.

I'm not embarking on this subject in order to boast about my bank account. I simply want to say what my experience has been for the benefit of young historians who think of venturing into print. And what a venture it is! When the historian has finished his or her lengthy research and expressed the results in a manuscript of four or five hundred pages, there remains the drama of getting it published. People consider me lucky in my career, but it has been a constant struggle from the time I first began writing up to my current venture. It doesn't matter how successful the previous book has been, the same sharp anxiety about getting the next one published is always there.

We live in a society where scholarly writing can't appear in print without a state subsidy. Before 1952 we couldn't even dream of such largesse. When government hospital insurance was introduced, Professor Luc Lacourcière suggested jokingly that there be a similar publishing insurance, at which we all laughed heartily. How times have changed! Even if copyright in Canada was for many years registered with the ministry of agriculture, there was no crop insurance for the products of our minds. Then came the day when we could hope for a grant to subsidize our manuscripts.

But what a painful process it is to get this subsidy! You submit your work to a publisher. His or her anonymous house reader accepts or rejects it. Once the manuscript has been approved, the publisher writes to a certain organization with an estimate of the cost of publication. This organization is slow to get going. It chooses three anonymous jury members to whom it sends the manuscript. They take their time. Long months go by. Sometimes all the jury members say yes, and then your luck is in! Sometimes they all say no. Or sometimes—as most often happens—one of them suggests corrections. There are always those who have the bright idea that chapter nine would be better in place of chapter four, or who remember that someone in some obscure university wrote a master's thesis on a portion of the same subject. The candidate is then asked to rework his manuscript and submit it afresh. Do you appeal the decision? In that case you'll lose more weeks explaining yourself before nameless evaluators. I learned something about this when I submitted my manuscript for *Les débuts du régime seigneurial au Canada*. One of the jury members didn't agree with my interpretation of the seigneurial régime prior to 1663, thus questioning a good part of the book. I didn't succeed in convincing this nameless, faceless jury member. Rather than have my intellectual freedom suffer, I preferred give up the chance of a grant.

Another time one of the evaluators, a former archivist, criticized me for using copies when I should have worked with the originals that were in his custody. He was making a serious mistake. *My* sources were the originals; it was his "originals" that were the copies. But how much precious time I lost in proving this!

These battles at least had the merit of steering the granting body toward more flexible rules that nowadays provide the candidate with greater fairness and more intellectual freedom.

When the grant is at last approved, the author is still at the starting gate. It must be decided whether publication of the manuscript fits in with the publisher's "calendar." The manuscript can be lying around in somebody's in-basket for a year or two. You'll have time to finish another.

Book publishing is practised according to three traditional methods: self-financed if your pockets are well lined; at the publisher's expense if you can find a house that will do this and give the author a ten percent royalty; or you can, as it is elegantly called, "waive royalties to the first edition." As it is always the only edition, this means the author simply gives away his manuscript. I have used all three methods.

My first work on Voltaire and French-Canadian literature appeared in 1945, published at my own expense, thanks to the kindness of my uncle who paid for everything and left me the revenue. As I quickly recuperated the $2,000 invested in this book, I could conclude that it was a success in the bookshops. The equivalent of a year's salary—a 1945 salary—fell into my coffers. The novel *Vézine*, my second book, appeared in 1946 at the publisher's expense. It sold fairly well, but we mustn't exaggerate: it brought me a total of $600. All the same, adding to this the receipts of the preceding book, literature was providing a worthwhile means of making up my income. My pen was earning something.

These two successes made me overconfident when it came time to publish my first Canadian history work in 1949, *Louis XVI, le Congrès américain et le Canada, 1774-1789.* I was a university professor and thought myself famous because of my earlier books, imagining that every publisher would pounce on my manuscript. I had the noble thought of offering it first to my university, which had just established a publishing service known naïvely then as Presses universitaires Laval. This encouraged all kinds of hopes. Professors could simply immerse themselves in research without worrying about finding publishers. Alas, the bursar of the Quebec Seminary (which still financed the university) replied that my book, a highly specialized study ("Congratulations."—"Thank you very much."), aimed at too small a readership for this university press. My illusions were rudely shattered.

The second self-publishing venture then began. Why wouldn't I be as successful as before? I got in touch with a young Quebec City publisher who asked me for $1,000 for a run of a thousand copies. A thousand seem a bit small. "I'll easily sell two thousand copies," I said to myself. "Let's go for $2,000." And so I doubled the run. Unfortunately my annual salary was only $2,600. I went to the Quebec Seminary, which was willing to lend me the money at six percent interest. Interest? "If the university wants its professors to publish their work, it should give them some help!" I protested. Monseigneur Parent spared me the six percent. The book appeared, the first thousand copies sold well, but the second thousand were left on my hands. I got rid of them by selling what had cost me a dollar at twenty-five cents a copy. And to think that today the rare survivals of this edition are offered for sale in "antique" shops at seventy-five dollars a copy! I emerged from this venture with a small surplus of about a hundred dollars.

This failure taught me a hard lesson: as a writer of history, I was an unknown. Either the public wasn't interested, or I wrote very badly. Still, I thought, there'll be another book to cause a sensation. This was *Le Régime militaire dans le Gouvernement des Trois-Rivières, 1760-1764*, a subject unlikely to bring crowds running to the bookstores. As I was still carrying my debt to the seminary, and because this manuscript dealt with an even more limited subject than the previous one, I didn't even try the Laval press. At the time Abbé Albert Tessier in Trois-Rivières was involved in publishing as many books about his region as possible. I made him a gift of the manuscript that was lying heavy on my hands. The book appeared in 1952 and gave me no bother, neither in spending nor getting.

For the years 1945-1952 my four books brought me, all in all, a sad little surplus of $700 for seven years' work—not even the equivalent of two months' salary in 1952! Luckily I was able to replenish my cash flow right away by taking part in the production of a textbook entitled *Histoire du Canada par les textes*. Academic textbooks are a well-known goldmine and the only way for a writer to survive. This one was published in 1952 and brought in a good income each year. At the end of the golden age of textbooks (ah! if it would only come back!), I had earned $20,600, an enormous sum at first sight but only equal to my 1968 annual salary.

I could have done several textbooks like this one, but it was merely a sort of by-blow. Only scholarly work interested me. I devoted myself to the subject of the Military Régime, although this didn't prevent me from going down another by-road and writing the Chiniquy biography for pleasure. Once the question of religious censorship had been satisfactorily dealt with, I again had the happy thought of offering my manuscript to the Presses universitaires Laval, since it might be a commercial success and would help them. The response was that the subject was not entirely suitable for the high standards of this publishing house. Decidedly I didn't have heaven on my side. In 1949 my subject was too scholarly; in 1955 it smelled of *Allô Police*.

I went back to Trois-Rivières where my previous publisher agreed to bring out the manuscript at his own expense. To judge by the talks that I'm asked to give everywhere on Chiniquy (in the Lower Saint Lawrence, the Montreal region, Abitibi, and even in New England), my book ought to have sold like hotcakes when first published. Was the sales distribution badly managed? Was there a boycott somewhere? This book, which is impossible to find nowadays, only brought me about a thousand dollars. Still, it was some consolation for the failures of my "scholarly" works.

My woes were not at an end. Let us take a quick look at booklets. *Le régime seigneurial* was a twenty-page monograph that I ceded to the Historical Society of Canada for $50. My 94-page *Champlain* was written for a collection brought out by Fides. It earned me a little over $500. In 1956, having just wiped out my 1949 debt, I had in hand a manuscript entitled, *L'Église canadienne sous le Régime militaire, 1759-1764,* to be published in two thick volumes. I thought once more of the Presses universitaires Laval, since this time there could be no connection between this ecclesiastical subject and *Allô Police*. The answer was no: I was told the press was not on solid enough ground to take on such a massive study. The printers of *L'Action catholique* agreed to publish the first volume on condition that I waive all royalties and contribute $500 of my own, in other words give away a manuscript and pay for the privilege. I borrowed the $500 from Canon Groulx, who was launching a collection called *Les Études de l'Institut d'histoire de l'Amérique française.* This was the second time I had borrowed in order to get my work published.

Now I had to get the second volume published. I had a stroke of genius, imagining very naïvely that I could get up a subscription among the curés of the old parishes along the St. Lawrence that were discussed at length in my book. Given the importance that I attached to my subject, I was sure they would help me to a man. "To a man" was right: there was only one. I had prepared fifty letters personally addressed to each of the curés, every letter accompanied by a stamped, self-addressed envelope. All the curé had to do was slip a cheque into the envelope and drop it in the mailbox. I sat back and waited for the gold to rain down. There were three replies: one curé bought a book, another excused himself on the grounds that he was constantly asked to give money for charity but assured me that I had his prayers. The third also excused himself, but without the prayers. Fortunately Laval agreed in the meantime to publish the second volume, still on condition that I waive all royalties. I gave away a third manuscript. It was not to be the last.

From my two books on the Roman Catholic Church under the Military Régime, I finally netted a slight deficit of $200. Then, for a while, the lean kine were succeeded by the fat. My *Esclavage au Canada français*, published by the Laval press at its own expense, brought me about $1200. The *Atlas historique du Canada français* (1961) brought in $1000. *Les vaines tentatives*, the first volume of my *Histoire de la Nouvelle-France*, published in 1963 by Fides at their expense, sold fairly well. I received $3,200 plus a Quebec literary prize of $4,000. The next volume, *Le comptoir*, published in the same way in 1966, was even more of a monetary consolation. It brought in about $4,400, in addition to two prizes totalling $5,000. Never had a book earned me so much, although this one was as dry as a dictionary. Yet, for a work that cost me three years of writing and editing, the royalties didn't amount to four months' salary.

The good years continued, thanks to the production of textbooks. In 1967, *Canada: Unity and Diversity*, a combined effort published in French and English, enabled me to bank about $9,000. In 1968, *Initiation à la Nouvelle-France* brought a little over $28,000, and the *Atlas de la Nouvelle-France*, a complete reworking of a preceding atlas, $4,800. In 1969 *Canadian History Textbooks: A Comparative Study,* published and French and English, brought in $5,600. People had repeatedly told me, "Do textbooks: it pays." I fully realized this, but though there is pleasure in adding to one's income, where is the scholarly gratification? I should add for this profitable period $5,200 in royalties for *The Beginnings of New France,* my English abridgment of the first three volumes of the *Histoire de la Nouvelle-France*, and $1,700 for the *Terrier de la Nouvelle-France* (1973), which also brought me a small French prize, the Montcalm, worth 800 francs.

This was something to help me forget that I'd once given away three manuscripts. However in that very year, 1973, history began to repeat itself. I had to give away a fourth manuscript in order for *La population du Canada en 1663* to appear in print.

Other works produced some receipts. In 1974 *Les débuts du régime seigneurial au Canada* brought in $2,000; and in 1976 *La révolution américaine* (a revised edition of a 1949 book) produced under $1,000. Alas, in the same year, 1976, I ceded a fifth manuscript, *Montréal, la formation d'une société*, for nothing.

At the time of finishing these memoirs, the two books making up the third volume (*La seigneurie des Cent-Associés, 1627-1663)* of my *Histoire de la Nouvelle-France* are still being sold. The first, *Les événements*, has produced $2,900 so far; the second, *La société*, $1,400 plus a $2,000 prize. Also on sale is the *Catalogue des immigrants*, for which I have received $1,800 to date.

As I always have a good supply of manuscripts to publish, I am now anxiously waiting to learn whether my *Dictionnaire des esclaves et de leurs propriétaires*, a thousand-page manuscript, will be published, or my three-act play *Onontagué*, describing the adventures of the French in Iroquoia in 1658, or this manuscript of memoirs.

Leaving the booklets aside, let us say that for a total of twenty-six books I had to give away five in order to get them published. The others have brought me the sum of $73,200. Add $15,000 for various prizes, and $20,000 for the Molson Prize, awarded for my work as a whole. This gives a total revenue from royalties and prizes of $108,200.

This sum appears impressive at first glance, but when you calculate that it represents over forty-one years of writing, it breaks down to a modest income of $2,600 a year. In 1949 this amounted to a year's salary at Laval. In 1962 it was no more than two and a half months' salary. In 1982 it would cover no more than two or three weeks.

One cannot live by one's pen, clearly. Writing only brings in tips. But even if it brought in nothing (as was the case of the five books that nevertheless required years of research), it must be remembered that I got pleasure from writing them and at the same time felt I was fulfilling a duty toward my university, which was paying me a salary to teach and do research.

Publication contributed to both the university's prestige and my own reputation. Indeed, I worked at building a reputation throughout my career. Why not admit it—is it something to be ashamed of? The fact of having some thirty publications to one's credit becomes impressive, raising the author above the crowd in terms of quantity at least, even though it would be preferable to be distinguished for quality. I aimed for quality, but in writing as in anything else you give only what you can. Critics have pointed out weaknesses in one or other of my works, but I know of plenty they didn't catch. If further editions should appear, I would correct, delete, and begin again. When you do a task honestly, you're well aware of your own shortcomings and revise your work constantly. Then if you're lucky (few authors get this far), you appear before the pitiless tribunal of posterity.

12

Before the Sand Runs Out of the Hourglass

THE SUCCESS OF A CAREER, I have often been told, is to realize the dreams of youth. My career is a success in these terms. It is true that I first dreamed of being a Greek scholar, a calling I would have followed while becoming the Balzac of French Canada. Youth tends to be more than daring in its vision. What I wanted, in fact, was to teach and write.

Circumstances led me from Greek and the novel to the history of Canada. I was confident that I could handle the demanding intellectual program for which a spartan adolescence had prepared me. When becoming a career historian, still at an age when one's dreams are great, I set my objective: to produce a massive *oeuvre* of books that would appear every two or three years, rich in learning. In short, as in my college years my goal was to reach the top. I don't feel guilty in the slightest about having had such dreams.

I don't know what place I actually deserve or the final mark to be handed down, but I've written the books I wanted to write—numerous, thick, each page built on a foundation of notes and references, books that leave nothing to be added. And what about the reader? Ah, the reader! I admit that I've rather forgotten this person, as the actor forgets his audience.

I write primarily for the pleasure it gives me, and to tell myself about a slice of history. If it pleases me to linger over small details of the past as I revisit it, I'm glad to do so, and when my pleasure is satisfied I continue my analysis. To colleagues who asked me whether I bought a lot of books, I replied, "very few; I write books for myself." They took it as a good joke, but it was no joke. I do write books for myself, as one talks to oneself. It may seem a refinement, but I'm no dilettante who puts his writing in a drawer and thinks no more about it. From a very young age the idea of publishing a book fascinated me. I want what I write to be published. Am I the only one to confess to this vanity? For me it has always been the most pleasant of tasks.

But is the historian happy in his profession? Since history is a scholarly pursuit, is he satisfied with the knowledge it has brought him? After being an active historian for forty years and hoping to continue for another ten or fifteen, am I still as enthusiastic as in my early years? Someone, I forget who, said at the end of a career, "I have written too much history to still believe in it." Perhaps he wrote badly. In any case, I haven't yet reached this point.

Everything has surely been said against history. Valéry's judgment is well known: "History is the most dangerous product that the chemistry of intelligence has ever concocted." Raymond Aron's recent summing up was no less harsh. He said, "History aims at an object that not only has passed by, not only has disappeared, but that only reaches us through the mind, and changes as we do."

The historian is in fact badly placed to achieve a genuine reconstruction of the past. He aims to be a faithful witness of a vanished society, but he's a man born two or three centuries after what he wishes to describe. He has grown up in a completely different world. He speaks a language with words that don't always mean the same thing. His outlook has little or nothing in common with the mentality of the past. He is part of an economy, the conditions, laws, and practices of which are alien to the old economy that he purports to study. He is from a country where the frontiers are no longer the same and relationships with neighbours have changed. The homeland itself no longer signifies the same thing. Since humans are logical, the historian tries to find a logical development in the course of history, although we know that facts aren't governed by the rule of reason.

To reach this past, the historian has only documentation. If he is studying the recent past this isn't a problem. There is plenty of documentation, although the wealth of information may possibly mask what is important to retain. The historian therefore has to make a choice. By what authority can he decide to keep this rather than that? Will he not unconsciously retain what he is looking to prove and not what leads to the truth? And if the information is only rare and fragmentary, isn't he in danger, by trying to get the most out of it, of giving it more importance than it really deserves?

This is why I'm still uneasy about what I have written, including, among others, my writings on seventeenth-century New France. Archives for the first two-thirds of this period are maddeningly sparse. For the first twenty

On June 6, 1999, Marcel Trudel received an honourary degree (D. université) from the University of Ottawa.

years, which I called *Le comptoir*, we have scarcely more than a single witness: Champlain. He tells us only what he did and what he considered worthy of interest to the reader of his time—which is only to be expected. For the next thirty years, that is, the period of the real founding of New France, there is the same dearth of information. We no longer have the administrative documents of the Company of One Hundred Associates, the enterprise responsible for the colony's development. In these circumstances how can we follow its work and evaluate its role? Also gone are the personal letters between people in France and Canada, as well as notarial acts, many of the registers, and numerous account books. And we claim to be reconstructing seventeenth-century New France and to speak of it as though we'd been there? It's true that we've managed to establish the existence of some events through a variety of documents, but what are they all but brief instants in a century of social interaction?

Looking at seventeenth-century New France, I'm like a spectator separated from the stage by a wall. Through this wall, thanks to a few chinks, I get glimpses of what's happening. I walk back and forth along the wall, lingering at various openings through which I can see better, but I never get an overall view of what's going on. All I see are isolated segments of the show. There are plenty of people on the other side of the wall, but how can I count them? How can I describe people when I only see bits of them? I hear voices, but the words are unintelligible. I'd like to ask questions, but they can't hear me—they aren't even aware I'm there, trying to get to know them. And I claim to know this society?

Must the historian therefore give up, must he no longer believe in his profession? In my view he must embark on his career by performing an act of profound humility. He has to admit that his resources are very slender, refuse to state anything beyond what can be substantiated by documentary proof, abandon all preconceived systems, and be as wary as possible of any ideology. If not, the past he purports to reconstruct will simply be his own present.

Marcel Trudel

Chronological Bibliography

L'influence de Voltaire au Canada. Montreal: les Éditions Fides, 1945. 2 vol.: 221p., 315p. Prix David, 1945.

Vézine. Montreal: les Éditions Fides, 1946. 264p. Novel. Reissued 1962 in the "Alouette bleue" collection, 286p.

Louis XVI, le Congrès américain et le Canada, 1774-1789. Quebec: Les Éditions du Quartier latin, 1949. 259p. Prix David, 1951.

Histoire du Canada par les textes. Montreal: Les Éditions Fides, 1952. 297p. With Guy Frégault and Michel Brunet. Reissued in 1962 as 2 vols., the first with Guy Frégault.

Le Régime militaire dans le Gouvernement des Trois-Rivières. 1760-1764. Trois-Rivières: les Editions du Bien public, 1952. 236p.

L'affaire Jumonville. Québec: les Presses universitaires Laval, 1953. 43p. Published in English in 1954 as *The Jumonville Affair*, 33p.

Chiniquy. Trois-Rivières: les Editions du Bien public, 1955. 339p.

Le régime seigneurial. Ottawa, la Société historique du Canada, 1956. 20p. Revised edition 1971. Published in English as *The Seigneurial Regime.* Ottawa: Canadian Historical Association, 1956. 18p. Reprinted 1967, 1973.

Champlain. Montreal: les Éditions Fides, 1956. 94p. "Classiques canadiens" collection. New, revised edition 1968.

L'Église canadienne sous le Régime militaire. 1759-1764. 2 vols.:Vol. I: *Les problèmes.* Montreal: les Études de l'Institut d'Histoire de l'Amérique française, 1956. 362p. Vol. II: *Les institutions.* Québec: les Presses universitaires Laval, 1957. 490p.

L'esclavage au Canada français. Histoire et conditions de l'esclavage. Québec: les Presses universitaires Laval, 1960. 432p. Prix Casgrain, 1961. Reissued as extracts by Éditions Horizon, 1963. 125p.

Histoire de la Nouvelle-France. Montreal: les Éditions Fides, 5 vols. Vol. I: *Les vaines tentatives. 1524-1603.* 1963. 307p. First prize for the Concours littéraires et scientifiques du Québec, 1963. Reissued 1965, 1968, and 1971. Vol. II: *Le comptoir. 1604-1627.* 1966. 554p. First prize for the Concours littéraires et scientifiques du Québec, 1966; Governor General's Award, 1967. Reissued 1971. Vol. III: *La seigneurie des Cent-Associés. 1627-1663,* in two books. Book 1: *Les événements.* 1979. 489p. Book 2: *La société.* 1983. 669p. Prix Macdonald, 1984. Vol. IV: *La seigneurie de la Compagnie des Indes occidentales. 1668-1674.* 1997. 894p. Vol. V: *Le Régime militaire et la disparition de la Nouvelle-France, 1759-1764.* 1999. 612p.

Canada: Unity and Diversity. Toronto: Holt, Rinehart, and Winston, 1967. 529p. With P.G. Cornell, J. Hamelin, and F. Quellet. Published by same publisher in French in 1968 as *Canada: unité et diversité,* 578p. Revised French edition 1971. 622p.

Initiation à la Nouvelle-France: histoire et institutions. Montreal: Holt, Rinehart, and Winston, 1968. 323p. Published in English in 1968 as *Introduction to New France,* 300p. Reissued 1972.

Jacques Cartier. Montreal: les Éditions Fides, 1968. 94p. "Classiques canadiens" collection.

Atlas de la Nouvelle-France. Québec: les Presses de l'université Laval, 1968. 219p. Bilingual edition, co-published with University of Toronto Press. Reissued 1973.

L'histoire du Canada: enquête sur les manuels. Ottawa: Information Canada, 1969. 129p. No. 5 of Studies of the Royal Commission on Bilingualism and Biculturalism. With Geneviève Jain. Published in English as *Canadian History Textbooks. A Comparative Study.* Ottawa: Queen's Printer, 1970.

The Beginnings of New France. 1524-1663. Toronto: McClelland and Stewart, 1973. 323p. Vol. II of The Canadian Centenary Series. Translated by Patricia Claxton.

Le Québec de 1663. Québec: la Société historique de Québec, 1972. 24p. No. 4 of the "Textes" series.

La population du Canada en 1663. Montreal: les Éditions Fides, 1978. 368p.

Le terrier du Saint-Laurent en 1663. Ottawa: les Éditions de l'université d'Ottawa, 1973. 618p. Prix Montcalm (France).

Les débuts du régime seigneurial au Canada. Montreal: les Éditions Fides, 1974. 313p.

Montréal: la formation d'une société. 1642-1663. Montreal: les Éditions Fides, 1976. 328p.

La révolution américaine. Pourquoi la France refuse le Canada. 1775-1789. Québec: les Éditions du Boréal-Express, 1976. 291p. Revised edition of earlier work, *Louis XVI, le Congrès américain et le Canada. 1774-1789.* 1949.

Catalogue des immigrants. 1632-1662. Montreal: Hurtubise HMH, 1983. 569p.

Mémoires d'un autre siècle. Montreal: Boréal, 1987. 312p. Médaille de l'Union des Éditeurs de langue française (France).

Au Canada français. Dictionnaire des esclaves et de leurs propriétaires. Montreal: Hurtubise HMH, 1990. 490p.

François Dollier de Casson. Histoire du Montréal. Montreal: Hurtubise HMH, 1992. 342p. New, critical edition with Marie Baboyant.

La population du Canada en 1666. Recensement reconstitué. Sillery: les Éditions du Septentrion, 1995. 379p.

Le terrier du Saint-Laurent en 1674. Montreal: les Éditions du Méridien, 1998. 912p. 2 vols.

Les écolières des Ursulines de Québec. 1639-1688. Amérindiennes et Canadiennes. Montreal: Hurtubise HMH, 1999. 434p.

Le Régime militaire et la disparition de la Nouvelle-France, 1759-1764. 1999. Vol. V of *l'Histoire de la Nouvelle-France.* (See above.)

Mythes et réalités dans l'histoire du Québec. Montreal: Hurtubise HMH, 2001. 325p.

Saint-Narcisse de Champlain. Au pays de la Batiscan. Saint-Narcisse: Municipalité de Saint-Narcisse, 2001. 214p.

Chiniquy. Prêtre catholique, ministre prèsbytérien. Montreal: Lidec, 2001. 62p. "Célébrités" collection.

Other Dossier Québec Books

They Were So Young: Montrealers Remember World War II
Patricia Burns. Foreword by Desmond Morton

Painting Friends: The Beaver Hall Women Painters
Barbara Meadowcroft

Montreal of Yesterday: Jewish Life in Montreal 1900-1920
Israel Medres. Translated from the Yiddish by Vivian Felsen

Through the Eyes of the Eagle: The Early Montreal Yiddish Press 1907-1916
Edited by Pierre Anctil. Translated from the Yiddish by David Rome

Renewing Our Days: Montreal Jews in the Twentieth Century
Edited by Ira Robinson and Mervin Butovsky

Putting Down Roots: Montreal's Immigrant Writers
Elaine Kalman Naves

The Passionate Debate: The Social and Political Ideas of Quebec Nationalism 1920-1945
Michael Oliver

Yellow-Wolf & Other Tales of the Saint Lawrence
Philippe-Joseph Aubert de Gaspé.
Translated from the French by Jane Brierley

Véhicule Press
www.vehiculepress.com